Taken Away

Taken Away

The Ordinary Life of a Lama

Doboom Tulku with
Sudhamahi Regunathan

BLOOMSBURY
NEW DELHI • LONDON • OXFORD • NEW YORK • SYDNEY

BLOOMSBURY INDIA
Bloomsbury Publishing India Pvt. Ltd
Second Floor, LSC Building No. 4, DDA Complex, Pocket C – 6 & 7,
Vasant Kunj, New Delhi 110070

BLOOMSBURY, BLOOMSBURY INDIA and the Diana logo
are trademarks of Bloomsbury Publishing Plc

First published in India 2024
This edition published 2024

ISBN: PB: 978 93 56408 81 4; e-Book: 978 93 56408 82 1
2 4 6 8 10 9 7 5 3 1

Typeset in Fournier MT Std by Manipal Technologies Limited
Printed and bound in India by Thomson Press India Ltd

Contents

Preface

My Life, a Note

I did not plan my life. That is why I decided to title my memoirs, *Taken Away*. At a very young age, I was identified as a reincarnation and taken away from the home where I was born. And the rest of my life unfolded similarly. My monastery, my horse, my country – to name just a few – were all taken away over time.

Despite that, when I look back, I find I am unable to say which period of my life was the happiest. I have always been happy. I have enjoyed every day of my life, notwithstanding all that was taken away. There was so much left for me! I am often asked which were the best years of my life. I am at a loss to reply. Every day has been the best day of my life.

Do I not miss my country, I am asked. Of course, I do. That was a sad separation. But life continued to be full of variety and showed me new things along the way. I think, had I not left when I did, I would now be a nomad perhaps, tending to animals. Maybe I would have been just as happy but I definitely would not have had the good fortune of being so close to His Holiness the Dalai Lama. I would not have met all the scholars and interesting people from across the world that I did.

My exposure would have been narrow. I would not have experienced oneness and nothingness in my day-to-day life. To give a small example, when I was in Doboom Ritro, my retreat in Tibet, I used to watch marmots peeping out of their burrows. They were very adorable. Some of them stopped being scared of me and became my friends. For many long years after I left the place, I did not see marmots at all, till I saw one in Switzerland. A marmot brought Switzerland close to my heart.

My memories of childhood and my experiences while growing up urged me to document them. So I started writing down all the incidents that came to my mind. Soon I realised I had quite a lot of material. One day, the well-known historian Narayani Gupta suggested just what was in my mind – to give form to what I had recorded. 'Why do you not write your memoirs?' she asked. Her daughter Niharika was ready to help me. She spent ten days with me in my late friend Swami Veda Bharati's ashram in Rishikesh and worked on my notes. She also had a good time laughing over my English. However, she got busy with other things and for more than four years after that, there was no progress.

It was then that I contacted Sudhamahi Regunathan, whom I had known for many years. We had worked together when she was editing a volume on sacred music for Tibet House. She had helped to transcreate – not merely translate – my two books of maxims into English. In 2017, we started our work on my memoirs and the exercise became very elaborate. We spent many afternoons at the India International Centre, when she would ask me questions and lead me down memory lane. I found I had so much more to tell! Between tea and cheese straws, not to mention cinnamon cookies and lunches, I relived my life. We worked for over five years, meeting for ten days every three months.

Just as many people, places and instances have made me what I am, many people and places helped to build these memoirs and bring them to this shape. I am now looking forward to seeing all these efforts as a book, edited with the nuanced pencil of R. Sivapriya of Bloomsbury. I must express my thanks to Krishan Chopra for seeing value in my memoirs.

I cannot finish this without thanking Chungkey, my personal secretary, my medical attendant, my cook... Her unstinting hard work, her conviction that my life story needed to be told and her ready laughter have added to making this whole experience yet another enjoyable event.

Doboom Tulku
5 November 2023
New Delhi

Part I

TEHOR (1941–54)

I

What I Had Not Prepared For

As geographical knowledge of the terrain to be traversed
eases one's journey,
knowledge of the ground and path
facilitate on the path to liberation.[1]

At some point, my home tutor told my attendants, 'None of us can recognise his mother.' I waited to see how they would find a solution to this problem for I, too, could not recognise my mother. Then my father said, 'Don't worry, I will show her to you.' This is the dominant memory I have of my first journey to Lhasa.

We were on horseback. The bells were clanging, one after the other. One bell was at a lower pitch and sounded far deeper than the others. The sounds came from the bells tied around the necks of the mules, which were ahead of us and carried our luggage. Generally, each mule had three or four bells around its neck. They were musical when all of them sounded together. Our horses had smaller bells that were high-pitched when they jingled. With the peals of the bells and the galloping rhythm of the horses, we rode across green pastures en route to Lhasa. I was being taken there to pursue further studies at the Drepung Monastery.

A drone of prayer wafted by softly in the winds. Somehow the peals and the prayers caught each other's rhythm. A wave-like musical tune emerged. It sounded like our prayers were swinging in the air.

Whenever we rode, we always chanted prayers. The chanting was usually a prayer to Tara.

Om tare tuttare ture svaha
Om Tara, I entreat you, O Tara! O swift one! Hail!

Goddess Tara is an important figure in Tibetan Buddhism and appears as a female Buddha. She ensures success and achievement of the task at hand. My other favourite prayer was:

Om sarva tathagatosnisa sitatapatre hum phat hum mama hum ni svaha

O Bhagavati Sitatapatra, please pacify all illnesses and evil interferences of myself and all others and bestow all attainments. I prostrate at the feet of the One renowned as Usnisa Sitatapatra, the goddess with the white parasol, undefeatable by others, the most sublime goddess, who took birth from the Usnisa, the Supreme mark of all the Buddhas.

This prayer is said to be particularly good for warding off evil. I chant these prayers to this day.

I was all of twelve years old when I undertook that journey. Identified as a 'tulku', I had been taken away from home when I was barely two years old. This was the first time that I was going back to the place where I was born. It was on the way to Lhasa from Tashi Dargye, where I had spent the last decade.

As we rode, nature seemed to be watching us. Our prayers drifted upwards through the air. The sky was clear. The pastures green. Mountain silhouettes spiked the bluish-grey horizon. We could see no one for miles ahead. When the winds grew strong, they would scoop sand from the surface and scatter it into the air with limitless abandon. It was the territory of the wind – sometimes shared with the clouds, the rain and glimpses of the sun and the moon.

I was riding my horse, Dragyal. I was very fond of him. I loved to rub my hands around his neck. Most of the time we would canter, but occasionally, we would break into a gallop for short distances, just for fun. There were two bags hanging on either side of the saddle, both full of treats such as homemade cookies and dry fruits that I could munch on as we rode. I was well taken care of. My parents were nomads. They lived in Ga Shiwu in the Kham[2] region of Tibet, where I was born. They lived in warm, black tents made of yak hair. They pitched their tents uphill in summer and downhill in winter. They had dri and yaks with them. The dri gave them milk and cheese, while the yaks helped them carry luggage when they moved. I was told that I had three brothers and one sister, all younger than me. I was going to meet them for the first time.

We had been travelling for ten days. On the tenth day, we saw some horsemen riding towards us. We feared they were robbers, but actually they were coming to welcome us to their area. My father was among them.

I recognised my father, Tashi Paljor, as he had visited Doboom Ritro, where I lived, a few times. He was not a very tall man, maybe about 5 feet 5 inches or 7 inches. He had shoulder-length hair, like most men of that time. It was combed back and he wore it in a single plait at the back. He was clad in the typical attire of Khampa men which was a long, thick garment with loose sleeves and a cord as a belt at the waist. You can imagine it as a bathrobe, but longer in length. His huge robe was loosely worn over the shoulders, pulled up a little below the knees and tied at the waist, thus creating a bulging space around the waist and chest which served as a bag to put things.

I do not think I looked like my father. Some people remarked that I, perhaps, looked more like my uncle, my father's brother.

Though I recognised my father, I had no idea who the rest of the family were. I had no mental image of my mother. It was then that I realised that I had not prepared myself for this meeting.

We usually made arduous preparations before we undertook any journey. The date of my departure would be fixed after keeping many factors in mind, including an auspicious date for travelling. The date would then be made public and anyone else interested in going along could seek permission to travel with us. A large group would thus be formed.

All of us had prepared for two eventualities. The first was natural calamities. If a river starts swelling due to incessant rain in a valley further up ahead, it causes a new stream to emerge, literally from nowhere. So we had to learn to navigate the waters and stay on the horse while it swam and reached the other bank. I was scared of such an eventuality, and what I feared, we had to face on this trip.

We were just about to cross a mountain when the waters started rising rapidly. What were we to do? Should we turn back? After some deliberation, my entourage decided to go ahead, since the waters had just started to rise. My horse and I crossed over. However, one of the mules loaded with a special package of white *khatag* scarves for the entrance ceremony celebrations at Drepung, was swept away by the current.[3]

A group of experienced travellers among us ran ahead, jumped into the river and managed to pull out the mule, but its baggage was soaked. Luckily, the next morning was sunny so the khatags could be spread out and dried, though their crispness was, of course, lost.

The second eventuality that we had prepared for was to face robbers. Conditions were difficult in those days and so to survive, people adopted any measure, even robbery. Small groups of people came together to travel as one large group because of the fear of robbers. It would be easier to defend themselves if they were more in number.

We did not meet any robbers during our entire journey, though we always viewed anyone who came in contact with us with suspicion. Such chance encounters happened to us twice and the experienced among us suspected that the persons were actually robbers who had come under the pretext of selling us horses to check our strength. On one such occasion, my friends arranged a shooting competition among us to impress upon the strangers that we were also prepared.

In fact, one member of our group had been a robber himself. He came from a place called Nyagrong. He kept advising us on how to deal with strangers. His group was one of the smaller groups that had joined us.

We had prepared for both these kinds of events. But I had not thought of, and therefore was not prepared, to meet my mother. My father held out some hope!

Usually, we rose very early and began our journey so that we could set up camp by noon. The animals would then be left to graze and rest till the following day. Our tents were white and light, unlike the nomad tents which were made of yak hair and therefore black and far heavier. We had so much load to haul that we used mules which could carry heavier loads than yaks. People travelling long distances, whether for business or pilgrimage or other work, would generally travel on horseback and their luggage would be loaded on mules. Yaks were used for travelling by people like my parents who moved short distances, maybe twice a year. On our mules we carried everything that we required, for if we did not take something along, we had to do without it.

We were nearing my parents' camp. This was the first time that I was visiting my parents since I had been taken away. Before reaching the place, we had to cross a mountain pass which was not too high. Soon, we reached an expansive green pasture where a few families had pitched their tents. When we neared this place, they all came out to greet us.

Wherever we went, people looked after us and my requirements were always given top priority. For instance, I was aware that butter, milk and meat were the main foods of the nomads. In the monastery, too, meat was served, mostly dry meat brought from nearby areas. Tibet was a cold country and it was difficult to get vegetables all through the year. So dairy products and meat, together with barley flour, formed the staple food. During our journey I did not want our hosts to serve any fresh meat. I did not want anybody to butcher any animal for me. My entourage conveyed my sentiments wherever we went and people respected it.

Other than this, what I remember distinctly about that day was that I waited uneasily to identify my mother. Generally, women in Tibet were shy and soft-spoken. Once I was identified as a tulku, people kept a certain distance from me. Even my mother did that. So, of course, I was not expecting a hug or any such display of affection.

There was some kind of curiosity in me to see what she was like. My mother's name, I had been told, was Loyak. 'Loyak' literally means 'good harvest' and is an uncommon name.

I saw all the people waiting for me in front of the tents. As my eyes scanned them, when we came close, even before I dismounted from my horse, my father pointed out my mother. 'This is your mother,' he said. She was like any other Tibetan woman, with a soft complexion and high cheek-bones. She just looked at me with greater fondness than those gathered there. She wore a loose shirt and a thick robe, much like what my father wore. Women wore their robes long, till their ankles. Men wore their robes a little below their knees, over their trousers. All the women had a rosary in their hands.

I met my mother for the first time then, after our long separation. I later realised that I had also seen her for the last time. I met her and parted, just like anyone else who was introduced to me on any journey.

2

What I Was Being Prepared For

To tell you why I did not grow up under my mother's care, I must recount a few stories.

There was a *geshe* whose name was Kalsang Tenpa.[4] It was later in life that I read about him in an ancient manuscript propitiating protective deities. The text said that Geshe Kalsang Tenpa was a highly respected man and some very well-known monks of that period like Zigyab Lobsang Palden Choekyi Wangchuk were actually his disciples. Geshe Kalsang Tenpa was considered to be the first Doboom.[5]

My predecessor, Lobsang Tenzin Gyaltsen, was the second Doboom. I am told he was a good practitioner and had followed a strict daily regimen. He built the hermitage called Doboom Ritro, which was linked to Tashi Dargye Monastery in the Tehor province. Doboom Ritro was about a ten-day journey from the place where I was born. It was from Doboom Ritro that I had been travelling with my entourage to Lhasa when we passed through the place of my birth. This was when I met my mother.

In time, Geshe Kalsang Tenpa, the first Doboom, passed away. In the same area there was another well-known monk. He was very accurate in divinations, predictions, telling the future from dreams and so on. He was considered to be realised. When he died, some people had the idea that they should try finding his reincarnation. The lama they consulted told them that if they were really eager to recognise a tulku, they should try to find the reincarnation of Geshe Kalsang Tenpa, not this monk. So accordingly, these people collected the names of children in that area and sent them to Zigyab Lobsang Palden Choekyi Wangchuk, who gave his seal to one name on the list.

The search party approached the family directly, without warning. They barged into the house and asked, 'Where is your son?' He was grown up by then, maybe about twelve or thirteen years old, and they were told he was tending to the cattle on the mountain slopes. The search party came upon the boy collecting dried yak dung. He was carrying a willow basket on his back in which he was placing the yak dung for use as fuel at home. With great excitement, they immediately grabbed him and put him on their horse. When the boy protested about the yak dung being left behind, they just threw away the basket of dung and prepared to ride on without it.

On that particular day, it is said, the boy had also found a knife, an old rusted one. He pointed to the knife which was lying close to his basket. A person in the search party put it in the dung basket and abandoned it though a knife was considered to be a good omen. It was believed that finding a knife meant the intellect would become as sharp as a knife's edge, and to abandon it was not a good thing. That is how the second Doboom Lobsang Tenzin Gyaltsen was identified.

One of the second Doboom's important gurus was Tehor Dagkar Lama, a great scholar and one of the rare lamas who had a non-sectarian approach. Tehor Dagkar Lama was a very learned Rinpoche, and unlike some other famous lamas of his time, his approach to Buddhist traditions was unbiased. His fame spread, so did the number of his followers, and that caused jealousy among a few lamas in the region. Some people were of the opinion that the second Doboom was greatly influenced by Dagkar Lama and was broad-minded when it came to questions of traditions.[6] He was also not one who would easily bow down under pressure.

Traditionally, one or two years after a lama passes away, his followers and the community approach a senior and well-respected monk to find out where the lama had reincarnated or been reborn. The monk mentions the area or region where the new incarnation can be found. He also specifies the particular time period within which he should have been born. Those searching for the reincarnation then start collecting relevant data from the area of the time period mentioned by the monk. A list of names is prepared. This is then submitted to him. By divination, dreams or any other method he wishes to use, the monk identifies the reincarnation and puts his seal on the name of one child from the list, who then becomes the tulku.

What does tulku mean? In the Buddhist doctrines there are *trikaya* or three types of bodies:

The Dharmakaya or 'truth body' which embodies truth

The Sambhogakaya or body of completeness which is perceived only by the Buddha and by highly realised boddhisattvas

The Nirmanakaya or the created body for the good of the common people

Tulku is the equivalent of the Sanskrit word 'nirmanakaya'.

When I was recognised as the reincarnation of the second Doboom Tulku, I must have been about two years of age. I could barely walk. In those days children did not seem to walk early – they were kept swaddled, perhaps to save them from the cold.

Generally, when reincarnations are identified, it is said that nature also sends signals, perhaps to confirm that the choice is right. There are always many stories of unusual happenings associated with the identification of reincarnations. In my case, I was born the day after Losar, the Tibetan new year's day. It is customary to light butter lamps on that day to welcome the new year. I was told that the small butter lamps lit by my family, which normally lasted a few hours, burned through the night.

Also, unusual formations of clouds and rainbows appeared when I was taken to the Doboom hermitage.

I was born on 17 February, the second day of the Tibetan new year, Losar. The year, I was told, was 1942.[7] It was the year of the horse. I do not know what my parents named me – I have no way of finding that out either. When I asked some of my relatives as I was writing this, none of them knew. I guess my parents must have lovingly called me 'anyog' for some time, as people often call babies in my region. When I was recognised as a reincarnation, I was given the name Lobsang Tenzin Phelgye.

It came as a surprise to my parents that so many monks belonging to the Gelukpa sect were visiting them in their nomad's tent. My parents belonged to the Kagyupa sect.[8] And they were nomads whose religious involvement almost ended with visiting and offering prayers at the local monasteries. By and large, it is true that many families in Tibet gave one of their sons to the monastery to become a monk. But this was not a practice among nomads. So, in every way, the tribe felt honoured and surprised to be chosen. When a senior monk declares the incarnation to be the child in a certain household, no questions are asked.

We lived very far away from Doboom Ritro. In those days distance made a major impact on the decisions taken. To reach my parents' area, the horse riders would have taken many days. That the monks, in spite of the long distance, sought out our family made them feel even more honoured and blessed.

My first memories of my childhood are of the hermitage of Doboom Ritro. If I close my eyes, even now, I can see the mountain where Doboom Ritro was located. It faced the east. At the back of the Ritro was a rocky mountain with a cave and plenty of juniper trees. In the front were some green patches of land and a clear stream. There was not much to do in that place. It was quite remote and about an hour's walk from the valley.

Doboom Ritro was a mid-sized establishment consisting of three levels. It was called 'Doboom Rinchen Pungpa' or the treasure palace of Doboom. The top level had a few simple rooms for the lamas who came for retreats. My living quarters, two halls, a chapel and a storeroom were on the second level. On the first level, there was another chapel and quarters for staff. The ground floor was meant for livestock and fodder storage.

The size of the establishment, they said, was directly proportional to the respect the lama enjoyed in the area. Every tulku had his own establishment, usually in the mountains. There were seven tulkus in those days, including the Doboom in the Tashi Dargye Monastery. All of them had separate establishments but they were all attached to the Tashi Dargye Monastery.

The administrative set-up of a tulku establishment is called 'labrang'. The size of the labrang varies with the size of the establishment. My staff consisted of the general manager, Lobsang Namgyal; the maintenance manager, Aku Tsepak; his assistant, Kachey; the babysitter, Nongchung; and my personal attendant, Gaga. Yaya, the head of the nunnery, was also a part of the labrang.

There was also a cook called Jolu and a person called Amchoe who performed simple rituals. They stayed on the first floor. I remember Amchoe very distinctly because his handwriting was clear and elegant. I have preserved one of his handwritten prayer books to this day. Karma Dhondup looked after the livestock. He would take them out for grazing and be back by sunset.

I stayed on the second floor only for a short while. When I began running around, my staff was afraid I would fall over the edge of the floor and so built me a single-story residence just below the Ritro. In my newly constructed residence was a biggish hall – a multipurpose hall, so to say. We ate, slept and studied there. There was a separate room for my resident tutor. And there was a kitchen.

There was a beautiful garden lined with flower beds. There was even a makeshift swimming pool for me as I loved playing in the water as a child. It must have been odd that I should want to play with water in a place which was so cold that people hesitated before washing their faces. I loved to sit and pass time in the waters of the pool. They had made the pool in a squarish shape and lined it with slate stones which had been stuck together with some plant material. My friends Yamatso and Pematso would bring water to pour into my swimming pool. Of course, I could not swim in it – it was too small for that. At best it could be visualised as a jacuzzi pool.

That this love for water would remain with me was something none of us knew at that time.

3

Growing Up

There were three of them – Yamatso, her sister Pematso and their brother Karma Dhondup – who looked after the livestock. They were from a humble background. When they were very young, someone brought them to the Doboom Ritro asking if the labrang could look after them since their parents were no more. It was a common practice that when parents were not able to look after their children, they offered them to the hermitage.

The youngest of the three, Yamatso, was my best friend and she would help me carry pebbles to make small mud castles. I was not always nice to her, though. Sometimes I even made her cry. But she would always be on my side, whereas her brother and sister were not so easy to handle. If they got annoyed with me, they would go away and stop playing with me. In fact, before I left for Drepung Monastery, Karma Dhondup went missing.

We did not know where he had gone. We thought he had left for good. But we did find him later. I will come to that in time.

I am still in touch with Yamatso. She continues to live in the same place, between Doboom Ritro and the Tashi Dargye Monastery, in a village called Khargong. Pematso now lives in Lhasa.

As you can see, I grew up like any other child, very unlike a reincarnated tulku. Normally, tulkus are seen wrapped in silk and brocade from the time when they are very small. I grew up in the lap of nature, playing games with children of my age, with my own share of disagreements with them, too. I liked playing with water and pebbles and would occasionally climb the hill so that I could slide down the sandy slopes. In the evenings, I liked watching the vultures return to settle on the rocks after their day's hunt for food.

Some rabbits and marmots became my friends. I would often spot a rabbit or a marmot suddenly emerging from its hole in the ground. I found them very interesting and could watch them endlessly as they put out their two paws and called *pheepheepheepheephee!* before going back to their burrow. I did not see a marmot for many years after leaving Tibet. I saw one again later, in Switzerland, and their behaviour and call was the same.

There weren't many wild animals in the area as there were no thick forests. There were only jackals and foxes. I could hear them often and see them sometimes. There were plenty of sparrows, magpies, hoopoes, wing-necked pigeons, blackbirds with red beaks, cuckoos, wood thrushes, partridges, owls, kites, eagles and golden vultures. The Tehor region also had musk deer.

Once someone brought me a baby Tibetan roe deer as a gift. I loved playing with it, but it did not live long. Somebody also gave me a white rabbit. I think I was generally inclined to prefer wild creatures. There was a chart with pictures of birds and animals on the wall in my room. I remember browsing through it for hours in fascination.

Animals were an integral part of our environment. This may be evident from a game monks and nuns used to play. In fact, this was the only game they were allowed to play and that too, only on Losar. It was called 'Sa-lam', literally meaning 'the ground and the path', and was based on the Buddhist scheme of spiritual progress, the ten *bhumi*s and the five *marga*s.

The five margas or paths are the path of accumulation, the path of application, the path of seeing, the path of meditation and the path of no more learning. These five paths overlap. When I do something good, the merit that I accrue accumulates. That is the first path. The second path is to apply the power of meditation. The third path is the place from where the first bhumi starts. The bhumis are levels of realisation. Beginning with the third path, that is, the path of seeing, it expands and intensifies with every subsequent bhumi. After the tenth bhumi is the land of the Buddha – Buddha bhumi.

In the game of Sa-lam, one player after another throws the dice and moves his or her counter. They may land on a path leading up or be taken down to be reborn as an animal or even reach the bottom of hell. And so the path of spiritual progress was taught even before the participants truly understood it theoretically.[9]

As is true for people and cultures across the world, we too had our share of stories of spirits. One incident remains in my memory of those times. I was not even seven years old. It was dark and we were going to bed when suddenly we felt we were hearing goats bleat. But we knew there were no goats around. Where was the sound coming from? When elders were consulted, they told us of a possible reason – on the other side of the river, in the valley of Tashi Dargye, was a much smaller place for meditation called

Yokhyi Ritro that had at one time been associated with Doboom Ritro. Its local deity was Vajrasadhu or Damchen Garnag (meaning the 'blacksmith') who was shown riding a goat. They said the deity had come to our area because its own place had been neglected for long and there was no one there to perform propitiatory rites. Long after that, when I was in Tibet House in New Delhi, I learned from Denma Locho Rinpoche, who belongs to the area of my birth, that the local deity of his birthplace was also my birth deity, Jowo Sedpang Dorje. Birth deity refers to a spirit believed to be residing in a mountain, structure or any such place around one's birthplace.

Jowo Sedpang Dorje is said to be another form of Vaishravana or Kubera, the god of wealth. He bears the head of a goat on his human body. I wondered then, that if we were to associate what we had heard that night with supernatural elements, perhaps this was it?

A story that I heard in my childhood that left a deep impression on me was from the Jataka tales depicted on the wooden panels in the smaller of the two halls for prayer assembly in Doboom Ritro. This was a story about the Buddha born as a beautiful deer with golden fur. One day, the story goes, a man was drowning. Hearing his cries for help the deer jumped into the water and dragged him ashore. Beholden, the man fell to his knees and asked the deer how he could repay his kindness. The deer replied, 'You need to do nothing. Just remember, you should never ever tell anyone about me.' The man readily promised that he would tell no one.

It so happened that at about the same time, the queen of the region had a dream. And what should she dream of but a golden deer! She told her husband that since she had dreamt of it, it had to be somewhere around and that he should spare no effort to get it for her. The king was obliged to announce that anyone who could give any information about the location of such a creature would be richly rewarded.

The man who had been saved by the deer also heard the announcement. Greed raised its head. He did not think too much about the promise he had made to the deer. It is almost always true that when we make a resolve, a large temptation comes along to test how firm we are in our resolve. The man succumbed to temptation. He went to the king and revealed that he had seen the golden deer. He even agreed to guide the king's men to the place where he had been rescued and where he had seen the animal. When he took them there and when he spotted the deer, he exclaimed, 'Look, there it is!' At that very moment, his hand fell off from his wrist to the ground. It was divine intervention.

Looking at the paintings in the prayer hall, I would always think of how sinful it was to betray. Betrayal is a heinous act. I do not recall betraying anybody in my life; indeed, I cannot be untruthful and deceiving in my utterances or actions. Besides, I am not at all good at it, even when I might feel the need for such conduct in this often untruthful world.

In the same prayer hall there was also a statue of Goddess Marici in a chariot drawn by seven boars. She is equivalent to the Hindu sun god, Surya Devta, and her mantra is chanted at sunrise to ensure the day goes well. She holds a needle and thread to stitch up the eyes of the enemy. The altar in the larger hall had a statue of Tsongkhapa in the middle, flanked by his two chief disciples. In a corner of the room was a smaller chapel with a statue of Palden Lhamo or Sri Devi Remati. This larger prayer hall was used for occasional assembly of monks and nuns like during new year's day and Ngamchoe, the anniversary of Tsongkhapa.

As I mentioned earlier, there was a nunnery just below the hermitage of Doboom Ritro, under its supervision. There were some 20–30 nuns there. Remember Yaya, who was also a part of my labrang? She was its head. Every morning and afternoon a stone gong would be struck and the nuns had to go into their rooms to chant prayers and meditate until the gong sounded again. Then they would come out and prepare tea and food for themselves. I could see the smoke billowing from the chimney.

The nuns would go to a nearby stream to fetch water for drinking, washing and cooking during their free time, in between the prayer sessions. If relatives came to visit, they had to first get permission from the hermitage and then go to meet them on the other side of the stream where they would share whatever food their relatives had brought. Visitors were not allowed to enter the nunnery premises. Looking back, the rules appear to have been very strict.

Tashi Dargye Monastery was not very far from the Ritro, but it could not be seen from there because it lay behind a curve of the mountain. On the summit of the mountain, behind the hermitage, was the spot people believed was inhabited by the local protector deity, whose name was similar to mine, Amnye Doboom. He is depicted with a white body, riding a white horse, holding a banner in his right hand and a container full of jewels in his left. Monks from Tashi Dargye came once a year to offer incense to him and spent the day there, picnicking.

As a child, there were two events every year that I looked forward to – one was camping in the mountains in the summers and the other was Losar, when the nuns would greet me with homemade cookies, butter and sweets.

I would begin counting the days to the new year long before it actually arrived. I measured the time left by counting how many nights were to be passed before the dawn of the new year. I would say to myself, 'Sleep, get up; sleep again, get up again; sleep again, get up again – and it's new year.'

I enjoyed Losar for many reasons, not the least among them was that I did not have to study for a few days during these holidays. There were no great festivities while celebrating Losar. The maintenance manager Aku Tsepak would come at dawn carrying a butter lamp and tsampa (barley flour) mixed with butter and everyone would throw a bit of tsampa to the sky before eating it.

This was a symbolic offering to the Buddhas and the deities, as His Holiness was to explain to Mao Zedong when he was invited to a new year ceremony during his visit to Beijing in 1955. The Dalai Lama described how Mao responded by throwing some tsampa to the sky himself, and then, with a different expression, throwing some on the floor. Maybe that was for the proletariat.

4

Learning to Become a Monk

My education began very late. I must have been six years old when I began learning to read. I remember people around me remarking it was high time that I started my studies.

For the formal ceremony to mark the beginning of my education, Trungsar Rinpoche, high-ranking lamas from Garze and Dza Choeje from Dza Khog, were specially invited. Preparations to receive them began days before their arrival. The whole area in and around the Ritro was cleaned and spruced up thoroughly. At the entrance, auspicious symbols were drawn in white powder on the ground. These symbols, eight in number, were considered lucky signs – umbrella, golden fish, vase, lotus, conch shell, shreevatsa or the endless note, victory banner and chakra.

I once learnt a verse enumerating these eight symbols. Generally, I never had any problem memorising texts. I just had to chant the text a couple of times, sometimes alone and sometimes in a group, and it would get embedded in my memory. But this verse came with another distinction. It was customary in those days for rich people to invite monks and lamas to their houses and host them for five or seven days. The hosts would request us to conduct a ritual called Yangdrub for prosperity and auspiciousness. It was for this ritual that I learnt to recite the special Tibetan verse on the eight symbols and it never left my mind.

I must explain the meaning of the symbols. The umbrella signifies protection from the heat of negative forces, the goldfish represents the beauty of the eyes of the Mahapurusha or the ideal person,[10] the vase is full of good qualities, the lotus symbolises purity, the conch shell represents the endless teachings of enlightened people, the shreevatsa represents the endless collection of good qualities, the victory banner represents triumph over the negative forces and the chakra is the Dharma chakra or the wheel of Dharma.

It was natural that when the ceremonial teaching was to begin, all these auspicious symbols were drawn. It was arranged that on the first day, the senior lama, Trungsar Rinpoche, would teach me the first four letters of the alphabet – *ka, kha, ga, nga* – and the next day, Dza Choeje would teach me the next four – *ca, cha, ja, nya*. I was quick at grasping things, so on the second day, when the lama began with *ca, cha, ja, nya*, I repeated them after him and went on to recite the letters of the third row, *ta, tha, da, na*, as I had heard them before. This aroused a good laugh from the teacher.

My main studies started soon after. Geshe Yama Choephel was appointed as my home tutor. Yes, his name was Yama, after the god of Death, Yamraj. Traditionally, particularly in the Kham region, if a child died, the next one was named Yama. That was not only a reminder of the earlier baby but also a remedy for death itself, in the sense that people believed that by naming the younger child Yama, they would be able to ward off the god of Death.

Though he always looked grim, Geshe Yama Choephel was a good person. He was of medium height and build and had an impressive moustache. Impressive in the sense that it was not very bushy or long, but it was very well maintained. He never played with me, but neither did he ever scold or beat me. He always sat next to my bed to keep an eye on me and I can definitely say I was happier when he left the room, even for a short while.

Geshe Yama Choephel was not one of the most learned persons in the region. He had acquired a geshe degree from Loseling Monastery in Central Tibet more as a reward for success in a mission in which he was sent along with a senior monk to the northern plateau to raise funds. And yet, though he was neither famous nor a scholar of great repute, I realised his knowledge of literature and Buddhist philosophy was appreciable. I still have some of the texts composed by him, written as a long-life prayer for a lama of Dargye Monastery and to appease local deities.

Geshe Yama Choephel slept in the room next to mine. He would wake up early and prepare the offerings needed at the altar. As soon as I woke up, we would have tea and tsampa and then the morning sessions would begin. We did not possess any clock or watch. All our sense of time was drawn from the position of the sun.

The nunnery downhill would sound its gong to announce the beginning of its meditation sessions. We would also sound a small gong at the Ritro and begin our morning prayers. Similarly, a gong would announce the completion of its sessions in the nunnery and we would follow suit.

Geshe Yama Choephel led the prayer session every morning and the rest of us joined in. We sat cross-legged for the prayers. That was how we sat at all times. Even today, if you go to a monk's room in any monastery in India or Tibet, the monk will sit cross-legged either on the floor or on his bed.

The worship would commence with the invocation of Enlightened Beings, drawing their attention and requesting them in the prayer, 'Please come here. Be present here. Accept my offerings,' and so on. The interesting aspect of this ritual is that the Enlightened Beings are visualised as reflected in the mirror and a ritual bath is given by pouring water on the mirror. Prayers are chanted throughout the two stages of worship – the invocation and the rite of the ritual bath.

While in prayer, we imagine that the Enlightened Beings have arrived and are present before us. There are many kinds of offerings we can make to them, but the most common one is to offer them a ritual bath. This is conducted with a mirror, using a pot from which we pour water. First, we show the mirror to the statues and the scriptures arranged in the room and then pour water on the mirror saying, 'Enlightened Beings have no dirt but for my own sake, for the sake of cleaning my body, speech and mind (*kaya, vak, chitta*), I offer this.' After chanting several shlokas, we wipe off the water. In this ritual, we treat the idols before us as the actual Enlightened Beings. So we are gentle and offer all the variety in the worship as we would to a living being. That is the spirit of the ritual. The ritual becomes very extensive if the worshipper adorns the beings with ointments, new clothes, ornaments and so on, and the entire process is visualised in the mind.

Mental worship requires great concentration. It is done every morning so it serves two purposes. First, the day starts with the ritual as a discipline. This gives focus to our life and creates a calm atmosphere. The second purpose is to make us familiar with the verses and learn them. Today when I say the same prayers, I understand the meaning of the verses and the experience is different. The meaning of the verses is very deep. The import of it all is to say that you, the Enlightened Beings, do not need any of these offerings but 'I am offering them for my sake, to cleanse myself.'

Taking refuge in the Buddha Dharma Sangha[11] and generating the boddhichitta[12] in our minds, we also perform a saptanga prayer. This translates into English as the 'Prayer of Seven Limbs' – 'sapta' means 'seven' and 'anga' means 'limbs' in Sanskrit. I prefer to call it the 'Prayer of Seven Bodies'.

The prayer begins with a prostration followed by an offering. The third step is a declaration of our wrong deeds or a confession, followed by rejoicing in the good deeds of the Enlightened Beings, then requesting the Buddhas to light the lamp of Dharma. The next step is entreating the Enlightened Beings to remain with the worshipper for countless ages. The last is the dedication of all good deeds for the attainment of Buddhahood.

The idea of the routine I was made to follow was that I should learn all these rituals thoroughly, without having to memorise them, by observing them daily. After prayers came memorisation of root texts from the scriptures that would later form the main subject of monastic study.

There were breaks for meals and tea and also for some running around in the garden. When the sun set, there was a short session of prayers, followed by supper. The evening prayers were mainly offerings to the Dharmapalas or the protectors of Dharma, especially Palden Lhamo, that is, Sri Devi Remati, asking for protection from hindrances in the process of learning and practising Dharma in our everyday activities.

There were five boys around my age who came to study with me and became my playmates. Of them, Sonam Dhondup, is still with me. Lobsang and his brothers Tenzin Choegyal and Yigha, are now businessmen in Kathmandu. The fifth boy, Joga, died in Nepal some years ago.

My diet consisted mainly of dairy products like curd and milk, butter tea, dry meat and homemade cookies. The only vegetables available throughout the year were radish, turnips and potatoes. They were stocked underground to retain their freshness and to prevent them from getting frozen in the winter.

Each meal consisted of tea, wheat bread, tsampa made of barley flour and dried meat, be it breakfast, lunch or dinner. However, for dinner we often had one variation – a broth called 'thukpa' which gave warmth during cold days. And there was a special snack that others around me would have. It was a summer special because the mushrooms from which it was made would sprout out of the earth only when there was thunder and lightning in the summer months. These mushrooms were gathered, cleaned and then roasted directly on the fire while being held upside down. When the mushrooms were hot and burning, they would be pulled out of the fire and some butter would be spread on them.

The mushrooms were delicious, but my elders would not let me have them since they were scared they would upset my stomach. Sonam would have them and so would all others. I could not have them though I loved them very much. The one person who understood my desire was Sonam Dhondup. He would take two handfuls of mushrooms, eat a few, take the remaining in his cupped palms and move out of the building. He would place them on one of the stones of the boundary wall. After class I would sneak out, eat them all and walk in, looking innocent.

Being a cold country, we had a huge pot full of tea, always boiling on a stove that was fuelled by dried yak dung. Adjacent to the boiling pot was a cove which was used to store the dried dung. Before going to bed, the teapot was covered up to the neck with fiery red embers from the fire to keep it warm through the night. The tea was quite strong since it never stopped boiling, but that was the way everyone liked it. Water and tea leaves would be added to the teapot every now and then.

The boiling pot provided us with other opportunities too, such as boiling eggs. We would pierce a small hole on the top of an egg, tie a string in the middle of a thin sliver of wood and insert it into the hole. This way we could hold up the egg with the string. We would dip this dangling egg into the pot of boiling tea and let it cook. At times, the egg would break and the tea would have an egg floating in it. It took many such misadventures before the elders figured out what that errant white floating substance in the tea was.

Besides my home tutor, there was another elderly monk with me. He had been a disciple of the previous Doboom. His name was Tagtrug Dorjee and I lovingly call him 'Gaga' which means 'beloved one'. He was my personal attendant. Gaga was actually like a real father to me. He was always there with me while my father visited only a couple of times. In those days, there were no motorable roads and coming on horseback took a week or more from my birthplace, so my father's visits were rare. Both my home tutor and Gaga were very kind to me.

It is a common belief that young tulkus should have very strict and harsh home tutors by their side all the time. This constant supervision helps the tulkus progress well in their studies and their conduct becomes as refined as possible. But in my case, whether at the hermitage or the monasteries of Tashi Dargye and Drepung, my tutors were all very gentle and compassionate. I can remember only very few instances when they used harsh words or physical violence. This might also have been because I was not a naughty boy and was quick at learning. Of course, like many children, I was quite lazy.

A monk called Gen Thubten from Tashi Dargye Monastery used to come for retreat to the hermitage. In many ways, he was extremely good at teaching and making learning joyful. He became very friendly with me and I started regarding him as one of my teachers. He was extremely skilful in teaching and inspiring small children. He was also skilful with his hands, for example, he once made a 'telephone' by covering two small earthen pots with thick paper and stringing them together. He was very good at making and flying kites. Once he taught me a prayer to help in kite-flying. When there was no adequate wind for flying a kite, the following verses could be recited to invoke the Wind God:

O Vayu devta, the lord of wind, of the north-west
Mounted on a deer, holding a wind banner
Surrounded by a hundred thousand wind gods
Come here and wave a gentle wind.

Of course, now I know this is from the invocation of the ten Dikshapalas in Mahakala Sadhana to which he had made a slight change to suit the requirement of wind. I also know that Vayu Devta is a Vedic god in Hinduism.

Gen Thubten once fashioned a *saling*, a little clay flute with four holes. Years later, in 1992, when I went to Peru, I visited a place inhabited by descendants of the Incas. They had an almost identical flute like the saling and I bought it straightaway, remembering Gen Thubten's flute.

There were other interesting aspects of my life which bring a smile to my lips when I think of them today. First, let me tell you about my first encounter with jam. Yes, jam!

We lived a fairly secluded life and knew little about the world outside. I had heard of Kalimpong and Calcutta in India in the context of trade, and places in China from where goods were brought. Living in a remote place with few contacts with the outside world, anything foreign evoked a lot of curiosity. Once, when somebody presented me with a bottle of jam, nobody in the Ritro had any idea what to do with it. What was it? We had no idea that it was to be spread on bread. So Gaga would give me a spoonful every day, thinking it was like a tonic. I happily ate the tasty gel and would look forward to it.

Somebody brought me a toy piano on which I struck my fingers just to produce some sounds. I feel I might have developed some skills in music had I continued, but once I started serious studies, there was no time for this. One day, somebody brought a torch, which was a great gadget, but as replacing the batteries was not so easy, I don't remember having used it frequently.

I also remember seeing a cylindrical tin, probably a cigarette container, which displayed the British crown. To me the crown looked like half a vajra until someone told me that it was the crown of the English royals. England was known to us; we called the English people as 'Inji', a word that included Europeans. We had also heard of America, China, Russia and India.

In this context, one incident carries some import. As I kept hearing people talking about the previous Doboom, I could get a feel of him. I even got the feeling of déjà vu when some stories about him were related. I had been told he was short-tempered, but his anger did not last very long. I was also told he liked black tea. When I was very young, they gave me butter tea, which I used to like until at some point I felt I had had enough of it and asked for black tea, to which I would add milk myself – English style! The practice was unusual at that time in our area.

Summer was very pleasant, with a wide spread of greenery and wildflowers on the mountainside. We usually went camping for several days, carrying tents to the mountains. I was in the habit of observing the behaviour of insects around the hermitage and in the mountains. I would observe how the birds made their nests. On the mountainside were lakes, where I enjoyed spending time. Even today, my instinctive liking for water makes me think of a beach for a vacation rather than the mountains.

In this part of Kham, there was a tradition of *sonyom* or *b* (literally meaning 'begging') at harvest time, when tulku around the area along with their complete entourage. The region in Kham, where I was living, was particularly well k for very good harvests. We visited four or five village day and finally halted for the night in a house which offe hospitability. This went on for a couple of weeks at a stretc

We spent the nights with the families who were the supporters of the Ritro. People offered us grain; dependi their wealth and on their closeness to a particular lama, som a plateful of barley or wheat, some gave a basket of barley, and gram, and some others, the most prosperous ones, gave of barley, wheat and gram. Every family gave something, ho small, to the lama. The lama never returned empty-handed. families invited the lama for tea and he was expected to con short ceremony for the consecration of the family altar an blessings to the family and their relatives before leaving.

The practice of seeking alms started in India in the ti the Buddha. In those days, monks walked through the vi barefoot to seek alms for the day. As time passed, both the and nature of the practice changed. In my time, an entire ca of horse riders would go in a procession. The families at homes we spent the night expected us to give longevity ble before departing the next morning, so I know the tex longevity, the *Amitayus Tsewang*, by heart.

The practice of sonyom brought us grains, which tool of our food for the whole year. Some monks from the were invited to perform ritual worship in homes and offe little money. The general manager of the labrang was sup to do some business and bigger labrangs did bigger bus like importing tea from China and sending it onwards to L Later, modern devices like the toothbrush also became pro for business. Bigger labrangs were rich because of all the bu they did. Ours was a small-to-mid-sized labrang. All the

labrangs of Dargye Monastery were middle or small. None of them was rich when compared to some other labrangs of Kham and Amdo.

While still at the Doboom Ritro, I attended a series of ceremonies at the Dargye Monastery. The local monasteries had a tradition of inviting tulkus to preside over festivals. When I was about ten years old, I was invited by Tashi Dargye Monastery to preside over the Monlam Festival the next year. This festival, in the first month of the Tibetan calendar, lasts two weeks. It is still a very important festival both within and outside Tibet.

It was Tsongkhapa who had started celebrations of Monlam in Lhasa to commemorate the Buddha's miraculous performances at Sravasti. It is said that many non-believers in Buddhism had gathered and in their midst the Buddha performed miracles while he elucidated his teachings.

The miracles were awe-inspiring. When he placed a toothpick in the ground, it grew into a huge tree, when he spit out water from his mouth, it turned into a deep lake, when he looked to his sides, mountains rose and so on. He performed miracles for fifteen days and also delivered his teachings. The last miracle was when he made food appear and fed all the people gathered. When their minds and bodies were thus full, the Buddha told them why there was such misery in the world. Through his blessings they realised that their misery was self-inflicted, by their own deeds and they came to hold great faith in the Buddha and the Dharma.

These miracles are depicted in archaeological findings in many Buddhist shrines and the festival is celebrated all over Tibet. To preside over the festival was a great prestige. Every morning I had to undertake a session of teaching and in the afternoons I had to recite three prayers I knew by rote. Giving teachings meant memorising a few lines and delivering them to make it appear as if I was really teaching. The main challenge

was reciting the three prayers because they were not very short and I was not allowed to keep any text by my side to refer to it. If I got stuck sitting on that high throne in front of all those people – the thought scared me.

At that time I did not know that, if stuck, I should not show that I had forgotten something and instead move on to a passage I remembered, for the majority of people would not notice. But I was not smart enough to think of that then. Luckily, I did not have to face such an embarrassment.

A year or two later, I presided over Tsogchod, which commemorates the 5th Dalai Lama and is second in importance to Monlam. The burden of recitation and challenges of memorisation were of the same level as earlier. I still remember the first line of the text of the *Lam-rim* I used for the morning teaching – a salutation to the Buddha, '*Namo guru munindraye*' or salutations to the king of monks. Gen Thubten had explained to me the enunciation and meaning of the Sanskrit words.

The Tsogchod festival was immediately followed by yet another ceremony called 'Jangwa' – purification for the deceased ones – lasting a couple of days. I also presided over an annual event where people gathered in one of the larger villages and a group recited the Mani Mantra. I was asked to preside over the 'shower of auspiciousness', an annual consecration ceremony performed in an elaborate manner in the tantra hall, lasting three days and ending with a *homa* or fire puja. Since it was a tantric ritual, I was required to have completed a retreat, or the chanting of mantras which usually takes a few weeks or a month, but I did an abbreviated retreat along with my home tutor and learned the mudras to go with the ritual texts. The sadhana used was the 13-Deity Yamantaka.[13] What my elder helpers were most worried about was that I would be holding a vajra in my right hand and a bell in my left, and did not know how to keep the vajra in place with my thumb. When I threw the grain into the sky or the fire, I might accidentally throw the vajra with it and hit someone or let it fall into the fire. So they tied the vajra to my thumb. That was clever on their part.

I remember the melodious chanting of the monks at the assembly. This tantra awakened in me a feeling of inspiration and the feeling has endured.

5

Learning in the Hermitage

We travelled leisurely on horseback for an entire day. We were going to Garze for my initiation as a novice. In Sanskrit the word for novice is 'shramanera' and in Tibetan the equivalent is 'getsul'. Trungsar Rinpoche was to initiate me at his hermitage near the Garze Monastery.

Today we can reach Garze from Doboom Ritro in half an hour by a motor vehicle. Garze is now the name of not just a huge town but of a whole area – the Garze Tibetan Autonomous Prefecture. Tibet in those days was different. Most houses, even of the richest persons, were small, with a maximum of three floors. Of course, I am not talking about the big temples and monasteries. There were hardly any roads and the paths that horses trod on were dusty and rough.

My entourage and I enjoyed our time in Garze as we had gone as guests of the Trungsar Labrang. We were looked after with care and fed exotic and lavish food. I particularly remember the yoghurt they served every night before bedtime. It was truly delicious and I enjoyed it.

The ordination itself was a simple procedure with just three candidates – Nyaluzhab Tulku from Tawu Monastery, a monk from Garze named Gyurme and I. The whole ceremony took about an hour. My people suggested I strictly follow all the rules of the ordination for at least a week. These rules included making lunch the only heavy meal. During the day, I was not supposed to eat any solid food after lunch. This was a little difficult, not that I felt terribly hungry, but I felt a kind of a vacuum psychologically.

Gelukpa monks are expected to spend three or four years studying in one of the major monasteries in central Tibet. Depending on the monastery they are affiliated with, they spend at least four years in the Drepung Monastery or three years in the Sera Monastery in order to be recognised as a full-fledged monk upon returning home. To do so, monks from the Dargye area, as a rule, spend a year at Dargye Monastery, studying preliminary philosophical texts before going to Lhasa. This year-long study at the Dargye Monastery lays the foundation for future studies. So, when I was about eleven years old, I joined the Dargye Monastery. I participated in the *chora* (literally, 'Dharma court') and also started my preliminary studies.

There were sessions for recitations as well as debates in the chora. My main teacher was Gen Thubten, who guided me in learning definitions of various things, starting with the sense of vision – the four primary colours (blue, yellow, white and red), how other colours were formed by combining these basic ones and the forms of appearances grasped by the eye in terms of length and shape, whether the objects were high or low, straight or otherwise. Similarly, we were taught the objects of the other senses and the qualities grasped by the senses.

These concepts were not as simple as they appear. They actually gave an understanding of the world. And from there we moved to more complex things like the definitions of existence and of a human being. The definition of a human being was very interesting to me. Thinking of it now, this definition, something every monk knows, has a deeper meaning because the text says,

'The one who can speak and can understand.' In this context, 'to speak' does not just mean 'can utter words and phrases', but the ability to convey an idea or a thought; 'to understand' means not just to know whether, say, the food is good or bad, but to understand the situation relevant to the subject of reference – to communicate and understand contextually and fully.

There were two sessions, one in the morning and the other in the evening. For beginners, the morning sessions served as the basis for debate which followed in the evening sessions. Often a debate went something like this:

What is the definition of colour?
That which can be perceived as a colour.
How many primary colours are there?
Four.
Name them.
Blue, yellow, white and red.
Does white represent all the colours?
No.
Why?
Because there are colours which are not white.
Such as?
The colour of the Amoghasiddhi Buddha (green).

It was considered auspicious to mention Amoghasiddhi Buddha because the name means 'accomplishment of purpose'. Amoghasiddhi Buddha is one of the five wisdom Buddhas. These five Buddhas are the personifications of the enlightened qualities, which act as opponents of the five basic delusions. They are the central figures of many mandalas. For example, in the centre is Akhyobaya Buddha who is dark blue and against hatred, to the east is Vairocana in white against ignorance, to the south is Ratnasambhava in yellow against pride and miserliness, to the west is Amitabha in red against attachment and to the north is Amoghasiddhi for accomplishment of the Buddhist path and guarding against jealousy.

In Vajrayana Buddhism these are personifications of enlightened qualities. We live with our follies. There should be something that counters them. The purpose of imagining enlightened qualities as entities is to make it easy for the common people to understand them, rather than leave them as abstract intellectual concepts.

The debate went on, similarly, with each colour. For example, in the question about the colour red, when asked 'Are all colours red?' the reply was, 'No, for example, the conch shell.' In this manner, the way of debating was learnt. The use and symbolism of auspicious words was also thus cultivated in the learner.

The debating sessions were held in the evenings and that meant it was dark by the time the sessions got over. The hall where we sat for our debates was illumined by candles or butter lamps. There was no electricity in those days, nor were there many torches. Remember how my torch had fallen into disuse because of the lack of batteries? To get back to our rooms from there, we had to make our way in the dark. But tulkus had an advantage – lanterns were carried outdoors for tulkus. They were meant only for the tulkus, not for or to be carried by the average monk. Hence, lanterns were a status symbol for tulkus.

Around this time, I received the first teaching on *Lam-rim* from a very renowned ex-abbot of the Dargye Monastery, Gen Rinpoche Jampa Khedub, who had studied at Sera. He had promoted the tradition of studying philosophical texts in the monastery. Before him there had been traditions of rituals and so on. Some wealthy senior monks had even indulged in trade for personal wealth and owned horses that they stabled in the monastery. Such things gradually changed under Gen Rinpoche's influence. I came to know he had lived until the Cultural Revolution and died in a prison.

The rhythmic chanting of the guru lineage prayer before each session of the teaching was very inspiring. I particularly remember that Gen Rinpoche had a small ceramic pot with a spout, inside which I believe there were raisins soaked in water. He kept sipping this water so that his throat did not become dry. As a child, I wanted to do the same thing very much. I got a similar pot and kept imitating him.

The teaching of *Lam-rim* was requested and sponsored by Doboom Labrang. The teaching went on for a month or so. In the front row there would be six tulkus of my age group from the monasteries around Dargye. But as a child, I could not comprehend much. However, the tradition held that by just sitting there and hearing the teaching, a person received its transmission and imbibed it.

At the close of the annual summer retreat, the monastery held its annual picnic, which went on for a week or longer. In the wide plains behind the monastery, a huge tent was pitched for the monks to assemble. Around this were the tents of the tulkus with their attendants, and the well-to-do monks had their own, smaller tents. Other monks would walk back to the monastery at night and return in the morning. Those who could afford to camp would light their tents with lamps or candles and a few used gaslights that could be distinguished from afar as a symbol of wealth.

There was also a large space created for *lhamo* or opera dances, surrounded by tents for actors to dress and a large viewers' tent. During the day, a group from the monastery would perform lhamo, based on the stories of the kings Norbu Sangpo and Drimed Kunden, which were similar to and perhaps adaptations of the Sanskrit tales of Sudhana and Manohara and Harishchandra.

During the performance, the narrator stood in the centre, reading out the story. Unique to this art was the *namthar* song or operatic singing, where the actor drew out each syllable in waves, the chorus providing support when he paused to catch his breath. Performances were often modelled on those by different troupes from Central Tibet. Masks and costumes were made within the monastery. Although monks also played the women's parts, since the word 'lhamo' means 'goddess', it may be that when this dance form was invented by Thangtong Gyalpo in the fifteenth century in U-Tsang province of Tibet, there were more women performers than men.

Another large annual event in the Tashi Dargye Monastery was the Cham dance, which was held towards the end of the Tibetan year (December–January). It was also an important social event because virtually everybody from the villages around made it a point to attend. Tulkus were given a special place for viewing and the best of food was served to them. There would be one day of rehearsal, followed by three full days of performances. The costume on the first day would be best described as monks' dresses of the finest quality, such as a brocade tonga; the second and third days' performances were in full costume and on the third day special kinds of gilded masks were worn. During the intervals when costumes were being changed, jesters would amuse the audience, mimicking people known to the audience, such as those in the monastery's managing staff. The event ended with the ritual of *torma* throwing, when a twenty-foot sculpture made of tsampa was cast into a specially prepared structure of dry grass, which was then burned to symbolise the destruction of negative forces.

On the last day we had to reach there at dawn, when the performer acting the part of Gonpo Dramzug or Brahmanarupa Mahakala proclaimed the power and greatness of the monastery. Even as a child I used to enjoy this spectacle. Decades later, once I sneaked out from a hospital in Chennai to take a walk in the streets in my hospital clothes when I came upon a huge crowd before a cinema hall and for no particular reason, there entered in my mind the scene of Brahmanarupa Mahakala with his costume, mask, topknot of long white hair and a long beard. Suddenly, from amid the noise of the crowd, I heard what sounded like a high-pitched call, 'Rinpoche!' from behind me. I knew there was no one there who would call me so, but when I looked behind me, I saw a tall sadhu, just like Gonpo Dramzug with a long white beard and hair tied on his head in a knot. It made my hair stand on edge in trepidation and excitement. What created such a mix of feelings was that when I turned back to look at the figure again, it had disappeared. I do not suggest this was a supernatural incident, nor am I superstitious, but it was certainly a rare coincidence.

Other than being given a special seat in monks' assemblies and being exempted from physical labour like fetching water and sweeping the floor, tulkus were not treated differently from other students. The Dargye Monastery was exemplary in that, among the seven tulkus, no one was placed above the other. Seating arrangements were according to seniority, but no one was higher than the other and no one held the power of administration or running the monastery. Elsewhere in Kham, as also in Amdo and other parts of Tibet, there was a system of hierarchy that eventually led to discontent and divisions. People naturally respected tulkus more than other learned monks, irrespective of whether the tulkus were learned or not. Since in the Dargye Monastery no lama was the head lama, there was plenty of scope for the monastery to function like a modern democratic system.

The monastery's administrative committee comprised two senior monks from each of the three sub-divisions in Tehor Dargye (a sub-region of Tehor) affiliated with it. These six monks, along with the Lama Tripa (head of monastic administration) and the Gekoe (disciplinarian), formed the regular working committee. Other senior monks who had formerly held significant positions were also called for meetings if an important issue arose, such as a conflict with neighbouring monasteries or dealing with the Chinese. The decisions were made, more or less, democratically, with tulkus having no role except, if sought, in an advisory capacity or sometimes to use divination. This avoided a situation where there was one senior lama at the top and, naturally, a danger of his becoming authoritarian. The selection of monks from each of the sub-divisions also satisfied everyone and provided a sense of equality.

Another positive feature of the Dargye Monastery was that it did not have an oracle, unlike some others, including some nearby monasteries. I found later that in many cases such oracles played a major role in crucial situations and sometimes created conflicts and confusion. But the monastery did have its own protector deity for each locality. The deity, Aku Dalha or Uncle Warrior, was represented as a typical Khampa warrior riding a horse, holding a spear in his right hand and a noose in his left. Monks tended to rely on him in all crises, propitiating him before proceeding on any mission. There were many stories of how he had helped people overcome difficulties.

I had a fixed seat during the afternoon chanting sessions in the Dharma court, from where I could see a painting of Dakini Simhamukha on the opposite wall. Since then, I have seen many other paintings of the lion-headed female deity, but I remember this one vividly because though its face was coloured white in keeping with the Tibetan notion of a snow lion, its hair was green. I took it to be just the imagination of some Tibetan painter, but decades later, when visiting an old Hindu temple of Vishnu on the way while travelling from Thiruvananthapuram to Kanyakumari, I saw a similar lion-headed female deity with a white face but yellowish-brown hair, which made me think the Tibetan iconography was somehow linked to some ancient Indian tradition.

Tashi Dargye Monastery was in the middle of a valley, facing the road, with a big river named Zachu flowing at the rear. Of late, Chinese trucks had started to come to lay a road in front of the monastery. Sometimes when I went to the river, I could see tree trunks floating down. Further up the forest, the Chinese were felling trees for use in construction, throwing the trunks for the river to carry down, some of which got stuck by the banks. If I came out after dusk and looked across to the other side of the valley, there was a point from where the headlights of Chinese military trucks fell directly on a small glass fixed to the window of my room in the monastery. I must have shown some interest in these trucks, for a monk who was very skilled with his hands made a small wooden model for me that looked exactly like a dark green Chinese army truck. I played with it in the corridors.

It was also at this time that I saw a telephone for the first time. The Chinese were setting up a telephone line for their exclusive use. I saw some of them using a black instrument which looked to me like a yak's horn. However, I did not have any interaction with the Chinese. They were mainly road-layers who were probably from the People's Liberation Army (PLA).

Part II

LHASA (1954–59)

6

Moving to Lhasa

I did not turn back to take one more look. Would that have helped soothe my feelings? I do not know. I was leaving for Lhasa. Leaving Doboom Ritro.

It was natural that within a year of being at the Dargye Monastery, I should go to the Drepung Monastery in Lhasa. I did not realise at that time that this would bring about a major change in my life.

Let me tell you how this came about. An auspicious day was fixed for us to leave for Lhasa. The actual journey was undertaken a few days later, but on that day we made a symbolic departure and camped in a tent just below the Doboom Ritro for three days. This gave us the advantage of fetching things that we might have forgotten to carry along for the journey. On the actual day of departure, a farewell function was arranged for me by the monastery in the hall above the main temple, which all the tulkus, geshes and senior monks attended. Butter tea and steamed sweet rice with dry fruits were served. I remember Kushok Tripa Rinpoche made a speech, gave me a khatag and emphasised that I should do well in my studies and be mindful of my conduct at Lhasa.

All preparations had been made. Our caravan would have five groups. When the time came to leave, I happily went ahead, not bothering to look back. This was the last time I was to see Dargye Monastery of that era as subsequently, major changes took place due to Chinese occupation.

More than fifty years later, a small part of what was so familiar at that time and then almost forgotten, came back to me in a most unexpected manner. My friend Venerable Olande Ananda, a Dutch Buddhist monk who was ordained in Sri Lanka, went on a visit to Tibet. He made a special trip to Tashi Dargye. Venerable Ananda had to face many difficulties before reaching the Dargye Monastery as there was some confusion on the part of his guide. The first time, they missed Dargye Monastery and had to return all the way back from Derge, another area in the same province.

Once Venerable Ananda reached the Dargye Monastery, he made a special effort to go to the ruins of Doboom Ritro on foot. I felt sorry that nobody in Dargye Monastery cared to arrange a pony for him. When he reached the valley, he visited the family which had kept the belongings of Doboom Ritro safely. They were faithful devotees of mine. They had been taking care of some valuable religious relics such as a few thangka paintings, a bundle of manuscripts, some statues and the bed that was used by the previous Doboom.

On his mobile phone, Venerable Ananda[1] connected me to an old nun in the family. The nun was happy to speak to me and offered to send me anything I wanted from the collection. When Ananda asked me what he should bring back, I asked him to get me some thangka paintings and a few manuscripts. He took the risk of facing trouble at the airport and brought back five timeworn thangka paintings. Three of them were of Sri Devi Remati and the other two were of Bektse and Brahmana. They were handed to me in Bengaluru when I was there for a programme with Dargye monks at the study centre of Krishnamurti Foundation. I arranged a special prayer to welcome them and thanked Venerable Ananda profusely. I felt a great sense of achievement.

When I was leaving for Lhasa from Dargye, the motorable road had just opened and only army trucks were using it. Traditionally there were three routes, the first a short one with many passes, the second longer but easier to travel and the third was via the northern grasslands which took several months to traverse. This was used by traders bringing tea from China on yaks because there was plenty of pasture land on the way for the pack animals. We took the second route, which took something like two months. We did have to cross some passes, but they were not very difficult.

In my group were my home tutor, my personal attendant and a trader. There were also four attendants to take care of the mules, load and unload baggage and pitch tents. Our routine was to set out well before sunrise. Sometime after sunrise we would halt, make tea and have a breakfast of tsampa before starting again. The caravan would then stop around noon at a place where there was pasture, pitch tents and stay there for the day so that the horses and mules could graze and rest.

The horses and mules with their loads travelled in a single file. Usually, an able-bodied mule whose head was specially decorated was at the front of the line, led by a young boy with a good voice for singing, who chanted from time to time, '*Oooooooh sho sho sho sho*...'. The 'ooh' was long and drawn out. The 'sho sho sho (come come come)' was short. People would get down from their horses from time to time and walk so that the horses were not too burdened, but I rode most of the time.

The leader of the group decided where to the halt for the night. Everyone was pleased if the stopping place was a pleasant meadow. Each group then quickly unloaded its baggage, gathered wood and lit a fire for tea. Getting tea ready first would often turn into a competition. Whichever group's tea boiled first would take a ladle and throw a little of it towards the sky, calling out, 'Cho sho!' or, 'To the guardian!' Then the tent was pitched and the seating arrangements organised quickly, for experienced travellers did everything promptly.

The sight of the fire being lit at dusk was delightful because I knew that thukpa, a thick broth made of wheat flour, radish and meat, would soon be ready. We carried tsampa, dry meat and homemade cookies as provisions. We would sleep very early, as there were very few lamps and because we had to get up early.

Talking of lamps, we did not have electricity in those days in Doboom Ritro. So lighting of lamps was an offering and also a necessity in our daily lives. However, there was a difference. Those who could afford it would have gas lamps. They would go to the Chinese border and buy these lamps. We did not have one. We ate early and went to bed early for there was little else to do in the dark. We slept wearing thick robes to protect ourselves from the cold.

As for baths, in the winters we rarely got to bathe. Washing hands was a must since offerings had to be made. In the summers we went down to the river and had a bath. If we washed our robes, it took weeks or months to dry, so we had to be careful about that, too. We did not have soap. We used salt that was found collecting around the rivers in northern Tibet. It was a kind of a chemical. We had dry toilets while most people used the fields. While travelling, we did not have to worry about such facilities as a good bathroom.

Finally, we arrived in the Lhasa valley. At the city limits of Lhasa, a reception was arranged by Drepung Tehor Khangtsen.

7

The Title of Tsogchen Tulku

As I stood before the huge bronze statue of the Buddha in Jokhang, the main temple at Lhasa, my mind automatically recited these five verses:

It is by the grace of the Guru that I came across
the teachings of the all-surpassing teacher, the Buddha.
May all the beings be guided by the Sublime Guru.
To that I dedicate this merit.

May the teachings of the Benevolent One, the Buddha, be never shaken
by the wind of wrong notions.
May there be great many people, who having realised the mode of teaching,
gain faith in the Teacher.

May I never be at a loss in upholding
the system of the monk elucidating the teachings
of existing inter-relatedly,
even at the risk of deprivation of my body and life.

May I spend days and nights
contemplating the methods of promoting the teachings
found by the guiding Buddha
with immense hardship in his past lives.

When I strive for the cause of Buddha Dharma, with pure motivation,
may the Brahma, the Indra, the Lokapalas
and the Black Lord and other protectors of the Dharma
be always supportive.

My root guru in Kham was Gen Rinpoche Jampa Khedub. His advice to me during my last meeting with him before my departure to Lhasa was that whenever I went to see a statue of the Buddha, I should recite this prayer of five verses written by Je Tsongkhapa. Even today, wherever and whenever I visit a shrine of the Buddha, these lines immediately and instinctively arise in my mind.

I must explain who a root guru is. In my understanding, the root guru is the guru who inspires you the most. He or she is responsible for taking you to the right path. Sometimes the guru from whom you receive tantric initiation on the path of enlightenment is also called the root guru. It can also be the guru who initiated you into the sangha. Therefore, there need not be just one root guru.

The temple at Jokhang was built by Songtsen Gampo, the thirty-third king of Tibet. He had married a Chinese princess and it is believed that the central statue was brought as an imperial gift in the seventh century CE. The temple had an inner and outer circumambulation path. The outer path, called Barkor Street, was lined with shops and was the main shopping area of Lhasa in those days. A person had to go through Barkor Street to reach Jokhang Temple. I had never seen anything like the shopkeepers, including women, waiting for buyers. I looked at everything in wonder.

The PLA or the Chinese troops had arrived in Lhasa around that time. These troops aroused our curiosity. Not knowing the implications of their arrival, we also experienced a little trepidation. I watched with interest a small group of army men marching down the street, ahead of us. Mao Zedong's photographs were already being displayed at many places. A brand new experience lay ahead of me, with only the serene Buddha as the familiar thread.

I must tell you a little about the monasteries of Tibet before I describe to you the welcome we received when we reached Lhasa. The information that follows is a bit difficult to organise but we need to understand the classification that informs the colleges and their administration and resources. Drepung, Sera and Gaden, along with Tashi Lhunpo, were the main seats of the Geluk tradition in Central Tibet. Each of these was a combination of semi-autonomous units called 'dratsang', meaning 'college'. Monks belonged to a monastery only through their membership of a college. There was a standing committee called 'lachi' consisting of all the abbots and ex-abbots of colleges. Lachi was chaired by the seniormost ex-abbot who saw to the overall matters of the monastery. There was no abbot for the whole monastery but only for the individual colleges.

Each dratsang or college had its own administration and resources. Each of them consisted of important residential subunits or hostels known as 'khangtsen', which contained the actual apartments of their monks. The khangtsens had their own administration and, to a degree, their own resources. A monk had to enrol in a specific khangtsen depending on his region of origin. Different khangtsens were affiliated with different colleges. The colleges also often had a regional flavour.

The Drepung Monastery was like a township and had four dratsangs, two major and two relatively small. Under each were many khangtsens. My dratsang, Loseling, had twenty-four khangtsens. I belonged to the Tehor Khangtsen. To simplify this, we may understand it as Loseling being my college and Tehor my hostel.

That is why the reception at the entry to Lhasa was arranged by Drepung Tehor Khangtsen. The disciplinarian[2] and other senior monks arrived, bringing tea, cookies and steamed sweet rice. The disciplinarian was wearing a red upper garment and a jacket with brocade in the front and the back. I was impressed with his attire. In Tashi Dargye Monastery, the disciplinarians wore such garments and were high-ranking officials. So I thought this disciplinarian was also a very high-ranking monk. But then I saw the senior monks ordering him around. Later I found that the disciplinarian of that khangtsen was actually subordinate to the council of monks. The administrative hierarchy in Tehor Khangtsen was a council at the top, two disciplinarians and then the managers.

Arrangements for my stay in Lhasa city had been made by people from my locality. The place was somewhat simple and a bit shabby. It was on the ground floor of a building in the Banagszol area on the edge of Lhasa. This area was inhabited by traders who belonged primarily to the Tehor region. At that time Lhasa was still very small, but to me it seemed huge. I listened wide-eyed as I was told stories of newcomers to Lhasa getting lost in the crowd. Though there were no such crowds in the streets, to my imaginative mind even a gathering of twenty people seemed a crowd.

I must mention two events within a few days of my arrival in Lhasa that affected me very much. My horse, Dragyal, whom I loved very much, was sold off. Seeing him go was heartbreaking. The brownish-yellow animal was majestic and loving and he was taken away from me just as I was taken away from my parents. I would have liked to keep him in the monastery but that was not possible. All the animals were taken away by buyers and I watched sadly as he left. I bid him adieu with a farewell prayer.

The second memorable event was when I spotted a person I knew when I was looking out of the window one day. It was Karma Dhondup, who had gone missing just around the time we were to leave the Ritro. When we had returned from Tashi Dargye to Doboom Ritro, we had found that Karma Dhondup was missing from the Ritro and we had spent a lot of time and effort searching for him. We had not found him. I was surprised to see him in Lhasa looking shamefaced and trying to catch my attention.

He had been sure, when he was in Doboom Ritro, that he would not be a part of my entourage to Lhasa. So he had run away from there and by the time I saw him again in Lhasa, he had gained admission into the same monastery where I was to study. Since he was unlettered, he had to start from scratch. But he did look slightly less shabby and unkempt. In those days, not everyone had access to education. I am talking of the early 1940s. In Lhasa it was different, but in areas like where Karma and I came from, it was more difficult.[3]

Life was not easy for people like Karma Dhondup and his experiences at Lhasa truly educated him. He became a monk in three or four years and went back to the Kham region. He remained there till the Chinese took over. He gave up monkhood during the Cultural Revolution and became a part of the community. He even got married and settled down.

To get back to the beginning of my life in Lhasa, after a day or two we moved to a new accommodation. My home tutor, who had spent some time in Lhasa and Drepung earlier, knew some people and we moved to a very pleasant house which belonged to the manager of the Jokhang Temple. This was the house of a monk who had become rich and behaved like an aristocrat. Coincidentally, the second-most senior monk in the house was to become the disciplinarian of Drepung Loseling a few days later.

We spent several days waiting for an auspicious date to enter the monastery. We were also waiting for the concerned government department to approve the rank of tsogchen tulku for me. While those admitted as ordinary tulkus did not need government approval, middle-ranking tsogchen tulkus were recognised by the government. Above them were tulkus whose predecessors had been rulers of Tibet or received titles from ruling powers. The highest ranking tulkus included reincarnations of the regents ruling between the Dalai Lamas, or those holding the title 'hothogthu', a Mongolian term.

Here it may be remarked that Tibetans, especially lamas, loved titles in foreign languages. The term 'dalai' itself is Mongolian for the word 'ocean'. Again, 'panchen' in documents is written as 'panchen ertini', where 'ertini' is the Mongolian version of the Sanskrit 'ratna', which means the same as 'rinpoche'. But rather than ‘rinpoche’, people prefer to address the Panchen Lama as ‘ertini’. So the title of the Panchen Lama contains three languages in four words – ‘pan’ (the Sanskrit for ‘pandit’), ‘chen’ (Tibetan for ‘great’) and ‘ertini’ (Mongolian) and ‘lama’.

Though the previous Doboom had been an ordinary tulku, my labrang thought it would be good for my education to have a tsogchen rank approved, which entailed having connections in the government and being able to afford the ceremonies at admission. According to the government recognition, tsogchen tulkus were even higher than abbots. In Loseling Monastery, they were seated on a throne, while ordinary tulkus sat on the same level as the others. Tulkus of tsogchen rank and above were expected to take part in government functions, such as the processions accompanying His Holiness the Dalai Lama, where they rode a specially caparisoned horse.

When the government approval eventually arrived, we marched to the Drepung Monastery, five kilometres from Lhasa. The monks of Tehor Khangtsen were again waiting, this time outside the monastery gate. All of us then proceeded to the hall of the khangtsen, where I was made to sit on a throne. As always on a ceremonial occasion, tea and steamed sweet rice were served. I was then taken to the apartment that my predecessor had occupied and which was to be my home for the next six years. It consisted of a multipurpose room for studying, sleeping and dining, a room for the servants, an attached kitchen and something very few houses had – a terrace to sunbathe in winter, while in summer we put up a cloth canopy to protect us from rain. There was even an extra room for storage!

Preparations for the admission ceremony started in full swing. Tsogchen tulkus were called on by the abbot instead of them approaching the abbot for admission. I remember that the old abbot from Gyalrong Khangtsen, Jampel Samphel, came to see me and asked a few simple questions about what I had studied. On the appointed day, a monk-official representing the government arrived with his attendants carrying a pot of tea, supposedly from His Holiness's kitchen. Tea was served and when he put the sacred cord from His Holiness around my neck along with a khatag, I was made to rise from the throne to receive it as a sign of respect to His Holiness's gesture. He then handed me His Holiness's sealed gift, wrapped in red cloth. The gift contained dried fruits and rock sugar. This was how I was conferred the title of tsogchen tulku.

As per the tradition of the admission ceremony, I served tea and distributed money to the monks of the Tsogchen at the general assembly of Drepung Monastery where there were guests from Lhasa and people from Tehor. I also offered money to the monks of my dratsang and khangtsen. The expenditure for all these ceremonies was sponsored mainly by the family of Odong Tsang, one of the major supporters of Doboom Ritro.

After admission, tsogchen tulkus were required to present themselves to His Holiness at Norbulingka at one of the daily ceremonies of serving tea and steamed rice, where monk-officials of the government assembled and where announcements of promotions, demotions or transfers were made. This ceremony was called 'drungja' and lay officials were not required to attend.

The ritual in the presence of His Holiness had well-defined steps that I had to perform. I had to make three prostrations and squat before His Holiness's throne. The chief of His Holiness's kitchen would first pour a little tea from His Holiness's pot into the wooden cup I had with me. I had to drink that, dry my cup with a piece of cloth, put it back in my pocket and make three more prostrations. This ritual was called 'dhuk-sel'. It was said that this ritual originated from the time when ceremonies were sponsored and tea used to be served from the sponsor's home. The practice followed was that before offering the tea to His Holiness, the sponsor tasted it first to show it was clear of poison. I remember doing trial runs of the ritual several days ahead of the event.

I was young, just twelve years old, at the time, but I was overweight and must have looked very clumsy going through the ritual and His Holiness apparently remembered that. Six years later, when He saw me for the first time in India in Kushinagar, his first remark was, 'You were quite fat in Lhasa.'

8

The Routine at Drepung

On the first day at Drepung, my attention was drawn to the prominent statue of Je Jamyang Choeje Tashi Palden, the founder of the Drepung Monastery. He founded the monastery with just seven monks. That image of the statue stayed in my mind and in February 2018 I asked my friend and monk, Gyurme Choegyal, in Lhasa, to send me a picture of the original statue. He sent me a picture confirming that it was the original one. I can feel the presence of the lama even now.

Meanwhile, my home tutor stayed for a few months in Drepung. Although I never went back to Kham, occasionally I received letters from people there, through visitors to Lhasa. Communication was very slow, and sometimes by the time a letter reached me it would be smudged by the rain and difficult to read.

At Drepung, routine studies started soon after the admission ceremony. In the monastic system, the students chose their guru. They usually had one main guru though they could go to others for lessons. The first thing to be decided in my case was who my tutor would be; it could no longer be the home tutor and would have to be a really learned monk from the same college, usually the same khangtsen. After some consultations, Sonam Gonpo, a highly respected geshe from Drag-go Monastery in

Tehor province, who was also in Tehor Khangtsen, was chosen. He had taken only a lower level geshe degree and was not a Lharampa.[4]

Geshe Sonam Gonpo's knowledge was profound. He was a man of realisation who had chosen to take the Geshe Lingtse degree and not the Lharampa. After the Lharampa degree there was progression to higher recognition, like the throne of Lama Tsongkhapa.[5] It was the highest position in the Gelukpa tradition. But Geshe Sonam Gonpo was not interested in titles or positions. By choosing a lower degree, he was conveying his disinterest in public encomiums. He was more interested in the learning rather than the title. This impacted me and my attitude too.

I find such monks in the Tibetan monasteries in south India today. They are very learned and teach many students, but are not interested in name and positions at all. They are very different from the monks we hear of who are interested in making a name for themselves, even though their learning may not be deserving of it. I am reminded of a verse in Sanskrit:

Ghatam bindyat patam chindyat, kuryat rasabharohanam
Yena kena prakarena prasiddhaha purusho bhavet

Break a pot, tear your clothes, ride a donkey if you wish
But by hook-or-crook fame, you must attain.

Geshe Sonam Gonpo was a compassionate and inspiring teacher with many of the top geshe lharampas as his students. He could not have been very old at the time, but his hair had turned grey. I call him my root guru because he was the first and main guru who taught me my main subject of Buddhist teachings. He had many students at different levels and in different classes. Along with me were 10–15 other monks who went to him daily for instruction. When I think of it now, I wonder how he managed to sit through the whole day in the same position.

Since I had done my preliminary studies in the Dargye Monastery, I did not need to repeat them. On the first day itself, teaching started with the commentary by Panchen Sonam Drakpa on *Prajnaparamita*. In this, the first stanza starts with the word 'ku-sum', which means 'trikaya', and definitions of the three kayas were taught.

Most sessions were held in the monastery premises or the khangtsen. In the monastic calendar, there were study sessions and intervals. Intervals ranged from 15 to 50 days. Intervals did not mean breaks or holidays, they just meant time for self-study. But let me tell you the routine before I describe the intervals.

All through the year, monks gathered early in the morning in the main assembly hall of the Drepung Monastery where tea was served. This gathering was not compulsory and so not many attended. After this was a short morning session in the debate courtyard of Loseling Dratsang, followed by a tea session in the assembly hall, where three or four rounds of tea were served. On special occasions, a thin soup was also provided. Monks then went to their rooms to memorise texts or to their guru's room for classes as there was no tradition of separate classrooms. The main debating session was around midday in the debate courtyard of Loseling Dratsang. In the afternoon, there was a tea session in the khangtsen, followed by a short prayer session in the courtyard of the khangtsens. Around sunset, there was a session of prayers in the Loseling debate courtyard.

Tsogchen tulkus were not required to attend all these tea sessions and prayer sessions, but it was important for them to attend the noon debate session and the evening debate session that followed the evening prayer session. I found the evening prayer sessions very inspiring because the chantings were so melodious. I also liked the prayers because, during them, I could think about my subject of study quietly. This prayer session lasted at least two to three hours but for me it seemed to go on forever, possibly because I was very young at that time. Yet it was pleasant sitting in the open courtyard with beautiful apricot trees and rows of butter lamps.

The disciplinarian and the courtyard caretaker were in charge of the fruit trees in the debate courtyard and would distribute the fruits to monks once a year during an evening prayer session. When there was fruit distribution, tsogchen tulkus received the message, 'This evening fruits will be distributed.' I remember how the disciplinarian, a friend of my home tutor, made it a point to send me the message. He brought packed fruits and added some dry fruits from his own house for distribution to the tulkus, while only fresh fruits were given to everyone else.

By the time the prayers and recitations were over, it would be late, around eight o'clock. Many students stayed on till about midnight, debating in the main courtyard, others returned to sit on the terrace of their hostels, reciting the memorised texts. Those who returned to their rooms were not allowed to gossip or light a fire to boil tea or light a lamp for any other activity. Monks not engaged in study or teaching preferred to perform the circumambulation around the monastery in the early morning or evening.

For me, the most enjoyable part of the day was going to the debate courtyard, whether for a debate session or prayers, because I was then spared of having to sit alone in the room. There were no other means of entertainment. Apart from the new year's day and the break of a few days after the summer retreat, the events I looked forward to were the Monlam and the Tsogchod. These festivals brought some change in the monotonous monastic life where everything was quiet and strictly disciplined.

New year holidays were enthusiastically enjoyed, mainly because during those days we could talk loudly, be noisy and enjoy *khapse*. We were also allowed to dance in the courtyard of our hostels, though usually the monks were not permitted to sing or dance. The ritual dance that monks performed was called 'Cham'. But during the new year holidays that went on for about a week, monks were allowed to perform folk dances. They would tie their shawl like a skirt around their waist and dance. My favourite song was '*Choeying Tageai Phodrang*' (in the pure palace of the sphere of truth).

During intervals between sessions, there were no debating or tea sessions in the dratsang. The tea session in the khangtsen was held only if there were special sponsors. During this period, the emphasis was on memorising texts, while reciting the memorised text at night was optional. The most serious students would leave the monastery between sessions and stay in the caves behind, devoting themselves to memorising texts. I did that a few times. During the summer retreat, monks observing the rules were not supposed to cross certain boundaries without ritual sanction. When the retreat ended, there was a custom of going, in groups or individually, for picnics by the river, where the well-to-do would pitch tents, stay for several days and do the annual washing of the bulky robes and mattresses.

It would be incorrect to give the impression that every monk was a serious student or a learned scholar. There were monks who belonged to the monastery's aristocratic class, who had formerly served as managers, administrators or disciplinarians. There were others who had sponsored the ceremony of Choeze, which literally means 'one who practices the Dharma', with the implication that certain people would prefer to engage in serious practice rather than intellectual studies. It must have started as a ceremony allowing exemption from studies, but it later became associated with status, which monks coming from wealthy or aristocratic families could easily obtain. This class of monks mostly led a leisurely life.

Another group was of monks good at physical work but intellectually not sharp enough to study scriptures. They performed the various duties of maintenance, like preparing tea and stoking the fire in the kitchen. There was yet another category of those registered as monks who spent most of their time in their home in the village, coming occasionally for special ceremonies where money was distributed, which they collected and then went back to their homes.

Ironically, most of the serious students in these larger monasteries were from faraway regions like Kham and Amdo. Fewer serious students came from Central Tibet or around, especially from the vicinity of Lhasa. This might be attributed to the proximity of their home because of which they had more distractions and opportunities to take leave from college. They were also more familiar with the city and could indulge in mundane activities, whereas students coming from far away, after having travelled on foot for many days, were rarely tempted to move away from their main purpose, which was to stay in the monastery.

To be recognised as a full-fledged monk on return to the area from where they came, the students had to complete three to four years of stay in the monastery. In the Sera Monastery, the required number of years was three while in Drepung the student was required to stay for four years. This was an administrative requirement for admission into the local monasteries as monks.

9

Life in the Monastery

Studying at the monastery was not my only concern. The business of getting along with other people present there was also important. I vividly remember a tulku younger than me who sat beside me during the sessions. He belonged to an aristocratic family in Lhasa and was very naughty. He had access to such things as chocolates and chewing gum, which he would show off, but not share. He chewed gum during sessions and once, at the end of a session, just before getting up to leave, spat it out, placed it on my head, pressed it down and ran away. It took a long time to remove.

No wonder then, that I was warned by my elders to be careful not to indulge in unnecessary friendships while attending prayer and debate sessions, because some acquaintances could be tricky. However, I was relieved I never faced ugly situations like fights or disagreements. Some naughty fellows would play harmless pranks like the one I just narrated or maybe pull out some wool or thread from the robes of his neighbour and place it on the heads of the person seated in front of them. Those who saw the prank would laugh while the person affected would not know why. I was also naughty at times.

My root guru was Geshe Sonam Gonpo. My other guru was Gen Yeshe Thubten. After my root guru died – about a year before we left for India – Gen Yeshe Thubten was my main guru. I also received much tutoring from the abbot of Loseling, Gen Pema Gyaltsen. All of them were gentle, kind and skilful in guiding students. The teacher would not go through a prepared lecture as is done in modern universities. Instead, the student would be asked to read out a text, passage by passage, which the teacher would then explain, elaborating on points, expanding the context and raising questions.

Once Gen Pema Gyaltsen was elucidating on paramita in a big hall above the Loseling main hall, to a gathering of a few hundred monks. I was seated next to Dagyab Rinpoche, who was on a slightly raised seat because of his position as the head of the Dagyab area of Kham. He had sponsored the tea for that teaching session. We were expected to keep the text open in our laps and go through it during the teaching. After a few days we grew bored, and I decided to take a story to read. I do not remember what I took. Perhaps it was the teachings of Drukpa Kunley, which were block printed or handwritten in pothis.[6] It could also have been stories of Uncle Tonpa, the legendary rascal of Tibet, who tricked people and played dirty pranks on nuns. I cannot remember. Both these persons were wise, but in very different ways. Dagyab Rinpoche had his own book.

We started reading our stories while pretending to follow the paramita commentary text, but occasionally I would burst out laughing and would have to pretend to be coughing, burying my head in my robes. Surprisingly, though we were sitting in the centre of the first row, we were not caught.

Drukpa Kunley was an unusual lama, a historical figure who was very learned. He delivered good teachings and his thinking was revolutionary. His teachings were not in the traditional style but very engaging and were in the form of jokes and wry humour. His writings could be considered daring, like the modern-day Indian writer, Khushwant Singh. The depth of meaning in his work was more like Rumi. His voice was very original. For example, a verse he wrote about himself as an introduction to his autobiography goes:[7]

> Writing one's own biography may look strange to common people
> But others do not know my good qualities or my faults
> What I am going to do now in this book
> Is to expose my faults and hide my good qualities.

In another place, he said, 'These days the practitioners of Dharma leave Buddha's doctrine aside and look for profound advice in the teachings of lamas, but if a lama is saying something contrary to the Buddha's teaching, something must be wrong. In fact, lamas cannot say something which the Buddha has not spoken.' Thus, in a subtle way, he guided the reader back to the source.

About learning of the Dharma, Drukpa Kunley said, 'It should be done in the same manner as starving people eat food. They put one piece in the mouth, hold another piece in their hand and their eyes are on the third piece on the plate. In the same way, you should listen, think of the meaning and meditate at the same time. Otherwise, the lama may be giving a talk on a point about which he himself is not convinced and the disciples may pretend to be listening without really paying attention. That will look like a guard who is just trying to pass time when on duty.'

Uncle Tonpa's actions were different. It must be reiterated that while Drukpa Kunley was a historical figure and a lama, Uncle Tonpa was a figure of legend, a fictional character. Uncle Tonpa's stories were witty. Here's a sample. He was once found walking in an open area. He took care to walk around small stones, avoiding them without stamping on them. But when he came to larger rocks, he would jump over them. Someone watching him asked, 'Why are you jumping over the larger rocks and walking around the smaller ones?' He replied, 'That is what I thought I should do because the monks do something very similar. They are very careful about the smaller rules but do not care for the bigger ones.'

In another story, Uncle Tonpa went to a rich person and borrowed a bagful of barley. Barley is called 'ney' and wheat 'dro'. When the time came to return what he had borrowed, he went to that family and said, 'I cannot give back the ney but please allow me to give it back to you in dro.' The rich lender thought for a minute and agreed to accept dro instead. The borrower walked to the courtyard and danced for a while. After some time, he stopped, bowed and said, 'Thank you, I have repaid you.' Saying so, he went away. Dro is also the name of a form of dance, although the spelling of the two may be different in Tibetan.

Drepung was about one and a half hour's walk from Lhasa, facing south, at the foot of Mount Gephel, part rock and part vegetation, which formed the background of the monastery. A small daily market would be held in the morning in front of the monastery, where people sold tsampa, vegetables and dried cow dung for fuel. Two small streams on either side of Drepung were used for washing. Drinking water was always taken from the western stream, said to be better for the body as it came from the rocky part of the mountains, while the eastern stream contained substances from the vegetation around, which could harm the body and was known to cause goitre.

A little below the monastery, on the eastern side was the temple of Nechung Oracle, which itself formed a small monastery. The oracle and Nechung Rinpoche lived there, and so did monks who did the propitiation of the deity. Right in front of the monastery, lower down, was a small village called Danbag, by which name there was also a lesser oracle. Tenma and Balawa were two other oracles to the northeast and above the monastery. In the case of Tenma, the medium and the spirit were both women; in the case of Balawa, the medium was a woman but the spirit was male. A little further, behind the mountain range to the west of Drepung, was another oracle called Gadong. So it came to be said that Drepung was surrounded by oracles, Sera by hermitages and Gaden by *rangjon*, self-manifested letters and images. An oracle sometimes referred to a human into whom a spirit had entered. Sometimes it referred to the spirit itself. Basically, an oracle made prophecies.

Standing in front of Drepung, we could see the sun rise from Shari (eastern mountain) and set behind Nubri (western mountain). The spirit of Shari was believed to be benevolent, unlike Nubri. They said that Shari was subsiding and Nubri was growing at that time. On Nubri, the formation of rocks had some resemblance to an ogress who, they said, wanted to make sure that Dharma degenerated rapidly. She slept throughout the year, waking up just once.

During the summer retreat, there was a tradition of opera groups being invited to give performances in different places at Drepung, coinciding with Shoton, the Yoghurt Festival, which originally must have been a special occasion for serving yoghurt to the monks. Many people from Lhasa came to these opera performances, clad in new attire and ornaments. This was the time when the ogress woke up to see how things were at Drepung. She did not like to see religious activity in Drepung. When she saw so many laypeople in the monastery and all the festivities, but less religious activities, she would be satisfied and go back to sleep for another year. Now that the Drepung Monastery has only nominal religious functions, with very few monks and religious activities, she must be very happy always and sleeping well.

At a particular hilly point between the summit of Mount Gephel and Drepung was the Gephel Hermitage. The place was blessed by lamas of high realisation, such as Jamyang Zhepa of Amdo. There were a few nomads who tended the cattle living around the place. The yoghurt made from the milk of its dri (female yak) was known to be the most delicious and nourishing. I remember that its texture was almost like butter. Directly in front of Drepung were meadows and parks with trees, and further beyond flowed the Kyichu, a tributary of the Yarlung Tsangpo river which is known as the Brahmaputra in India.[8] Beyond the Kyichu river there was another range of high mountains which divided Lhasa valley from Lhokha valley, the southern part of Central Tibet.

Apart from the major oracles like Nechung and Gadong, there were minor oracles whose role was to attend to smaller matters like everyday household issues. One of these, not very far from Drepung, was Thangse, or the son of Thanglha, a well-known local deity in northern Tibet. He was known for sucking out solid things from inside the body.

I fell ill once, something that did not happen often. Despite the lack of awareness of the nutritional importance of vitamins and minerals, we did not see much illness in monasteries. My attendants had given me pieces of fried meat that I felt had turned bad but I ate them anyway. It took several days before I was cured and the method used was unique.

Thangse was brought to my room and he went into a trance. He used his thumb ring, which was something like a tube with a large emerald on it. He placed one end on my stomach and sucked from the other end. He spat out something into a small bowl, which looked exactly like what I had eaten. This was repeated once or twice and I got better. Later I heard of a person who had accidentally swallowed a needle and Thangse had sucked it out the same way. In India, I was to hear of someone from the Philippines doing surgery with no instruments but their bare hands and leaving no traces of any incision, which made me think there must be some common principle for such actions. There was a belief in Tibet that when you were sick you should neither sleep during the day nor drink water, and the helper tried hard to enforce this. This, of course, did not sound sensible to me.

During the new year holidays, monks gathered in the common hall in the evenings and one monk read aloud the biography of Milarepa, with two or three others joining in singing the songs. The intention was to inspire students towards austerity and the necessity of enduring hardship on the Dharma path. This is a good example of the basically non-sectarian approach of these monasteries, because Drepung was a purely Gelukpa Monastery, but while reading the biography of Milarepa, there was no feeling that we were listening to an alien philosophy.[9] Similarly, several chants featured prayers to Guru Padmasambhava or mentioned important gurus like Marpa. During the Losar holidays, monks even staged a very amateur production of a story from Milarepa's biography, such as 'Milarepa and the Hunter'.

Cham dances were not performed at Drepung, Sera or Gaden, because these were monasteries for study, particularly of esoteric subjects. Even the departments of tantra at Drepung and Sera did not conduct the dance. Gyutoe and Gyumed, the upper and lower colleges of tantric studies, did not hold Cham dance performances either, being more oriented towards study and rituals. The dance was performed by Nechung Monastery as well as some monasteries within Lhasa city considered specialised in such rituals. It is only now in India that the dance is performed in many monasteries.

Annual events included the Monlam and Tsogchod festivals at Jokhang Temple. Another annual event was Jang Gunchoe which took place in Jang, which was two days' walking distance from Drepung. A session of debating on Pramana, the Buddhist system of logic, was held there for about one and a half months, convened by the Rato Monastery. Students from all three monasteries around Lhasa, who had reached a certain level in their study on the subject, visited for a concentrated study of logic, with a focus on debate. The programme was extremely intense and the debate sessions carried on almost throughout the day until late in the evening. Participants attempted to outdo the reputed performers of other monasteries. These sessions were considered very effective in boosting the understanding of philosophy and logic.

Tulkus from Drepung Loseling also looked forward to another annual event when all of them went to an estate about an hour's horse ride away, to perform a thanksgiving ceremony to the Gadong Oracle, second in importance to Nechung. On that day, tsogchen and other tulkus dressed in their best and rode horses, accompanied by their servants. The horses were also decked up with ornaments. In the morning, we would go directly to the Gadong Monastery, where the oracle would go into a trance. We would offer him khatags and the monastery would consult him about the success of the work in the coming year.

We then went to the estate belonging to Loseling Monastery, not far from there, and spent the day picnicking. The best food was served – an elaborate feast of momos, thukpa, vegetables and sweets. This also led to some competition over the dress and the quality of brocade worn, especially among tulkus of high and middle ranks. Though on the scale of wealth I was nowhere near the regent tulkus, one year I wore a *tonga* said to have belonged to the previous Panchen Lama, who had gone on a self-imposed exile to China, and whose possessions were sold off. The brocade on the dress was from imperial Russia. As it was a picnic, we were allowed to take off our upper coats and display what we were wearing. Everyone was very impressed with what I had worn and it was informally accepted as the best. I was quite flattered. I later brought the tonga to India and, thinking it would be useless, sent it to Ladakh, where it sold for a pittance.

Lhasa was a small and very old-fashioned place at that time. In both material aspects as well as in the habits and conduct of people, it was quite different from the rest of Tibet. All kinds of people could be found there – traders, people coming for admission to monasteries, pilgrims and later, people escaping Chinese aggression in eastern Tibet. The people performed circumambulations around the city with its many historic temples, Jokhang and Ramoche, the Potala Palace and Chagpori, an important hill. At one point on the route, beggars would line up and be given donations.

Elsewhere, beggars adopted a unique way of begging. They would hold a long stick, like a fishing rod. To one end of this would be attached a miniature stupa mould. The stupa mould is generally a mould which is filled with clay to create a miniature stupa for the purpose of earning merit. The small mould of any sacred object is called the 'tsa-tsa'. In this case, the beggar would dip the empty stupa mould into water and when the water took the shape of the stupa inside the mould, he claimed he was creating water stupas. People believed that the greater the number of water stupas they created, the greater was the merit they earned. The beggar would then earn some money while giving pilgrims the feeling of having earned spiritual merit.

Although the language was the same all over Tibet, dialects were different and people newly arrived in Lhasa like me, found it difficult to grasp the spoken dialect. My khangtsen consisted of mostly people from my region, but I had to meet students from other parts of Tibet during the debating sessions. However, I soon overcame my problems of understanding what they said. One of the difficulties in communication was the use of several words in their honorific form while addressing superiors so that almost every word was substituted with another. It was common to attach a prefix to a word so that it became honorific. But in addition to this, the honorifics used in Lhasa were often completely different words. For example, the word for 'shoes' in my province of Tehor was 'lham'. To make it honorific, we would say 'chablham'. In Lhasa the honorific was a different word 'zhabchag' and the word 'lham' denoting shoes was no longer there in the honorific. The mouth, was 'kha', and the honorific was 'zhal' – the word was thus changed completely. It may be interesting to add here that honorifics were used for all the belongings of a person who was given respect. That was why the shoes of a venerable lama were also spoken of with respect.

People from Kham and Amdo usually considered the typical Lhasa native as very intelligent and clever. At times they felt they were looked down upon by the people from Lhasa. There was a degree of regionalism, with the Khampas thinking the Lhasa people were too clever to deal with and the people of Lhasa referring to the former as 'these stupid Khampas'. In fact, there was a dormant feeling among people in some parts of Kham that they had been discriminated against for a long time. The main reason for this was the failure of the Lhasa government, for many centuries, to unite the whole of Tibet.

This sense of discrimination was only partly reflected in reality because in the larger monasteries around Lhasa, the majority of abbots, senior scholars and monks on their way to attaining Gaden Tripa (the highest position in the Gelukpa tradition) were Khampas or Amdowas and no discrimination was apparent. And there was a uniting force, for in the mind of every Tibetan,

Lhasa was the centre of religion, the symbol of spirituality and culture, not merely a political capital. The holy statue of Buddha enshrined in the main temple and the Dalai Lama were universal sources of inspiration.

As I close this chapter, I recall the four other tulkus in my class – Dagyab Rinpoche, Losempa Tulku, Jampa Rinpoche and Togden Rinpoche. Dagyab Rinpoche now lives in Berlin and is the patron of Tibet House, Frankfurt. Losempa Tulku is one of the 'three tulkus of Tibet', influential in various ways at a point in history, and at a time when the system of lamas becoming regents between Dalai Lamas was not introduced, so they were the highest tulkus in at least the Lhasa area.

It may be observed that there has never been a clear third position after the Dalai Lama and Panchen Lama (likened to the sun and the moon in their importance ever since the Panchen Lama, who was the guru of the 5th Dalai Lama, played an important role in history), though this point would be relevant only to seating formalities at official ceremonies of the government. Most of the high lamas required to attend the Dalai Lama's ceremonies sit on cushions at different levels, with a select few on thrones – the Dalai Lama's tutors, the regent during the Dalai Lama's minority and the prime minister, who has high status but not the power vested in the cabinet. The obligation of attendance does not apply to the Panchen Lama and Sakya Trizin, whose family lineage is accorded importance for historical reasons, and whose palanquin is permitted to come up to the inner pillars of the Potala Palace.

Jampa Rinpoche did much to build the newest assembly hall of the Drepung Loseling Monastery in Karnataka. He was the main person who shouldered the responsibility of bringing it up. In the process, he sacrificed a lot. Whenever he travelled, he chose the cheapest mode of transport. He stayed in the cheapest accommodation even when he came to Delhi. He used to carry a kerosene stove with him and cook for himself when out of town. He was also a very knowledgeable person and people would often seek his advice. I felt that during the inauguration of the hall, his efforts were not adequately recognised.

Jampa Rinpoche suffered from diabetes and liver problems. Somebody volunteered to sponsor his treatment in the USA but he refused to go, saying that if the sponsors were willing to spend that much money, they should give it to the monastery so that poor students could be sponsored. He passed away in March 2011. He left a will clearly instructing that no ceremony be performed before his body, stating that he wished to be cremated as an ordinary monk without arrangements for a special urn and wanted no reincarnation to be recognised. It seemed to me he was reacting to the recent trend of recognising so many tulkus and the sickening politics associated with this. His will also indicated that little money (about ₹6 lakh) was being left behind. I thought this was very exemplary. These days, monks have much more money.

I was much moved and composed a prayer of seven verses the morning after hearing this, which I emailed his disciples, who told me that the prayers were chanted the same evening. I hold Jampa Rinpoche in high regard as a selfless and genuine practitioner of Dharma. We had been not just classmates but had also studied together under Geshe Sonam Gonpo for many years. Two years before his death, during a visit to Mundgod, he came to see me. He presented me with an old statue of Buddha and a text of *Jamphel Tsenchoe* (*Manjusrinamasangeeti*) written in gold on black paper. It appeared to me as though he was disposing of his important possessions.

Lastly, about Togden Rinpoche, who was very good in his studies. He is very learned and highly respected, yet remarkably humble. He gives extensive teachings, especially on transmissions of voluminous Buddhist canonical scriptures such as Kangyur and Tengyur. Kangyur consists of over a hundred bundles and Tengyur of over two hundred bundles. He lives in the Drepung Loseling Monastery in Karnataka.

10

Living in Lhasa

In addition to my studies, I was also imbibing much from the culture around me. For instance, along some of the paths to Lhasa, I would see men leading donkeys which were carrying heavy loads. Sometimes it was just cow or yak dung, sometimes it was mounds of vegetables. This was how goods were transported to Lhasa. There were no vehicles in those days and it was not easy to arrange a horse. But walking had its own romance. Frequent travellers and industrious traders on these roads needed periodic refreshments and there were small tents along the route where bread and yoghurt in earthen pots were served. I do not know why or how, but the taste, combination of food items and the exotic earthenware made it all very inviting.

In the later years of my stay in Lhasa, traders visiting Kalimpong and Kolkata brought back Indian-style sweet tea, which started growing popular slowly and became an upper-class fashion, so we would come across 'sweet tea' shops. Alongside these shops were people selling what they called 'sweet water'. A pill was put into a glass of water and sold. The pills, I now realise, were nothing but sugar-free sweeteners.

It was also when I was in Lhasa that I saw the first movie in a cinema hall called Dekyi Odnang (meaning 'light of happiness'). The cinema hall belonged partly to Tsepon W.D. Shakabpa, who was a very famous official in Tibet and figured prominently in modern Tibetan history. At that time, he was one of the finance secretaries of the old Tibetan government. Shakabpa was famous because after the Second World War, a delegation led by him was sent to the victorious nations with congratulatory messages in the form of letters from the Tibetan government. The nations he visited stamped their visa permit on that letter. So those who argue in favour of an independent Tibet say the reason why many nations stamped their visas on the letters was because they recognised Tibet as an independent country. The cinema show I watched was a documentary depicting the fight between the Chinese and the Japanese. Since movies were very new, there were no rules forbidding monks to watch them. The year was 1959.

Outside the khangtsens of Drepung, there used to be occasional sales – what North Americans call a 'garage sale' – for disposing of belongings of monks returning home or those deceased. At one such sale, I picked up a slate that was used in primary schools in India in those days, thinking it would be a nice toy. Later I happened to look into the room of a monk I knew who was artistic and good at painting and calligraphy. There I saw a small book *Teach Yourself Hindi* by Babu Tharchin from Kinnaur. Tharchin used to publish the first Tibetan newspaper from Kalimpong called the *Melong*. I borrowed the book and started practising the script and some sentences on the slate. Later, as we travelled through Chu-dangmo, Tawang, Bomdila and through the plains in India to Missamari, I was able to impress people by saying a few sentences in Hindi. I must also mention that it was in Drepung that somebody gifted me a clock from India. Till then we estimated the time by looking at the position of the sun.

Although I did not go to Lhasa very often unless there was good reason, the walk from Drepung Monastery to Lhasa was quite pleasant. During one of my walks back from Lhasa, I noticed some representatives of the Muslim and Nepalese communities in Lhasa, whom I recognised by the caps and beards and by the tilak and white dress. They told me they were going to receive the Panchen Lama. I decided to walk with them to see what the Panchen Lama looked like. The Panchen Lama arose as an institution during the period of the 5th Dalai Lama. The Dalai Lama is the head of the state and also the religious head. The Panchen Lama is only a religious head, second to the Dalai Lama.

We had to wait quite a long time at a park called Kyitsel Luding. A Chinese military band was also waiting and must have received a message that there would be a delay, for their members had started playing cards. Finally, the Panchen Lama arrived in a motorcade. He was not dressed in monks' robes but in travelling clothes of yellow brocade. The band played the often heard song, 'East is Red'. It was a song that was the de facto anthem of the People's Republic of China during the Cultural Revolution in the 1960s. The lyrics of the song was attributed to Li Youyuan, a farmer from northern Shaanxi, and the melody was derived from a local folk song. Li Youyuan is said to have got his inspiration upon seeing the rising sun in the morning of a sunny day.

That was the first and the last time I saw the late Panchen Lama. At that time, he was not popular in the Lhasa valley because his predecessor had bad relations with the Lhasa government. Also, his establishment was perceived as siding with China and had, in fact, sent a congratulatory telegram on 1 October 1949, the day of the founding of the People's Republic of China. But after the complete takeover of Tibet by China, he gradually emerged as the most patriotic leader of Tibetans, standing up for their culture and identity, and loyal to the Dalai Lama. His sudden death in 1989 was a great loss to the Tibetan cause.

His Holiness the Dalai Lama's visit to China in 1955 to participate in the National People's Congress caused great anxiety and worry to Tibetans, who imagined that the Chinese would not let Him return. He was away for almost a year. Tsogchen tulkus took part in the procession of both His departure and arrival, riding decorated horses. I particularly remember the welcome, because there was heavy rain and we were made to wait a long time in the cold and wet on our horses, before the procession started. Long speeches by the Chinese in their language and the military band are all I recall of the elaborate ceremony in the famous 'Great Tent of the Peacock', a tent of bright yellow colour, a colour used only for the Dalai Lamas.

I do not remember much of His Holiness's visit to India in 1956 at the invitation of the Mahabodhi Society of India to participate in the celebration of 2,500 years of Buddha's *parinirvana*. It was a sudden departure so no processions were arranged. I did hear that the Chinese government was not keen to send Him and when they finally did, they sent a written speech which they wanted Him to read. I read in His Holiness's book later that He had kept the speech aside and spoke what He wanted to say.

I remember hearing of the time when His Holiness went to spend a few months in Chumbi valley which, though in Tibet, shared its border with Sikkim. He went there to avoid certain pressures from the Chinese government. That was also the year a high-ranking delegation arrived from Beijing. It was headed by Marshal Chen Yi, who held the important position of vice premier in the Chinese government. He resembled Mao Zedong and some simple-minded people suggested he could be Mao in disguise.

On the day of his visit to Drepung Monastery to sponsor a prayer session, he even followed the tradition where the sponsor, carrying incense, weaves in and out of the lines of monks. Among the gifts distributed was a Mao Zedong badge. On the morning of his arrival, tsogchen tulkus had to receive him at the monastery gate with khatags and they had learned to say 'Tashi Delek' with the Chinese pronunciation, 'Zashi Dele'. The words of greeting meant good health and auspiciousness.

Chinese magazines containing propaganda in Tibetan were sent to the khangtsens in the monasteries. They printed images from China and events like the Korean War and all the glorious stories of the Communist Party. It was there I read about the setting up of the Preparatory Committee for the Tibet Autonomous Region, of which the Dalai Lama was the chairperson. I remember seeing pictures of senior monks who were asked to clap in welcome when His Holiness arrived. In Tibet, clapping is traditionally symbolic of driving out evil. So how could they clap when His Holiness entered? They just brought their palms together in salutation. But when the Chinese officials came in, they clapped.

The Preparatory Committee had Ngapo Ngawang Jigme as secretary, a brilliant and competent cabinet minister, who played many important roles before and after the Chinese takeover, including as the head of the delegation sent to Beijing and who signed the 17-point agreement. He died in Beijing in 2009, aged nearly 100. After His Holiness left Tibet in 1959, this Preparatory Committee became the Government of the Tibet Autonomous Region and the Dalai Lama was replaced by the Panchen Lama.

I heard many years later that His Holiness the Dalai Lama had been invited to China for Panchen Lama's funeral in 1989. His Holiness wished to go, but due to some reasons could not. This was seen by many as not the right move to further the Tibetan cause. The late Bakula Rinpoche – who was the seniormost lama of Ladakh and one of the Loseling tulkus – told me that when he went to Beijing, he met Ngapo Ngawang Jigme, who told Bakula Rinpoche that His Holiness's not attending the funeral was a great mistake.

History teaches many lessons. One such lesson is connected to the reincarnation of Panchen Lama. A search party for the reincarnation of the Panchen Lama was constituted in Tibet. The committee included senior Tibetan monks. They identified a boy but this was kept a secret. The Dalai Lama was aware of the developments. Though I could not discern if they picked the boy and sought His Holiness's approval or if it was the other way round, but I know that His Holiness fully agreed that this boy was the right person. He even went ahead and wrote a long-life prayer, which was to be quietly and unobtrusively transmitted to the Tibetan community.

I do not know what transpired after that, for one day I saw an announcement in the media that the new Panchen Lama had been recognised ceremoniously. This infuriated the Chinese authorities and weakened the already frail thread of connection and hope that Tibetans had with the Chinese government.

11

Memories of Historic Events

I have talked about my tutor earlier, the highly respected Geshe Sonam Gonpo, and in that context had mentioned the four categories of success in the geshe examination. It was among the greatest occasions of my life when I attended one such examination. It was also the last major event I attended in Tibet, but I did not know it then. This was the Geshe Lharampa examination taken by His Holiness the 14th Dalai Lama.[10] Only a few people get the opportunity to experience an event of this kind.

In 1959, the main ceremony of His Holiness's Geshe Lharampa examination was to take place during the Monlam festival at the main temple in Lhasa. Before that it was customary for His Holiness to visit Drepung, Sera and Gaden and conduct an initial examination. In Drepung, His Holiness the Dalai Lama was seated on a throne with two of His tutors seated on either side. This took place in the courtyard of the general assembly hall of the Drepung Monastery, which was filled to capacity by officials, monks and visitors. There was grandeur everywhere.

It gives me goose pimples as I recollect those moments. I was sitting quite near the throne so I had a very good opportunity to see His Holiness from very close quarters. I closely observed the way He was dressed and delivered His teachings.

A lot of preparations had gone into making the event a success. Cleaning and decoration had started well in advance. New curtains were made for all the houses, the frames of the windows facing the street were polished jet black, the streets were cleaned and the golden roofs over the main monastery and other assembly halls were polished.

The ceremony in Drepung lasted three or four days, including the day of the actual examination, the day when His Holiness distributed gifts and tea, and the day of thanksgiving by the monastery. Most government officials were moved into Drepung, and the middle-ranking and lower-ranking officers were given some quarters there, while those of high rank rode back to Lhasa in the evening and came back early morning.

After the longevity ceremony, there was some talk that His Holiness had not liked the conduct of some high-ranking tulkus during one of the ceremonies. All tulkus who were still students were summoned along with their tutors. Given the society of the time, this was frightening to everybody. We were all practically shivering in our shoes, wondering what might happen and imagining the worst. But in the waiting lounge adjacent to His Holiness's room, the Grand Chamberlain just gave a long lecture on behalf of His Holiness, speaking in general terms about the importance of study and good conduct, while we were made to stand, bowing down. It was a relief, yet we heard that afterwards, when His Holiness went to Sera, the sermon was not delivered. People like to speculate whether Sera was his favourite of the two.

On the day of distributing gifts, each monk received money in a handmade paper envelope. There was calligraphic writing on what the envelope contained. A coin-sized mould of Yamantaka was also gifted.[11] This clay coin-sized image was said to have been blessed by the 13th Dalai Lama.

There was also a ceremony for foreign representatives held in a medium-sized hall where His Holiness did not appear, but His robe was placed on the throne as was customary. It was during this ceremony that I saw an Indian couple for the first time in my life. They were probably from the Indian consulate in Lhasa. They were sitting just next to me and I noticed, in particular, the lady's sandals. I had never seen someone wearing shoes where one could see the toes and it seemed funny to me. Due to the cold weather in Tibet, we always wore fully closed shoes.

The Chinese general, Zhang Jingwu, would not sit down but put a scarf on the throne and went straight out.

On the third day, during the official ceremony for longevity, everybody filed past His Holiness. While monks of all ranks could expect His Holiness to touch their heads in blessing with His hand, laypeople were blessed with a small cylindrical yellow silk suspended from a handle. When the Muslim representatives approached the throne, this was removed as they were not expected to receive blessings, though they raised their hands to their foreheads in salaam. I felt at that time that this was a nice gesture of showing respect for other religions and cultures and it is significant that this was how it was perceived even under the old society.

A couple of months later, at the main temple in Lhasa, the day of Monlam dawned. Festivities were everywhere. Lhasa was full. At a conservative estimate, around a hundred thousand people were present. In Tibet, we believe that if one lakh people gather, which by itself is a very rare occurrence, a halo of sound engulfs the place. All devout people, of any religion, have the habit of reciting some prayer quietly, to themselves. In Tibet everyone chants mantras. *Om mani padme hum* is a commonly chanted one. Generally, it is done quietly. Many recite their prayers with a rosary in their hands. Here I am talking of the laypeople. All monks always have their rosaries in their hands.

I was full of anticipation. It was the tradition that on the full moon day of Monlam, His Holiness gave a teaching in the special, partially open arena adjoining the Jokhang temple. His Holiness took His seat at the appointed time. Directly in front of where His Holiness was sitting was a huge building that had belonged to the aristocratic family of Samdub Phodrang. They had sold it to the Chinese.

Since I was a middle-ranking tulku, I was seated on a higher platform, quite close to where His Holiness was seated. I could see the roof of Samdub Phodrang's house. The Chinese had put up sandbags on the roof of the building and we could see machine guns pointing directly towards His Holiness's throne. And even as ceremonies of such grandeur and colour were going on, keen eyes were watching His Holiness. From where I was sitting, I could also see huge posters. I remember two of them. One showed the PLA killing American president Eisenhower and the other said 'Taiwan Must Be Liberated'. To me and to all those who had gathered, His Holiness shone far brighter than all those guns and so we had no fear.

But trouble was already beginning. During Monlam, the Chinese authorities sent His Holiness an invitation to a theatrical performance by a Chinese dance troupe. The show was to take place in the Chinese military headquarters. The people of Lhasa were suspicious about the designs the Chinese had – why would they invite him? Would they take him hostage? These questions had a background and a history.

The person who had invited His Holiness was General Tan Guansan. He would often visit His Holiness and advise him to tell the Tibetan army to quell the rebellious group's uprising. The rebellious group was called Chushi Gangdruk. They were mainly people from the Kham region. There was a reason for their resistance. The Chinese had infiltrated the Kham region and behaved badly with the people there. Many high lamas were arrested. The people became indignant and rose in protest against the actions of the Chinese. The Chinese did not want His Holiness to come to the region in case His visit became a trigger for a revolt. They came both to warn Him and to see Him. This was the context in which His Holiness went to take the examination.

Typically, the morning of Monlam began with debates. There are many methods of conducting a debate but generally the one who asks a question stands and places his left foot in front, claps his right hand on his left and asks the question. After he finishes asking the question, the right hand moves to the right shoulder and the left downwards on the left side. The foot is also withdrawn. Before he claps, the monk would hold his rosary and pull it back to sling it on his left shoulder. It was very interesting to watch. If there were three of four questioners, there was a kind of a tussle about who got to ask first. If the one who had asked the question was completely dissatisfied with the answer given, he took his rosary, circled it around the one who was answering (symbolically) and wore it back on his left shoulder. This showed he did not agree with the answer.

The same method was followed with His Holiness also but, of course, it was done with respect. The abbots and ex-abbots asked His Holiness questions. Later, He put questions to them and assessed the validity of their responses. The question–answer session lasted about two hours and included some ceremonies like serving tea and sweet rice. To add to the tumult, as a part of tradition, the oracle of Nechung went into a trance and threw a philosophical question at His Holiness for symbolic effect. I could feel everyone in the gathering holding their breath. The occasion was very exciting foreverybody, an opportunity not everyone would have in their lifetime. His Holiness answered questions from *Pramana* in the morning, *Prajnaparamita* and *Madhyamika* at noon and *Abhidhamma* and *Vinaya* in the afternoon. Then He gave His teachings.

As a part of the celebrations at Jokhang, there were huge mounds of ceremonial cookies and khapse. Towards the end of the very dignified ceremony, all the sweepers of Jokhang temple were allowed to go to this pile and take as much as they could, causing great fun and chaos that I enjoyed as any young boy would. His

Holiness's huge bodyguards tried to control the commotion with a kind of a whip.

Monlam concluded with two ceremonies which were hugely enjoyed by the visitors and the people of Lhasa. On the second-last day was torma-throwing, where monks of the Namygyal Monastery and the Tantric College of Drepung formed a very impressive procession, reciting mantras. With them were the Nechung Oracle and the Gaden Tripa, the official head of the Gelukpas. The Nechung Oracle shot an arrow at the structure of dry grass into which a huge Tibetan ritual cake with a special shape called torma was thrown and burned. Simultaneously, cannons were fired at a mountain across the river. The idea behind the festival was the destruction of evil and victory of the good. The burning had a similar impact on the people's minds as the burning of Ravana's effigy in India.

On the last day, a statue of Maitreya was taken around Lhasa, halting at various spots while chanting mantras. The idea was to remind people of the coming of the future Buddha. Yet, on the whole, the ceremony left me with mixed feelings, knowing it had been a very rare experience, and somewhere sensing that this would be the last event of its kind.

Another great occasion, which took place in 1954, was when His Holiness gave the first Kalachakra initiation at Norbulingka. Everybody went to attend the teaching, which lasted several days. Kalachakra is a Buddhist tantric system which covers subjects such as the whole structure of the universe including the sun, the moon, Mount Meru and the stars. It also covers the relationship between the various elements – the five elements, the sky, wind, fire, water and earth – and living beings. So it has a big message for today's world in terms of the interconnectedness and interdependence of the elements and living beings.

When this teaching was given, I think I was too young to understand all of it but I remember the idea of interdependence because of how it was made easy for the common people to understand. It was explained in terms of layers – the bottom was the space or sky and was called the sky mandala, on top of that was the wind mandala, on top of that were the fire mandala, water mandala, earth mandala and then the living beings. The human being was presented as being on top of all these mandalas. The presentation made it easy to understand and visualise. However, the real message was one of interdependence and that if one layer or mandala was destroyed, the whole system would get dissolved, and so it was very essential to keep them all healthy.

This is a message for today's world. These layers are not created by anyone, nor by a supreme power, nor are they composed of microorganisms. In science, quantum physics also talks of the possibilities of interconnection of all particles. Newtonians talk of the world as composed of small indivisible particles and gravitation. But in this teaching, the world was not like that. Here, everything was explained as being interdependent. Even if something happened far away, its effects will be felt here.

Kalachakra also talks of symbolic wars between the meritorious and the sinners. The defeat is always of the sinners. Kalachakra is unique and different from other Buddhist tantric systems because the other tantric systems are based on the conventional way of thinking. Kalachakra is the latest system of Buddhism. It came from India, became popular in Tibet and became a part of Mahayana Buddhism.

I also remember His Holiness spoke of the feelings of animals. He recollected that during His visit to a village, He had seen some villagers tending to yaks and cows. He told us of how the animals responded to the calls of the animal herder. They recognised the tone of his voice – angry or happy – and reacted accordingly. He was talking, I think, of the importance of compassion.

For a few days, we went to Norbulingka every day and came back in the evening. Then, some monks and I arranged for tents and organised a camp in a park nearby so that we did not have to return to Drepung every evening. The programme was conducted in a grand manner. Apart from the teachings, there were the comings-and-goings of grand lamas, well-dressed lay- and monk-officials, ladies of Lhasa in their finery, thickset Khampas looking brave and rough, Amdo people in their bulky outfits and yogis with matted hair.

Although I could not follow all His Holiness's teachings in 1956, the whole environment, the presence of His Holiness, as well as the numerous senior lamas including His Holiness's tutors, made it an occasion of inspiration and provided a great sense of fulfilment. On the last day, His Holiness was dressed in grandeur with royal and yogi's[12] ornaments over His monk's dress. That was the first time I had seen Him wear them. For some reason the Chinese did not interfere throughout the entire ceremony. As a young monk, I enjoyed myself and tried to imbibe all that His Holiness said.

Behind the scenes, grave situations were developing. Members of the Chushi Gangdruk group had organised the Kalachakra teachings. The people from Kham, who were mainly traders, had organised themselves to raise funds for presenting a golden throne to His Holiness. In the course of collecting donations and having the throne built, the Khampas had an opportunity to discuss what could be done about the threats facing Tibet and the Dharma, which eventually led to the formation of their guerrilla resistance movement.

Part III

IN TRANSIT

12

Flight from Tibet

I was finding it difficult to climb. Visions of my warm bed made me feel all the more cold. The Gephel mountain that we were climbing lay behind the Drepung Monastery. As it was night, we could not see very well. When the moon came out from between the clouds, visibility improved somewhat for the full moon was just six days away. But first, let me explain to you how and why I was climbing the mountain.

We had returned to Drepung from Lhasa on 6 March, when the festivities ended. Within a few days of our arrival, reports of trouble brewing around Lhasa area started reaching our quiet monastery. The period between Monlam and Tsogchod was usually relaxed. Even though regular sessions took place, there were no special events or excitements.

In the classes, Tsulkhang Lama Rinpoche, one of the greatest teachers of Drepung Loseling, known for his profound knowledge of Madhyamika subjects, expounded on a very important text by Tsongkhapa, *Legshey Nyingpo*.[1] There were many pauses between the class. These were not due to profound reflections but out of fear. We kept hearing of different incidents. One was about a fashionable monk named Sonam Gyatso who belonged to Chamdo. When he came for a formal tea ceremony at Norbulingka, a ceremony that all monk-officials had to attend every morning, he saw a huge crowd outside the palace. These people were there to protest. They felt that His Holiness should not agree to go to the cultural event in the Chinese military camp. Even though His Holiness had assured them that He would not attend the cultural function, they were there to guard Him. For some reason, Sonam Gyatso rushed back to his house and changed his clothes. He dressed like a Chinese person, complete with a mask, picked up his pistol and rode his bicycle at great speed towards Norbulingka. The people gathered there thought he was a Chinese and mob mentality prevailed. One man threw a stone and everybody followed and finally Sonam Gyatso lost his life.

In another incident, a cabinet minister was stoned and he got injured on his head. The Chinese reportedly took him to the hospital and arranged his treatment. He survived. Such rumours and reports kept pouring in. Fear and uncertainty about the future had gripped the monks, who were valiantly trying to study, in spite of it all.

The teaching was conducted in the hall of Gozhima (meaning the 'House with Four Gates'), one of the hostels of Tehor Khangtsen. The hall was next to my room. That was why I was attending the classes, along with many senior and learned monks. I could sense that most monks, though physically present, were distracted by the disturbing information. At the end of class, one day, Lama Rinpoche said, 'We will carry on as long as the Triple-Gem's blessings keep us here,' indicating that we might not be able to reach the end of the text.

A few days later, trouble started. Still a young boy, I did not understand the details of the problems in Lhasa area. One night, around midnight, I heard the sound of big guns. At first, I thought it was test-firing or something like that, but it quickly became clear that it was something more serious. I heard monks rushing up to the terrace to look towards Norbulingka.

We could see lights thrown up to the sky, which we knew was the Chinese military camp signalling the direction of attack to the other regiments. This went on all through the night and the next morning. By daybreak, we saw it was unmistakably a scene of war. In the late afternoon, we saw horse riders coming from the side of Norbulingka Palace and some of the old monks started shouting, 'Now is the time for the victory of the gods!' believing that the Tibetan horse riders were coming out to attack the Chinese camp. We saw the members of Chushi Gangdruk, the rebel group, coming out of Norbulingka on their horses. We were happy. Now we were rising in protest.

Our hearts sank as we saw them riding towards the Kyichu river. Crossing the Kyichu river meant that they were fleeing, for that was the direction southwards and out of Tibet. They were not racing against the military camp, they were running away from it. The sense of fear doubled in all of us and a feeling of helplessness set in. Everybody's concern, understandably, was about His Holiness's safety: What could have happened to Him?

As the tension was reaching new heights, we received a message saying that the monks had no need to fear and that everyone should stay calm; there was no cause for worry. The message claimed that they (the Tibetan fighters) had Lhasa and Norbulingka Palace under their control and would soon attack the Chinese camp. Soon it became clear that the message was definitely not from the Tibetan fighters. It had actually been spread by the Chinese spies because they feared that while monks were obviously unarmed, a provocation would lead them to rush to the Chinese camp carrying sticks, stones and perhaps kitchen knives. For the Chinese it would be an awkward situation – killing so many thousands of unarmed monks would be a serious matter.

I went to see my teacher Gen Yeshe Thubten in Tsulkhang Khangtsen, who did not say much, but all indications were that things would not be the same in the monasteries. I then went to the terrace and saw Tsulkhang Lama Rinpoche standing there taking in the terrible scene in the valley. I approached him; he registered my presence but did not utter a word. He looked very depressed. He was a great guru and respected by the monks, but some people had a notion that his way of thinking tilted towards socialism. After the suppression of the uprising, he was given a nominal post and put in charge of setting up a school for studying the texts of Buddhist philosophy in Nechung Monastery, just below Drepung Monastery. He died in 1984.

Around this time, a member of Chushi Gangdruk called on me. He was from my area, Dargye, and so came to pay his respects to me. He said in passing, 'Now we do not have to worry about His Holiness's safety.' I did not understand why and how, but later came to know that His Holiness had already left Tibet by then.

The next evening, I attended a small prayer session in Tehor Khangtsen and when I came back to my room at dusk, my attendants had already made preparations for departure. Things were packed and everybody had taken off their monks' robes and dressed like laypersons. It was a great shock to me, but I quickly realised that this was the only way. They asked me to wear my best monks' robes, so that they did not become an extra burden to carry. I had no time to think about what to take – I got hold of my daily prayer book at once, and my eyes somehow fell on the *Teach Yourself Hindi* book which I had borrowed. Something told me that it would be useful and I wrapped it with my prayer books. Later, I thought something inside my head had been telling me that I was heading towards India.

With me were ten of my attendants. The point of our exit had already been decided. Obviously, we could not come out from the front gate because although it was night, the road led towards the main road and Chinese camps were spread throughout the valley. Leaving from the back, we began climbing the Gephel mountain.

It was 19 March 1959 (Earth Pig Year, 10th day of the 2nd month). My climb was also hampered because I was wearing my heaviest robe. I had no experience of climbing mountains and certainly not in the dark. Somehow, we managed to reach the western pass before daybreak. Inside an area fenced off by stones, probably used earlier by herders, we started a fire for tea, making sure that it could not be seen from the valley.

My attendants told me to hurry up. We finished our tea quickly and before we started the descent, I had my last glimpse of the monastery. We hurried down to Gadong Monastery. The descent was not as difficult as the climb and we reached by mid-morning.

I had been to this monastery several times earlier with the Loseling tulkus for the annual festivals. It now bore a deserted look. I think the oracle had left the previous night. Somebody gave us tea and food. We spent the night in the monastery and there is a story about our stay.

It was a time of fear and escape meant that you were holding your breath till you actually escaped. Rumours and fears were always floating around. No sooner had we settled down, someone said that the bridge which we had to cross to reach the Kyichu was going to be blocked by the Chinese. Shelling was going on in Lhasa. The atmosphere was charged with fear. My attendants were eager to cross the bridge right then. 'If we do not cross now, we may never be able to escape,' they said. Gaga was crying. My other travel mates were very worried. I was tired and sleepy. I told them we would cross only in the morning. They tried to convince me, make me change my mind, but I think I just wanted to sleep and refused outright. I had not experienced the havoc the Chinese had wreaked in the eastern part of Tibet and so was not so scared, while my companions had heard about it and were fearful.

Next morning, we proceeded towards the old iron bridge over the small river which was a tributary of the Kyichu. Everyone was apprehensive that the Chinese may have already blocked the passage, but the Chinese troops were concentrated in the Lhasa and Norbulingka area and the bridge appeared clear for us to cross. Today, people look back at this incident and wonder if I knew more and that was why I had said we would cross in the morning!

Then we got even more lucky. We met Mingyur. He was a villager who used to supply firewood to Tehor Khangtsen. We made an arrangement with him. In exchange for a letter which authorised him to collect whatever he wished from the store of my labrang in Drepung, we took three mules and a horse from him. That was of great help and I was able to travel on horseback.

In the late afternoon, we reached the banks of the Kyichu river. Luckily, there were boatmen available. We got into boats and led the horse and the mules, holding the reins, through the water. At one point, one of the mules turned irritable and tried to spring away, creating a momentary panic that it might overturn the boat, but we managed to get to the other side. By then it was getting dark and we spent the night at the boatman's house. The next day, we continued our journey. We stopped at a house in a larger village and from the people there we heard the story of His Holiness passing that way. His Holiness had left Lhasa three days earlier.

Early next morning, we set off again. Soon, we were facing another mountain. It had a trail along which we had to climb. That was most difficult, for it meant going up one step and slipping back two steps on the sand. By now, we could see many people on our route, both monks and laypersons, all fleeing Lhasa valley. After struggling for a while, we reached some kind of a path that was free of sand, and it became easier to journey. When we reached the edge of the pass, we looked back towards the Lhasa valley to bid farewell.

13

Navigating Snowy Mountains

I soon realised that our adventures had only just begun. I had never imagined I would be climbing a snowy mountain on a dark night when even the moon had gone into hiding behind the clouds or that I would learn to make a bed in snow. I had never anticipated that I would have a guide who would rely on a large boulder to be his landmark – a boulder that would, in that wintertime, be covered with snow and not be found! And so we were lost along with our guide. On one side were the physical and emotional challenges that we were faced with. On the other side were the comic interludes provided by people like our guide. Many may wonder how I could laugh given those circumstances of fear and oppression. I always laugh easily. But let me take you back to the mountaintop from where we had filled our eyes with our last impressions of Lhasa.

It was already late afternoon when we started descending. We decided to spend the night at an old temple before going on to the Lhokha valley. Though we feared that we might lose each other in the dark, we managed to stay as a group and reach the temple. The next day we crossed the river at the point where Kyichu from Lhasa and Tsangchu from Tsang met and reached a village where there was a temple called Kangyur Lhakhang. The locals there invited us inside and served us tea and food. We went on to a small town, Chedezhol, in the middle of which was the Sakyapa Monastery. With an intent to assess the general situation and discuss it with those involved, we decided to spend a few days there. The monastery put me up in the main room above the temple and attended to us well.

I understood that the town was the local headquarters of the Khampa resistance movement, and some people from Tehor who were a part of the resistance met me. They were true fighters and so were not ready to accept defeat. They were constantly speaking in terms of continuing the fight with the Chinese. Some suggested that instead of spending time in a place like that, I could find a remote hermitage or monastery, away from villages and towns and continue to stay on. Others even suggested that I should try to find my way to Bhutan, whose culture and religion was similar to Tibet. Its prime minister, popularly known as Kumar Sahib, was friendly with some nobles of Lhasa. But to me all these sounded optimistic assessments of our situation.

The monks of the Sakyapa Monastery also apprised us how His Holiness had visited the monastery and described vividly how He passed through the area dressed like a layperson in a maroon *chuba*.[2] During our stay there, many of the younger monks from Tashi Dargye at Drepung arrived in the town. It was now becoming clear there was no going back to the monastery and the old way of life and these monks decided to make their own way. I felt sorry for them They would have to confront huge challenges and hardships ahead, but I could not do anything beyond giving them blessings, touching my hand to their heads. I learned later that many of them joined the resistance movement.

While staying there, I visited another monastery, Sungrabling, over an hour's horse-ride away. The name was familiar because a very highly respected hermit, Tehor Kyorpon Rinpoche, had left Drepung some years earlier to stay in Lhokha and had given a teaching there. The son of Sungrabling's head lama had been my classmate during the teachings given by Geshe Sonam Gonpo. He had ears that stuck out prominently and I used to playfully imitate him by putting my two palms behind my ears. Unfortunately, he was not at Sungrabling, but we were received warmly and served tea and what seemed then to be a banquet, in the main room above the hall that served as a room for receiving special guests in the monasteries.

Before reaching the monastery, we came upon Gyalrong Khensur, the ex-abbot of Loseling, who was in a state of great despair. He asked me whether we were going to the monastery to consult the oracle. We said we might do so. Then he gave an interesting piece of advice, 'All right, do that and then do exactly the opposite of what he says. This is the time of negative forces in the higher realms because of which all the oracles and divinations are also going in their favour.'

We did, in fact, consult the oracle, both the main and the secondary deity, but did not get any clear answer. It was believed that the deity entered the monk and spoke through him. That monk was called the oracle. First, the main deity entered the human body and left it. Then the secondary deity entered. Normally, the secondary deity did the talking. But in this instance, the secondary deity became very violent and started hitting out at his attendants with the blunt edge of his sword while uttering something that was not audible to us. I thought the deities were also expressing their helplessness and frustration by becoming wrathful and aggressive.

After ten days we left Chedezhol and headed towards Dranang. We stayed at Dathang Gonpa overnight. From there we proceeded to Yarlung to reach the Chode-Og Thosam Dargyeling Monastery, which was connected to Ling Rinpoche, senior tutor to His Holiness. Its first impression was of a very well-maintained and disciplined monastery. I was again given a room above the temple. Even at that time they were continuing the evening debates and prayers in the main courtyard as if nothing had changed. They treated me well, perhaps because I belonged to Loseling Dratsang as did Ling Rinpoche. After an overnight rest, we moved on to the Chode-Gong Thosam Dargyeling Monastery, also connected to Ling Rinpoche, where we stayed for a few days.

We continued travelling in this fashion, trying to spend the nights in monasteries. There was no worry about having enough rations, because we were passing through villages and I was still wearing my tulku's robes, so people came forward with offerings. We crossed the Yartoe-dagla pass and travelled through areas of Nyal for another two days and finally reached Tsona. The Lhokha area was clear, thanks to the resistance movement, so there was no immediate fear of capture.

We essentially followed the route taken by His Holiness towards Tsona Dzong, the last dzong of the Tibetan region according to the then-existing political geography. It was also the headquarters of the eighteen dzongs or districts of Lhokha under the Lhasa government. Its chief held the highest position among the district heads. We planned to stay the night at Tsona. We found a house to stay where our hosts made us comfortable and served us hot tea.

However, as soon as we finished our tea there was a rumour that the Chinese were coming. No one wanted to take any risks at that point, when we had travelled so far and would soon enter Indian territory, so we decided to leave immediately. It was dark and snowing. My attendants quickly loaded our mules with rations for the journey ahead. The man of the house agreed to come with us as a guide and he carried a big bag of wool on his back, saying it might prove useful to exchange for food on the way.

We had to climb a snow-covered mountain, and with more snow falling continuously, it became more difficult and more dangerous to make the climb. There was very little or no moonlight, which increased the likelihood of someone falling over the edge. What was worse was that our guide floundered with the directions as the landmark he knew, a big boulder, was by now completely covered under heaps of snow. None of us had any idea of the direction we were heading. At around midnight our guide said it was too dangerous to proceed. We unloaded the mules and tried to sleep in the snow. For me, the elders had provided warm clothes, but I cannot imagine how the others would have slept, chilled to their bones. The animals were also shivering and tried to draw nearer to the humans to get some warmth. Fortunately, in the early morning we saw a long line of yaks approaching, loaded with what might have been grains. Our guide said confidently that these yaks were coming from Tsona Dzong. We quickly loaded our bags and decided to follow the yaks. That was a good decision, for their passage made an easier path in the snow for us to follow. And as luck would have it, we had been following more or less the right path at night.

After some time, we started to descend. This took several hours and the snow became thinner as the day progressed. After a time, the air also felt warmer. The area became more and more green and we realised that we were already in Mon. In Tibetan history books, the term 'Mon' referred to Bhutan as well as the land whose major part falls in Arunachal Pradesh, though it now refers exclusively to the latter. Technically, however, we were still in Tibetan territory, so if the Chinese were indeed behind us, they could still capture us, but the likelihood of that was now almost nil.

After almost a month's travel including a few days of halt at some places, we reached Mangmang, the first village in the Mon area and the last village that fell in Tibet. This was the first time I saw houses made of bamboo, for in Tibet even village homes were made of handmade mud bricks and stones, with a wooden frame. The cattle in these homes were usually housed at the ground level, with people staying on the level above and the third level was used for storing food and grain. The sight of green shoots in the fields was very pleasing because they were yet to emerge from the buds when we had left Lhasa valley. The scenery we had passed till then had been rather dull and grey. We stayed in Mangmang for one night and the next day we reached the border.

14

Arriving in India

The first sight of the Indian tricolour flag on top of a small check post gave me hope for the future. I really felt it was the start of a new life. We had arrived at the Indian border at a place called Chu-dangmo (clear water), now in Arunachal Pradesh. All I had seen in Tibet were the red, five-star Chinese flags or prayer flags or, occasionally, the Tibetan military flags. But it was not that I was seeing the tricolour for the first time because I used to receive some magazines printed in Gangtok in Tibetan language and I had seen the tricolour in them. But when I saw it then, it came with a different kind of feeling for I had come to the land of the Buddha.

We had fled from Tibet, escaping the danger. Danger of all sorts. There was the constant fear that the Chinese would capture us. There was the hitherto unknown experience of travelling through wildernesses, climbing and conquering snowy mountains peaks and crossing difficult passes. All that time, I did not really pause to think. I did not make the decision to leave – I was too young for that. Once the decision had been made and we had set out, there was no choice but to reach some place where we could live a life similar to what we were used to. What made every experience acceptable was the fact that His Holiness had passed that way and our journey was just to follow Him.

The challenge now was to start a new, safe life, but I could sense that the immediate future was not going to be easy or smooth. At that time the feeling was that I had left behind my country and was entering another country, which we considered and still do, as the source of Buddhism, the place of Buddhism's origin. Tibetans regard Mahatma Gandhi as a Boddhisattva. I had come to the land of Gandhi. And I had left behind a country that would be fully occupied by a different kind of people.

We had reached a narrow gorge with thick vegetation on both sides and a river in between. The person in charge of that post was of Tibetan origin and he was sympathetic. He promised to arrange rations for us. He explained that we would have to be stationed there for a few days. We were among the first to arrive there from Tibet.

I felt at ease because at least we could go to the river and wash our feet and face and feel somewhat clean. I don't remember how many days we were held up at the border, but I do remember my attendants worrying that our tsampa may not last long. No rations arrived. There were no villages in the vicinity from where we could hope to buy food. So we literally lived on diluted soup of tsampa. Hundreds of people continued to arrive each day.

Eventually we were formed into groups, each group consisting of a hundred members, the first consisting of tulkus, abbots and senior monks. Each group had a leader and we set out on the road again. Travel was primarily on foot, carrying our own baggage. From Chu-dangmo, the first stop was at Gorsam Chorten, after having trekked the whole day. The next day, we arrived at a slightly bigger village and halted for the night. The local people were the Monpas of Arunachal, who spoke some Tibetan and were Buddhists. They were very kind and welcomed us with incense and even cleaned up a space for my stay. A few older Monpas had tears in their eyes while expressing sadness at the helpless situation. They offered us food like roasted rice and dried blackcurrants. I enjoyed eating them. However, there were always mischief makers who spread the rumour that these Monpas were of a ritual cult that poisoned others so that all their wealth and power could be grabbed.

The journey was not easy. The further we went down the gorge, the more the river widened and we had to cross some shaky, makeshift bamboo bridges and planks placed on rocks high above the river. It was very frightening and we were extra careful as we had heard that a few times mules and horses had fallen off into the river, along with the bags on their backs.

After about four days we reached Tawang. Tawang Monastery was small by Tibetan standards, but there was a persistent myth with no apparent basis that it was the biggest Buddhist monastery in the world! Tibetan monasteries had thousands of monks living in them in the old days, but in Tawang we did not see more than a hundred. Its interiors did not have many signs of it being a monastery. They had also piled up a lot of wood for fire. I stayed in the room of one of the monks.

To my surprise, even monks there possessed bows and arrows. The Monpas were known to have sharp arrows with a poisonous substance applied to the tip. I was amused to hear one of the monks boast, 'We will not allow the Chinese to come this side, because we have these poisonous arrows. We will protect our monastery.'

The situation in the monastery gradually changed for the better and more emphasis was laid on studies and other religious activities. While staying in Tawang, some rations arrived and for the first time, I saw an Indian aircraft, throwing rations down in an empty field. Many packets of rice and tins of Dalda (hydrogenated oil) burst open on the ground, having been thrown without parachutes. But the feeling that we were in a free country and breathing the air of freedom was a great relief and most enjoyable.

In the main temple of Tawang there was a Buddha, about two storeys high. The facial expression of the Buddha was not particularly striking or special but the strange thing was that on top of the Buddha's head they had placed a shikhar, the peak of a victory banner, instead of the usual Usnisa. At that time, I wished somebody would point this out to the people that this was wrong. But it did not look right that we point out a fault when we were their guests. Later, when the temple was renovated, the mistake was corrected.

We were then taken in groups to Bomdila, passing through a place called Jang. After crossing Sela pass, we descended and reached Senge Dzong. Then, we went on to Derang and Rawang and eventually reached Bomdila. A new township had just started being formed there, consisting of mostly bamboo houses. We stopped at the outskirts at a teashop and there I had the most delicious sweet Indian tea for the first time on Indian territory. Although we had reached the border several days earlier, at Bomdila I had the feeling of being at home in India, because the atmosphere in this new town was different from the Tibetan habitat and more Indian army personnel were visible. I cannot sketch the area of our camps as it was then. In the 1990s, when I went to Tawang to attend a seminar and passed through the area of the camps, I could not spot anything I recognised. The place looked different and had grown into a full-fledged town.

While coming down from Bomdila, most of the people were travelling downhill by trucks, but somehow somebody took pity on me and I was taken in a jeep, sitting next to the driver. The door in the front was low and I needed to hold the handle firmly all day for support, thinking that if the jeep took a sharp turn I would be thrown out. By the time we reached the Indian plains, my hands had turned numb. As we came down the mountain and drove through the forest, the climate grew warmer and more humid. In front of me, the vast plains of India with their green vegetation started to pan out.

Driving through the forest greenery was an experience of a new kind. Occasionally, I spotted black wooden cabins, perhaps checkpoints, by the roadside. The thick monk's clothes I had been wearing from Tibet started feeling thicker and heavier. I saw people dressed in clean, crisp white dhotis and when I saw those comfortable-looking clothes, I felt my robes becoming more of a burden. We stopped at a place where there was an army camp. We were given a place to sleep and provided food in aluminium lunch boxes.

The next day we left and reached the transit camp in the plains, at Missamari in Assam. It was May and very hot. We were all given shirts and trousers of some thin cotton fabric that I had never seen earlier, in shades of white, blue and pink. I too wore them but I must say I felt awkward. At that time, it must have looked like a huge prisoners' camp. We were told we should burn all the thick leather clothes or they would rot, which was not factually correct. I did not have any leather clothes so I did not have to burn anything.

The residential arrangements were in long bamboo houses with platforms on two sides of the rooms on which people were expected to sleep. Food was served and there was a special effort made to educate us on cleanliness and maintaining hygiene. Tibet was cold and bathing was not a daily habit. Also, since Tibetans lived with livestock, they must have carried their smell. In the old system of our thinking, cleanliness meant removing defilement, mainly inner dirt. On the clothes, we used incense to make them fragrant. It was said that if we placed our clothes under the stars at night, they would become pure. Sometimes people would sprinkle water and chant a mantra that was believed to make them clean. Washing was not always done to clean soiled clothes.

We remained at Missamari for about three months. There was no shortage of food. The rations included ripe bananas, which the Tibetans were not familiar with. I heard that some people tried to fry them like a vegetable or add them to broth. We laughed over this at that time, though I learned later that it was a common practice in some places in the world.

Part IV

India: Settling Down, Finding Ground

15

Missamari and the Idea of a Government-in-Exile

A whiff of Lifebuoy soap always brings back memories of my Missamari days. Our rations there included half a bar of Lifebuoy soap for each of us. Our drinking water came from tube wells. For bathing we went to a river nearby, the waters of which looked a little muddy but were cool in the heat of summer. Speaking of the river, I must confess, one day I was with some young tulkus, the youngest of whom must have been about eight. I took him across to a small island in the river, left him there and came away. I still remember his crying. He was the youngest among us and this was perhaps one way of welcoming him into the fold and having fun. He was later brought back and comforted. The Government of India looked after us very well and I believe some foreign relief agencies made significant contributions to the relief work.

Missamari had all kinds of people who were refugees from Tibet, not only monks. The first celebration we had there was His Holiness the Dalai Lama's birthday. Later regularised to be celebrated on 6 July by the Gregorian calendar every year, at that time it was calculated by the Tibetan lunar calendar – the fifth day of the fifth month. A temporary brick throne was made on which His Holiness's photo was placed and Kundeling Dzasag and other high-ranking officials of the old Lhasa government made speeches. It was the first celebration of His Holiness's birthday outside Tibet.

Home Minister Gulzarilal Nanda came one day and addressed the refugees. I understood he was giving assurance of the help the Indian government would give the Tibetan refugees and the Dalai Lama. It was my first experience of listening to an

Indian leader. Later, he became the acting prime minister for some days after the passing of Nehru. I believe he was a Gandhian. I once read in a newspaper that he did not have any house of his own and stayed in a rented house in Defence Colony in New Delhi. This made me feel that even though he was in such a big position, he did not crave wealth and property.

His Holiness's eldest brother Taktser Rinpoche, known in the West by his actual name, Thubten Jigme Norbu, also came one day and met the gathering. I don't remember whether he gave a speech, but his very presence was an encouragement to the refugees. At that time, I must mention, we all felt we would be going back to Tibet very soon. We took that for granted.

The leaders, about four or five of them, would work in one corner of the long makeshift structure, which people used to point to and call the cabinet. Among them was the Lhasa cabinet minister Surkhang Wangchen Gelek. Surkhang was a very impressive, handsome-looking man. I had seen him at the Monlam festival celebrations in Lhasa, looking most impressive, dignified and elegant among the important people sitting on the balcony.

Surkhang gave a speech at a meeting in Missamari. He began by saying the meeting was not like a meeting in Lhasa under Chinese control. I understood why he was saying this – at one point people in Lhasa had started suspecting he might be closer to the Chinese. They even said he had shared the same cigarette with Chinese officials!

He later joined His Holiness in Mussoorie and eventually went to Dharamsala. I remember when I went on a pilgrimage in 1959–60, I saw His Holiness for the first time in India in Kushinagar near Gorakhpur, and Surkhang was in the entourage. Later, in 1960–61, when His Holiness established the first government-in-exile with five departments headed by senior officials from the Lhasa government, Surkhang and another cabinet minister Yuthok were not taken. The public perceived this as the influence of Gyalo Thondup, His Holiness's second-eldest brother. Both Surkhang and Yuthok lived in Kolkata for some time and Surkhang eventually went to the USA where I heard he got a teaching job at a university. In 1971, both ended up in Taiwan, then ruled by the Kuomintang.

Surkhang and Yuthok were the most prominent Tibetans in Taiwan along with Lithang Jamatsang, a wealthy trading family from Kham. The Kuomintang's policy towards Tibet was peculiar – they wanted to treat it as part of China. Their official line, whether they believed it or not, was that they would recapture the mainland and grant proper status to Tibet and inner Mongolia. They even had a special bureau to look after 'Tibet and Mongolian Affairs'. The two former cabinet ministers were given special treatment and the status of 'Tibet Cabinet in Taiwan'. Tibetans in India opposed this strongly, because at that time everybody believed that the final goal was total independence from China. Since then, all this has changed in all respects. Surkhang died in Taipei in 1977 and the so-called Tibet Cabinet in Taiwan closed down a year later. The National Party came to power, which continued with the rhetoric of uniting with the mainland, but didn't make special efforts to use particular sections of the Tibetan people to further their own agenda.

I came in contact with Surkhang on some occasions. In 1960, in Kalimpong, I happened to meet him on the road and he asked me my name and then said he knew my previous incarnation whose brother was a friend of his. His father had been sent by Lhasa as the governor of the town of Chamdo in Kham. When monks from Dargye Monastery were fleeing from Chiang Kai-shek's army in the early twentieth century, Aku Tsundue, the brother of the previous Doboom Tulku, was prominent among them and he and Surkhang became friends.

I next met him at the Library of Tibetan Works and Archives (LTWA), for he was a man of letters and a skilful writer. He was said to have written extensively about the old Tibet systems of taxation and so on, but unfortunately, much of it has been lost. He must have written something critical of someone, probably that was why it conveniently got lost. In Merwyn Goldstein's great and vivid *History of Modern Tibet*, the stories of the inner circle were probably drawn from Surkhang, to whose daughter Goldstein was once married. And while working at the Private Office of His Holiness, a handwritten letter of Surkhang to His Holiness came my way. It had been sent from Taiwan to explain he had never played into the hands of the Taiwanese and never had an intention to do so.

16

My First Train Ride

Missamari was not going to be our place of residence for long. Soon plans were made for the different residents, depending on their inclination and aptitude. Arrangements began to be made to send people to different places in India. The younger ones with greater bodily strength were sent for road construction in Punjab, where Dharamsala was located. (at that time Himachal and Haryana were all part of Punjab). For the older people above sixty, plans were made to accommodate them in a cooler area. Children had to be sent to school. People were asked to register wherever they felt they would fit or would like to be.

For younger monks who had been studying scriptures in Tibet, a special transit camp was organised in Buxa Duar in Jalpaiguri district in West Bengal. It lay along the Bhutan border. Those who did not want to depend on this arrangement were to register under 'independent livelihood'. Most of these were tulkus or abbots. I chose this option and wanted to go to Kalimpong because I knew a few benefactors there, especially the Odong Tsang family. The Odong Tsang brothers had left Tibet before the uprising and had been kind enough to send word to me at Missamari, encouraging me to come to Kalimpong.

Soon it was time to leave Missamari and we boarded the train from the nearest railway station. The sight of a long, winding train drawing into the platform was bewildering and a little frightening. The Tibetan man in charge of putting us on the train tried to be very strict and instructed us not to mix the small groups he had made of all the travellers. He was holding all the tickets and was hoping everything would go in an orderly manner. But as soon as the train arrived, everybody rushed forward, and in the chaos, he did not know what to do. He handed me a bunch of the tickets saying, 'Go, go, go.'

It was only after I boarded the train and found myself and my three assistants – Gaga, Sonam Dhondup and Lobsang Ngodup – in an almost empty compartment, did it strike me that I knew to ask, 'Where are you going?' in Hindi, but I did not know how to ask, 'Where are we now?'

That was the first time I had seen a train, let alone travel in it. The romance of it totally escaped me since I thought I had been separated from the other Tibetan groups and was going into some unknown area where I would not be able to ask, 'Where are we?'

Some Indians were sleeping on our berths in the compartment. There were empty berths, but we did not dare to sit on them. We sat down on the bundles we were carrying. After some time, some Indian travellers gestured to us to sit on the berths. Things seemed quite all right, but the whole night I was worried because there was only my group in that compartment and we had no means of finding out where the other Tibetan groups were. In the morning the train stopped at Rangapara and I looked through the window and saw some Tibetans. That was a great relief because we might have ended up in totally different places.

Finally, we reached Siliguri. It was night and there was no way of knowing where to go, so we slept on the platform. The next day I went to Kalimpong by jeep with some others. This was again a new experience, to be riding through tea estates. Not knowing these were tea gardens, I thought someone was tending to the bushes even in the forest and had trimmed them evenly.

We went directly to a huge storage house which belonged to the Sadutsang family. In the good old days, this was used for the storage of wool transported from across the border of Tibet to India. The Ogdong Tsang brothers were living there. They were my main supporters from Tehor. They made arrangements for my stay in a nice bungalow outside the town, which belonged to a high Nyingmapa lama called Dudjom Rinpoche. The bungalow looked palatial to me, with its veranda overlooking a beautiful garden. It had a bedroom, a drawing room, a bathroom, a storage room and a separate kitchen. The Rinpoche and his family lived upstairs. We occupied half the ground floor. It was an unbelievable transformation of my living situation as compared to the past few months. It was like suddenly reaching heaven. The rent was ₹90 per month.

Later, another family moved in, occupying a smaller part of the ground floor. They were the Chogtays, whose names are also mentioned in Goldstein's history of Tibet. Chogtay was previously a fifth-ranking lay official in Tibet. Around the time of the conflict between Reting and Tagdrag (two successive regents between the 13th and 14th Dalai Lamas), Reting's side was defeated. He had been close to Reting and Tagdrag's regime kept creating trouble for him. So he resigned from service and came to India. He and his wife were quite young at the time, in their forties, and he had extraordinary knowledge of the outside world. He also knew some English and his knowledge of Tibetan literature was very good. He was a devout practitioner of the sadhanas of the Nyingmapa tradition and a close disciple of the famous nun, Shugshep Jetsun Rinpoche, believed to have lived for over a hundred years in a hermitage in Tibet.

Chogtay was very particular about hygiene, cleanliness and tidiness. He told me how he once saw a monastery in Bodh Gaya arrange butter lamps for pilgrims under the Bodhi Tree and had remarked that the lamps might cause the tree to dry up, a treasure of the world against which their few lamps were nothing. Why not offer from a distance? This offended the monks, who abused him saying he was an aristocrat who imagined he could still give orders.

He was strict to the point of being fussy about his diet. He was allergic to onions. Sometimes, if he had a headache after drinking milk or eating yoghurt, he would go to the extent of complaining that the cow must have eaten some onions. Every evening, he would invite me to his room and serve supper while listening to the Tibetan language bulletin on the All India Radio and also sometimes the Lhasa radio. We became very close friends and remained so even after he moved to Manali. Eventually, he moved to Orissa and built a hermitage on a small hilltop near the Tibetan settlement that was just coming up in Ganjam district, a few hours' drive from Bhubaneshwar.

Kalimpong was considered a very prosperous place. It was a small town at that time, with few telephones. Electricity was from a big generator for the whole town. There was no telephone in the bungalow I was staying in, but Chogtay took me with him when he was making a call to Darjeeling or Gangtok to show me how to make phone calls. In those days the procedure to make phone calls outside the town involved booking in advance and waiting. The wait could be for hours. I still remember the phone number of the Ogdong Tsang brothers. It was 45, just two digits. When I revisited Kalimpong in 2001, like all other places, it had changed beyond recognition.

I was in Kalimpong for a little over a year. This period was spent without any clear idea about what I should be doing and what should be, so to speak, my life's mission. The months passed in a leisurely fashion because I didn't have any engagements of study or any daily routine except eating and taking a walk in the beautiful hillside. I was about eighteen then.

I did not take up any course of study, but I observed people coming to obtain teachings from Dudjom Rinpoche, as he was a very highly renowned Nyingmapa master. At one time a foreigner, I believe a researcher, came to study the *Guhya Hriday* or the *Sangwa Nyingpo Tantra*. He could read Tibetan and was studying the text. This appeared incredible to me because the Tibetan tradition was to start at lower levels and gradually progress upwards. But this person was starting right at the top. *Sangwa Nyingpo Tantra* was not one of the texts found in the Kangyur,[1] and was accepted only by the Nyingmapa school. Later, I was informed that the original Sanskrit text had been found somewhere.

Dudjom Rinpoche was not a monk; he lived with his wife and three children. His behaviour was very refined, like a Lhasa aristocrat. He was kind to me and did not try to influence me with his tradition or way of thinking. Jadral Sangye Dorje, a lama from Kham who lived in Darjeeling at that time, was also a very well-known yogi, who used to visit Dudjom Rinpoche from time to time. He was extraordinary in that he did not use any vehicle while travelling and I believe he had to walk for days together to come from Darjeeling, which took only three hours by car. He was a great walker, a vegetarian and an ascetic. I heard years later that he had changed his stance and had started using vehicles.

One day Jadral Sangye Dorje suddenly said to me, 'You should embrace the Nyingma tradition because you seem to have a karmic link.' I must confess I did not take this advice seriously. He was very skilful in talking and negotiating with people. Once there was some conflict between the disciples of Dudjom Rinpoche. He made all of them sit on the lawn in front of the bungalow, talked to them and made them confess and even do prostrations. Common people knew him for his practice of saving lives like buying fish and releasing them in the river. He had a place somewhere near Siliguri. Sometimes he used to live in a hermitage in Nepal near his disciple, who would have been the successor of the Chogyal (king) of Sikkim.

17

Pilgrimage

Finally, there came a time when I had an opportunity to travel by train and enjoy it too. By then I had also learnt how to ask in Hindi, 'Where are we?' I experienced travel by another mode of transport also – a steamer. Better still, these travels took me to places where I felt the presence of the Buddha himself.

In the winter of 1959–60, I went on a pilgrimage to major Buddhist sites. One of my supporters, Lobsang Namgyal of Dongchung Tsang, who was the manager of Doboom Labrang when I was very young, took responsibility for making arrangements for the trip, which he sponsored as well. There were four of us and we took the train from Siliguri, travelling second class, which was quite comfortable compared to the crowded third-class compartments. Lobsang Namgyal brought along plenty of prepared food foreveryone. We also had a kerosene stove for cooking our food when we stayed at a dharamsala.

Unlike my first journey from Missamari which, as you know, was full of anxiety and uncertainty, I enjoyed this one. The last time we had travelled by night and could not really see anything outside the window. This time, during the day, I liked watching the vast fields in the Indian plains and the variety of scenes of people working in the fields and driving in jeeps and cars. The next morning, we reached a station from where we had to cross a river, probably the Ganga, by steamer. We had to walk on the sand to reach it. The coolie we wanted to engage demanded ₹10 to carry our luggage, which was a lot of money at that time. We managed to strike a bargain. This was my first experience of taking a steamer.

We had to wait a long time at the station, during which period I observed the beggars around us. It was an example of the great contrasts in India because just before that, in the steamer I had noticed some rich-looking people behaving like 'angrezi sahibs' or Englishmen.

Eventually we reached Gaya and took a tonga to Bodh Gaya. Bodh Gaya is considered by all Buddhists to be the place where all the Buddhas of all the three times – the past, the present and the future – attained or will attain enlightenment. The very sight of the tall stupa even before we reached the place filled me with joy and ecstasy. We easily found a room in the dharamsala run by the only Tibetan monastery there. The monks at the monastery had come to India a few years earlier, before the situation had changed in Tibet, and they were well-off compared to the new arrivals. They showed off their clothes a bit in front of us refugees.

We did circumambulations and prostrations at the main Mahabodhi Stupa. Sitting in front of the Buddha statue in the main temple, as well as underneath the Bodhi Tree behind the temple, gave me the feeling of fulfilment of a long-cherished desire. I felt very fortunate to be at the very spot where Gautama the Buddha had attained the state of full enlightenment. While sitting in the temple, I felt the presence of the Buddha amid the calmness and serenity around.

I was very impressed by the conduct of the renowned monk Zigyab Rinpoche from Kham Karze who had studied in Tashi Lhunpo. He sat under the Bodhi Tree every day and recited the five root texts of the five major subjects of Buddhist philosophical studies. I was told he did that in order to fulfil his commitment to his guru. Usually in places like these, people engage in prayers, not reciting philosophical texts over and over again. I met an elderly Buddhist monk who was actually Tibetan but ordained in the Theravada tradition. He told me that in the Theravada practice, monks were not supposed to wear any ornaments or decorative items, not even rosaries. Following the Vinaya rules in a more literal manner, there was an element of truth in his statement.

On a later visit after a few years, I found that renovation and more decorative elements had changed the look of the temple premises, which perhaps cast a shadow over the serenity. On my first visit, I never imagined that Bodh Gaya would become the crowded place it is now, with so many temples and guest houses and institutions. I felt greater sanctity then, in the vicinity of the outer parikrama path, despite it being dusty. And the same holds for the broken pieces of the old structure that were lying around, as compared to now, when there are a lot of repairs and renovations and replacements sponsored by wealthy people.

From Bodh Gaya we visited Niranjana river where Siddhartha had practised austerity and meditated for six years. We also went to the place of the Mahakala situated between Gaya and Bodh Gaya where, in a cave, there was a statue of the six-armed Mahakala standing on Ganesha, installed with a Tibetan style alter. I was surprised that no local Hindus had protested and wondered if they knew what it was. Subsequently it occurred to me that such images may be acceptable in Hinduism, where we see Kali stepping on Shiva, and may have a philosophical explanation which I was not aware of. Buddhists also gave an explanation that it was not a suppression of Ganesha but an attempt to put both on the same pedestal. We also went to see some temples supposed to be the site where a monkey offered honey to Buddha, but there were no signs of Buddhist shrines there.

Visiting Rajgir was another extraordinary experience because we always recited the Heart Sutra and other Prajnaparamita sutras, most of which were said to have been uttered at Rajgir and had descriptions of the places and the gathering of so many thousands of monks and arhats. The exact spot identified as the place of the turning of the second Wheel of Dharma by preaching Prajnaparamita is not important, and there are miracles interpretations and visions of great numbers, which may not be meant to be taken literally. The climb up the hill to the sacred site was a bit difficult for me as I had gained some weight then. Now a Japanese temple, beautiful as it is, has come higher up on the hillock and a ropeway leads directly to it. Pilgrims who take the ropeway reach the temple and then have to take extra trouble to go down the steep slope to reach the sacred site. Some unknowingly go back by the ropeway and miss visiting the sacred site.

In Rajgir, we had some difficulty finding a place to stay, because apparently a few days earlier, some Tibetans had come and had not behaved properly. A yellow-robed monk-in-charge of a dharamsala said many things to us in a raised voice, which I could not follow, but I got the impression that someone had done something wrong. Yet in those days finding a place to stay was never very difficult because there were fewer visitors and people respected pilgrims coming from other parts of the country or other countries.

Another place we visited was Nalanda. The sight of the ruins was very saddening, especially when we imagine the burning of libraries and smoke billowing for many days. The story reminds me now of the Cultural Revolution that Tibet was to experience in some years.

We then went to Varanasi and stayed at Sarnath. This was to be a place I would stay for three years as a part of the Acharya degree programme for monks who had studied in monasteries and Buxa Duar. The sight of the Dhamekh Stupa and the newly-built Mahabodhi temple which held the Buddha relic took me back to Tibet. I had seen a photograph of it in a magazine from India and it had stirred in me a desire to visit some of these sites. Next to the Dhamekh Stupa was a temple which all Tibetan pilgrims visited. The paintings on the temple wall, which were actually representations of Mahavira's life, also looked somewhat similar to certain stories from Buddha's life. Everybody took the main figure to be a statue of Buddha, in black stone. I learned later that it was a statue of Mahavira and that it was a Jain temple.

When we came to India from Tibet, we had an eagerness to see everything as a legacy of the Buddha, since this was the land of his enlightenment. So pilgrims would go to, for example, Amritsar, to the Gurudwara there. Guru Rinpoche in Tibetan meant 'the teacher'. There was some confusion between this and the word 'Guru' used by the Sikhs. Additionally, the langar provided free food, which made them stay even longer.

Now that confusion does not exist. People have become clever. From a devotional point of view, it is okay if people offer worship in different places, but we have to admit that Guru Rinpoche and the Sikh Gurus are not the same – the equivalence is faith without basis.

While staying in the Birla Dharamsala, I somehow developed a desire to learn Sanskrit, but circumstances did not lead to my doing that. I visited the Sampurnanand Sanskrit University, where four or five Tibetan monks were studying. Tara Rinpoche, one of the senior monks who later became the abbot of one of the tantric monasteries, was there at that time. I did not get the impression that they were very enthusiastic learners, but he told me that he somehow managed to pass the exams. He described how, when some students failed, they jumped before a train and killed themselves and he had jokingly told people, 'If I fail I will not be able to jump in front of a train or even a car, but I will lie in front of a rickshaw!'

As I mentioned earlier, at Kushinagar I had the opportunity of seeing His Holiness for the first time after He came to India and received the transmission of Gaden Lhagya, Lama Ngachupa and Thogthama in a tiny Tibetan temple next to the main shrine containing the reclining Buddha. I must have lost some weight by that time as this was where His Holiness remarked that I used to be chubby back in Tibet.

His Holiness made a short consecration prayer in that Tibetan temple which ended with the verses of auspiciousness from the *Chakrasamvara Sadhana*. I got an impression that this sadhana was His Holiness's main practice. In Gelukpa tradition, there are three main deities and three main sadhanas. The sadhanas are linked with the deities and are called Guhyasamaja, Chakrasamvara and Yamantaka. Generally, Yamantaka Sadhana is common among the Gelukpas. Manjusri is the deity of wisdom and Yamantaka is the wrathful form of Manjusri. The Gelukpas consider Tsongkhapa to be an emanation of Yamantaka, a manifestation of Manjusri. In Tsongkhapa's biographies, there is a reference to his conversations with Manjusri. Whenever he had any doubt about the scriptures, he asked her directly.

I also met the senior Ladakhi Rinpoche, Kushok Bakula, during my pilgrimage. He was close to Nehru and had been the minister for Ladakh Affairs in Jammu and Kashmir Government under Sheikh Abdullah. He was India's ambassador to

Ulaanbaatar for two terms and later became one of the trustees of the World Buddhist Culture Trust that I founded in 1996 and then managed.

18

Taking a Decision about My Future

Finally, we returned to Kalimpong and I moved into a smaller place. I went to a so-called school to learn English where my teacher, of Tibetan origin from a place called Domo or Yadung and a chain smoker with yellow nails and teeth, taught me the alphabet and some spellings. Classes of about an hour and a half were held at night. There were very few students in our class. D-O-G dog, C-A-T cat, apple means *seb*, dog means *kutta* – that was how I learnt the language. That was also all the formal schooling in English I ever had – of about two months.

One unforgettable memory during this time was the visit of Apa Pant to Gaden Tharpa Choeling Monastery and the school, founded by Domo Geshe Rinpoche Ngawang Kalsang, in 1912 at the hilltop in Kalimpong. We were made to line up to receive him. He was a descendant of the Raja of Audh, ICS officer and political officer in Sikkim.[2] His physical features and voice left a long-lasting impression on me. He enquired about the monastery's land and about the classes. In fact, this was not the first time that I was seeing him. In 1957–58 he had visited Tibet, accompanying the Chogyal of Sikkim, and he came to the debate courtyard of Loseling in Drepung Monastery in Lhasa. What I noted at that time was that there was a tall Indian officer and a few of Chogyal's bodyguards in British-style red coats. The Chogyal wore a brocade chuba and did not look any different from a middle-level officer of the Lhasa government.

Later I came to know from Apa Pant's writings and from other sources that he was a spiritual practitioner and practised yoga and meditation. He had two written books, one on Surya Namaskar and the other on mandala. The latter summarised his spiritual experiences and mentioned his guru, Jamyang Khentse Chokyi Lodro. I had the good fortune to invite him to give a talk on Tibet when I was in Tibet House. I remember introducing a Tibetan doctor to him for his physical check-up by pulse reading. At his advanced age, he was found perfectly fit. He passed away on 5 October 1992.

We still believed that we were just biding time and would soon be back in Tibet. We believed we would regain our freedom and our lands. At that time every Tibetan was told that our purpose of coming into exile was to regain the lost freedom. It was not like running away to escape some natural calamity. Around that time, I read His Holiness's advice to a group of road construction workers, 'We should direct all our activities for the future of Tibet. Even keeping yourself clean would make people think these Tibetans are a clean people. That will contribute to regaining Tibet back.'

There were many other tulkus and abbots at Kalimpong at that time, each with their sponsor or supporter. The sponsor or supporter was generally a businessman who had settled earlier in that place.

Once there was a letter from Dharamsala asking the tulkus to perform prayers for three days, with various rituals, for the future of Tibet. We assembled in the small Tharpa Choeling Monastery that had existed before our arrival. I don't know how much it helped the Tibetan cause, but it was a good occasion to meet people, especially the well-known lamas from Tibet. I saw Sakya Trizin Rinpoche there for the first time. He came to preside over a prayer session one day.

Around that time, Kyabje Trijang Rinpoche, His Holiness the Dalai Lama's tutor, visited Kalimpong and stayed at the Sadutsang House and I went to receive his blessings. As I was leaving, he gave me a one-line advice which has lingered in my mind forever. He said, '*Da mi da manang aah* (Don't do strange things).' He did not specify what the strange things might be, but given those days, I think what he probably meant were things like going to the cinema, eating in restaurants and so on.

So far, no clear idea of my destination for my life in exile in India had formed, but it became evident that I could not just keep hanging around in Kalimpong doing nothing. There were several possibilities. One was to go to school, for I was eighteen and still young enough. Somebody asked me if I wished to join the school that Freda Bedi had set up in Dalhousie for young tulkus, where they were taught English as well as traditional subjects. For some reason, I did not feel like going there. Some tulkus, like Chogyam Trungpa, who came out of this school became known internationally.

One alternative was to specialise in a particular discipline of traditional subjects. Gyara Rinpoche, a senior lama from Chamdo residing in Kalimpong at that time, whom I regard not as my guru but my role model and who had been a disciple of Geshe Sonam Gonpo, encouraged me to study Tibetan medicine and even gave me some Tibetan medical texts. Now looking back, I sometimes have regrets that I did not pursue that line. Obviously, there was always the choice of following the monastic line and my admirers were not in favour of any other idea. The obvious place to go was Buxa Duar, where the Government of India, with the help of the Central Relief Committee, had made arrangements for a camp exclusively for monks to continue studies they had started in Tibet, especially those from the three major monasteries around Lhasa – Drepung, Sera and Gaden. So it was decided that I should go to Buxa and I went there with my attendants.

19

At Buxa Duar (1961–69)

A small stretch of land between the hills with a narrow stream running through, Buxa Duar lies along the border of Bhutan in the Jalpaiguri district of West Bengal. Coming from a cold country, we dreaded the summer heat in India. We used to escape from the heat and humidity by dipping into a stream two or three times a day. The clean, cool waters dispelled our fatigue.

If we climbed further up from Buxa, we could reach a village called Paksamkha, inhabited by the Bhutanese. In Bhutanese literature, there was mention of the four *kha*s.[3] My hunch was that Paksamkha, which the Bhutanese pronounce 'Pasakha', became 'Buxa' during British rule.

The Buxa camp had about 1,500 monks, mainly belonging to the three largest Gelukpa monasteries in the Lhasa area. There were some from the other traditions of Nyingma, Kagyu and Sakya, too. There were some nuns from the Kagyu tradition. This area was to become something like a monastic settlement for the next eight or nine years.

There are four major traditions of Tibetan Buddhism, each of which have further subdivisions. When important gurus have a large number of followers, they form a tradition and start having their own texts, prayer books and so on. This is how so many traditions came into existence.

Nyingma means 'the old' or 'original one', established by Guru Padmasambhava and Acharya Shantarakshita during the period of the great king Trisong Detsen. Kagyu literally means 'the one who follows the order from Vajradharas'. Vajradharas are not human beings but Sambhogakaya.[4] Kagyu's human gurus are Tilopa and Naropa in India and Marpa and Milerapa in Tibet. Sakya literally represents the area of the root monastery. It means 'grey land'. The place must be grey and dry. They are the followers of the tradition of the great scholars Sachen Kunga Nyingpo and Sakya Pandita.

Tsongkhapa lived in the fourteenth century and his followers are called Gelukpa. Tsongkhapa's direct disciples were Gyaltsab Je, Khedub Je and the 1st Dalai Lama Gedun Drup. In the eleventh century, a great Bengali Buddhist master called Atisha Dipankara came to Tibet. His system, called 'kadamb', did not stay as a separate tradition because his teachings were assimilated into all the traditions.

The camp commandant at Buxa Duar was Lieutenant Colonel (retired) Pathania from Punjab. He was in charge of overall arrangements. Under him was a police superintendent and below him Mr Kalibabu. The camp was enclosed by a wire fence and had a watchtower. People believed it was a prisoner's camp during the British period (some even say Mahatma Gandhi was imprisoned there), but I have not come across any account of such a prison there. Apart from the monks and a few Nepalese and Bhutanese villagers, there were no other inhabitants or visitors. Occasionally, when the officers managing the camp had relatives or parents visiting, I would see Bengali babus in dhotis.

There was no assembly hall, but the monks would gather on a levelled and cemented ground, which must have been a tennis court or something similar. Later, somebody donated money to put up a cloth canopy above this, to be used on special occasions. The daily schedule was more or less like the monastic system in Tibet, except that in the beginning many of the monks did not have a complete set of robes, so they were seen wearing white shirts with a monk's lower garment.

The study programmes were carried out seriously. But in the first couple of years, my mind was not settled at all. I think this was because I had become a bit spoilt by the facilities available during my stay in Kalimpong. In the beginning the supply of rations was abundant, but gradually the amount reduced. The camp sometimes received old supplies and people were driven to complain about the quality and quantity of food. It was perhaps due to the substandard food that some monks developed tuberculosis. Although the conditions were poor, on the whole, everyone was happy and quite satisfied with the facilities available. We were told that back in Tibet, the conditions were very bad.

Buxa was a very remote place. We never saw any kind of vehicle, not even a bicycle. The nearest motorable road was about two hours walking distance down the hill, from where people would try to hitch a ride on the trucks carrying goods like road-building materials and then take a bus to the nearest town, Alipur Duar, which was also a railway junction. The nearest large town was Cooch Bihar. I managed to get away on some occasions on one or the other excuse and go either to Kalimpong or Shillong. Shillong was known as the 'Scotland of the East' during British rule. A few Tibetan businessmen had settled there and were running Tibetan restaurants and some businesses. They loved inviting tulkus and senior monks for vacations and I used to enjoy this kind of *chutti* (holiday).

A lady called Frieda Bedi did much to help improve the living conditions at Buxa Duar. She was the first Western lady to take full ordination in Tibetan Buddhism. She was called Sister Palmo at that time. When His Holiness visited India in 1956, she had escorted Him around the Buddhist shrines. Jawaharlal Nehru, the prime minister, had requested her to help the refugees. Among other things that she did, she introduced the young tulkus in Buxa to foreign penfriends, some of whom sent gifts and even money.

Before we move away from Frieda Bedi, it may be of interest to the readers that she was the mother of the Bollywood–Hollywood actor, Kabir Bedi.

My penfriend was Enna Decke from the small town of Lübeck in Germany. She would send postcards and photographs of the city. I looked at them again and again. In Buxa Duar nobody knew English. I would go to Mr Kalibabu with the cards and letters I received from Enna Decke and ask him to explain what was written in them and also write a reply. I doubt whether he was able to decipher the peculiar handwriting she had or the language either. But whatever he wrote in reply, I would send it off as it was.

Once I received a large packet which contained many small items like towels of different sizes, soaps, cards and objects to be placed on the table, all of which looked to me very luxurious. I heard that sometimes gifts were intercepted and hijacked on the way, perhaps followed by requests to send future packages to a new address. One young monk gained a reputation for doing this all the time. In the late 1980s, I took advantage of an opportunity to visit Lübeck. The town looked very familiar to me because of the picture postcards I had received from my penfriend. Unfortunately, she had passed away just a year before my visit.

I developed an interest in aircraft during my stay in Buxa. I would cut out the shape of a plane from tinfoil and string it across my room. I don't know if it was a sign that I would be flying all over the world later. I also spent days studying the behaviour of insects, some of which I collected in bottles. I would watch how wasps used mud to build small cylindrical structures in which they left a small hole and brought spiders and other small insects and stuffed them inside. They bit the insects' legs off without eating them and I would wonder why. The wasp then laid her egg inside, closed the opening and flew off, her job done. The insects stayed alive and fresh inside the structure, which seemed to act like an air-conditioned space. When the egg hatched, the young wasp would feed on the insects and gain strength to break open the structure. Today, this may seem commonplace information because it is freely available on the internet. But for me at that time, it was a revelation. I 'discovered' all this myself.

I spent some nine years at Buxa, during which time my dear Gaga, who had looked after me since I was very young, passed away. He had known both my predecessor and me. Looking back, I do not think he was that old, but at that time he seemed very old to me, though he looked after the details of my daily requirements very well. He did his daily prayers loudly. I learnt them from him without having to memorise them. The power of repeated hearing was so great. As a monk, he never had any requirements for himself. After finishing the chores, he would sit all day long in the room. He was with me all through my stay at Doboom Ritro, Drepung Monastery and then in India and through all the travels. He was like a part of me. I was very sad when he passed away.

A story he was fond of repeating was that once, when he was not at Doboom Ritro, a messenger came from the Dargye Monastery asking for Gaga. I was not there. He was told by Lobsang Ngodup, one of the boys who studied with me, that Gaga was not in the Ritro. When Gaga came back, I told him that a messenger had come and gave him all the specifics of where and when he was to go. Lobsang Ngodup was surprised because the messenger had not mentioned all those details. But all that I had said turned out to be correct! Gaga was very pleased for he felt it was something special about me that they had discovered. Losing Gaga was like losing a very important connection with my past.

In Buxa Duar, we had very little information about what was going on in Tibet. It was a remote place where newspapers took their own sweet time to reach. As monks, we were told that we were the seeds – we had to go back to Tibet and revive all the monasteries. There was no doubt that all the monasteries and monks would have been erased by then. We had to go and revive our culture. There were thousands and thousands of monasteries and even if all the 1,500 monks in Buxa Duar and a few nuns became abbots, we would still not be enough. So we concentrated on our learning.

Today, looking back, I realise only part of all that was true. The people of Tibet have remained devout and continue to pray quietly, in their own way. In areas close to Lhasa, they could not do so openly. Today, I find everything is flourishing, even the monasteries and there is monastic education being offered.

Part V

STUDIES

20

My Interest in Buddhist Studies

On reflection, I think he had staged this. In the class, my teacher, Gen Pema Gyaltsen, then the abbot of Loseling, asked us an important question on a philosophical point in the text he was teaching. There were many brilliant students in my class. The smart classmates gave great answers, but our teacher was not satisfied. He almost expressed his inability to solve the puzzle. Then suddenly he turned to me and asked, 'Can you answer this?' I said something without thinking. Then he brightened up and said, 'That is the answer, well done,' and praised me. I do not remember what the question was or what my answer was. But it had not been a difficult one. Maybe this was his tactic to draw my attention and stir up some kind of interest in studies. I may have seemed inattentive in class as I did not ask questions or voluntarily give answers like my other classmates. I must say his tactics succeeded. They provided a great boost to me to persevere with my studies.

My classmates were among the best students of Loseling College and also the whole monastic camp at Buxa Duar. Later, one of them ascended the throne of Gaden Tripa as the head of the Gelukpa tradition of Tibetan Buddhism. Another became the abbot of Loseling Dratsang in Karnataka, yet another was the head of the Buddhist Institute of Dialectics in Dharamsala. Another one became a teacher of Buddhist philosophy in the Namgyal Monastery in Dharamsala.

It was only in the latter part of my stay in Buxa that I developed some interest in studying the scriptures and texts of Buddhist philosophy. A part of the reason was probably the push Gen Pema Gyaltsen gave me. And as my intellectual faculties were not weak, I did not have much difficulty catching up with my classmates despite several years of negligence.

The subject I was most interested in was Madhyamika, Nagarjuna's philosophy of Emptiness and Interdependence. I worked hard, memorising the texts, attending classes and debating sessions, and also attending other prayer sessions, very regularly and seriously. The syllabus of my monastery, Loseling, included commentaries by Panchen Sonam Drakpa. I found the text very lucid, not unnecessarily extensive or discursive with too many quotations, but clear and to the point. I enjoyed memorising the text. I have never been a good debater, but I began enjoying participating in the debate sessions. Debate was a unique method of learning philosophy, because we debated every detail of the assertion, the refutation and counter-refutation. So the knowledge gained through debates stayed in the mind for a long time.

The Buxa camp included very senior monks, such as those who had served as abbots in Tibet or were presently abbots and other learned scholars. However, I took most of my lessons from Gen Pema Gyaltsen, just as in the monastic tradition where one individual goes for lessons only to a few scholars. I also took lessons from Gen Yeshe Thubten, one of my teachers from Tibet who later joined the camp after staying in Ladakh during the formative period of what is now the Central Institute of Buddhist Studies. He was highly respected by all the monks but not much feared, because he mingled with people more easily than other senior monks. He was later appointed abbot of Drepung Loseling Dratsang and contributed a lot to re-establish the monastery in Karnataka. Without a doubt, he was one of the greatest scholars of all time. His knowledge of Buddhist philosophy was so profound that every utterance and every word of his explanation carried important meanings that could open many doors of understanding.

There was also a very senior lama of Gaden Monastery, Kyabje Zong Rinpoche, who enjoyed the respect of many Gelukpas there. He was a special figure as he taught and played the role of a major guru rather than teaching just philosophical texts. He was erudite in both sutra and tantra subjects. I received many teachings on *Lam-rim* (stages of the path to enlightenment) as well as many Vajrayana initiations from him. He also specialised in ritual performances such as chanting and monastic music.

It was hot at the camp and as the facilities were very basic with no electricity, there was no question of a fan. But this senior lama had hung a traditional Indian pankah, or bamboo screen, and tied to it a cord that he would pull to and fro while teaching, to create a breeze. At times he could be moody. If someone made a mistake, he gave a sharp reprimand in front of everyone in the class – sometimes it may be necessary to exhibit our feelings as everyone is not good all the time. He was very particular about everything – chanting, on which part of the drum the stick should hit or how strongly to tap the drum and so on. I remember he once scolded someone who hit the drum too hard and produced a harsh sound. He instructed that the stick was not to hit the centre of the drum or around its sides. It was to be tapped on the lower part of the drum.

The drum was not played at all times but was associated with particular rituals, mainly propitiation of Dharma powers. We used a big drum which was played with a stick. That kind of drum was played along with two different kinds of cymbals – one kind worked sideways and the sound produced was very delicate, the other worked up–down and the sound was louder. Horns were also blown at this time. The text being chanted was generally from memory but sometimes, when the chanting was very long, texts were read and not recited from memory. There were some monasteries which specialised in chantings and rituals. They did not use texts.

Watching Kyabje Zong Rinpoche play the cymbals was a great feast for the eyes and ears. His playing seemed effortless as if he was not doing anything and the cymbals were playing by themselves. As I write this, his reincarnation, who studied in the Gaden Monastery in Mundgod, is set to become a shining example of an exemplary lama. He is good in his studies and has earned the respect of many people. This was not only for his scholarship and good conduct but also for maintaining a low profile and for not projecting himself unnecessarily.

His Holiness the Dalai Lama's junior tutor, Kyabje Trijang Rinpoche, also visited Buxa Duar in the winter of 1960 – the senior tutor, Ling Rinpoche, had visited a year earlier. Kyabje Trijang Rinpoche was put up in a simple wooden cottage – a forest inspection bungalow, just outside the camp. He gave the initiation of the 13-Deity Yamantaka to the monks and the blessings of the Vajrayogini to a smaller gathering of which I was a part. He told us that we should start reciting a sadhana of Vajrayogini every day without fail. It could be of any length and composed by any lama, Geluk or Sakya. I remember this because he was generally considered a very orthodox Gelukpa teacher but this was a very unorthodox advice. To a select few he gave the initiation of Chintamani Tara.

The group for the Vajrayogini blessings included senior non-Gelukpa lamas like Drugpa Thugsey Rinpoche, a very senior lama of the Drugpa Kagyu system. Addressing Thugsey Rinpoche, particularly during the initiation, Kyabje Trijang Rinpoche emphasised the preservation and promotion of all the traditions. He said it was known that in the olden days the tradition of Drugpa Kagyu was spread over an area that required 18 days' flight of an eagle to cover. It had now shrunk and needed to be revived and promoted.

His thoughts remained in my mind and much later in the 1980s, when monasteries were struggling to establish themselves in India, I had an opportunity, however small, to contribute to the preservation of the monastic tradition of Drugpa Thugsey Monastery. I will detail it later.

In 1963, I made my first trip to Dharamsala to receive my bhikshu ordination from His Holiness the Dalai Lama. This was the most important event in the life of a Buddhist monk. It was an ordination for full-fledged monkhood. I travelled by train with a group of monks in the unreserved compartment because at that time I did not know there was such a thing as reservation. I did not find any of the food items sold at the stations or inside the compartments edible because they were either too spicy or too oily. But when we reached Jalandhar, I managed to get some yoghurt which I took with some chapatti, which was delicious and nourishing.

In Dharamsala, I stayed in a room above a small restaurant and after a few days I had audience with His Holiness. He was staying at Swargashram. His official attendants from old Tibet were there to present the sacred cord and other items. The person who conducted me to His Holiness was a familiar face – Rinchen T. Sadutsang. He was from a well-known trading and philanthropic family of Kham, Tehor, who had made many offerings to monasteries.

The ordination ceremony was held after a few days. After the preparatory ceremonies, people were to go to His Holiness in threes. I was among the first three, with Kirti Rinpoche and Takbar Tulku. The three of us were symbolically handed ceremonial clothes and begging bowls. Being among the first three saved me from an uncomfortable situation, because the rest had to remain squatting on a piece of brick, a position I found very difficult because I was quite bulky. I was impressed by the simplicity of His Holiness's accommodation because the Swargashram was just a single bungalow and I believe His Holiness's mother and other family members were in the rear half.

While at Dharamsala I also went to seek blessings from His Holiness's two tutors. Ling Rinpoche was staying in Chopra House and Trijang Rinpoche in Naoroji Kothi. Both of them followed the philosophy of simple living. I also met Serkong

Tsenshab Rinpoche, one of the debating assistants to His Holiness in Tibet. Later, though Serkong Tsenshab Rinpoche was not conferred the title of tutor, His Holiness received some rare teachings from him. At the time I met him, he was working in the Council of Religious Affairs.

The first set of offices or councils set up by the Tibetan Government-in-Exile were Religious Affairs, Education, Home Affairs, External Affairs and Finance. Most of them functioned from an old bungalow called Mortimer Hall, where each department had just one room. As the heads of these offices were from the old Tibetan aristocracy, they might not have had much of an idea of the new world and how to deal with people other than Tibetans, but they maintained a certain dignity. Later, when I was working in the Library of Tibetan Works and Archives in Dharamsala, I came across an old file. I was amazed to find that they used to send official notes to each other, although their offices were just next door to one another, and had arguments over seemingly trivial issues such as certain offices not getting enough firewood in winter to heat the room.

While coming back by train from Pathankot to Alipur Duar, one of my attendants, Sonam Dhondup, got down at a railway station for some reason. The train started moving and he was left behind. I felt I would never see him again. But at the suggestion of some fellow travellers, we got down at the next station and waited for him. He did arrive after some time. He is still living with me.

At that time people were very afraid of thieves in trains and took elaborate precautions. I heard the story of someone who cut a hole in a bar of Lifebuoy soap, stuffed it with whatever currency notes he had and smoothened out the surface with water!

During my stay in Buxa Duar, I travelled to Varanasi to spend a month or so for the Vajrayogini retreat at Sarnath, then a small, peaceful village. I had a pleasant room in the Sangharama, run by a Buddhist organisation. His Holiness's senior tutor Yongzin Ling Rinpoche was also staying in the same compound. One day there was news that India's prime minister Pandit Nehru was coming to Sarnath. I was very excited because I had heard about him since my childhood in Tibet and was eager to get a glimpse of him.

Pandit Nehru came in an open jeep waving to everybody standing at the roadside, throwing back to the crowd flower garlands that were offered to him. I managed to push myself through the crowd to have a look. I felt satisfied as this was the first time I had seen a world figure. During the same period, Burmese prime minister U Nu also visited Sarnath. One day I saw him walking into a house next to where I was staying. People said he was attending a lunch meeting. He appeared so simple that an onlooker would hardly think of him as a leader of a country. I was impressed by his simplicity. I credited this to his being Buddhist though now I realise that not all Buddhist leaders are necessarily simple and humble.

21

Monastic Study Continues

In the past, writing was not essential to the transmission of knowledge in the Tibetan monastic tradition. So many monks did not learn how to write. They could read, memorise long texts, deliver lectures, debate and even explain the meanings of complex concepts, but they could not write. This was the oral system of education. Many abbots and great scholars belonged to this tradition. With the coming of the modern systems, this had to change.

Naturally, any change calls for adjustments. The monks started settling down in Buxa Duar. Each of them had to try to maintain his traditions. They had to make some changes in their living style to be able to restore their way of life which they had almost lost. The monks continued their study of Tibetan texts in the traditional manner for six years. Buxa Duar functioned like a monastery in terms of daily schedule including prayer and debate sessions, studying the traditional way and following the traditional way of discipline, making adjustments dictated by the availability of material such as full robes and so on.

At that point, a change came. The place that had till then functioned as a monastic institution was proposed to be converted into a school or college. The thinking behind this was that in a changing world, monastic institutions may not be relevant to the people for long. The appearance and way of functioning should be that of a modern academic institution, while the subjects of study should be Buddhist philosophical doctrines. I don't know who initiated this, but around 1966–67, a delegation from Dharamsala brought a recorded message from His Holiness which emphasised the necessity of this move.

At this point I would like to reminisce about our first experience of listening to recorded sounds. When we were in Drepung Loseling, Yapa Sonam Topghyal from Sikkim brought a spool tape recorder and recorded the chanting in the debating courtyard.[1] At some point he told the chanting master to stop and he played to us what he had recorded. We were all dumbstruck. The effect was great, indeed. We had known of the gramophone but that was the first experience of a tape recorder.

Later, a Japanese academician came to record the debate procedures at Buxa Duar. When he played the recording back to us, we were not very surprised, but still excited. By the time the message came from His Holiness, we were familiar with this mode of communication. The recording was played again and again to the monks. It conveyed the impression that traditional monasteries now belonged to the past and that for the continuation of the tradition of Buddhist studies, it was necessary to make this place function in the style of modern schools or colleges.

For many monks, especially those of the older generation, it was not easy to accept this new idea, but as His Holiness was talking about it, everybody felt it must be good for the Buddha Dharma. The idea of establishing a centre for higher studies was also slowly taking shape by then. After some time, the camp was converted into a school.

Many of us felt that the monastic way of life would soon be lost forever. One of the monks said he felt he was travelling by a train, leaving behind everything he saw through the window. At that point I too thought it would soon belong to the past. But that has not happened and the monastic way of life has come back in a big way. Huge monasteries have come up both in India and Tibet. But some changes have remained. The nature of the study centres has changed, which has impacted the guru–shishya parampara or the teacher–student relationship.

Mahayana Buddhism, and Tibetan Buddhism in particular, placed special emphasis on the traditional relationship between a guru and his disciple. This relationship was considered very sacred and was considered to be the foundation of all subsequent spiritual growth. There is a lot of literature dealing exclusively with this relationship and the qualities that a guru should possess. There are also lists of the qualities required for a person to be a guru. Basically, the guru should be well trained in his or her spiritual subjects and practices and should have special skills to lead their followers and students by setting their own example. The guru should not be self-seeking. I am sorry to observe that these days many of the gurus who promote or market themselves are ready to do anything for their own gain and fame and to increase their possessions. The guru–shishya relationship has changed and it is certainly not in the traditional mould at all.

However, the main change that has come about is that while in the traditional way, the spiritual aspirants studied and learned the philosophical scriptures one by one, in the new system, parts of all the five main texts are covered in one day in different sessions by different teachers. Pandit Jagannath Upadhyaya, from the Sanskrit University, Varanasi,[2] was the key person for framing the syllabus. Fifty-four senior monks, including abbots and ex-abbots, were selected and sent to Mussoorie to undergo emergency training programmes that would enable them to become lecturers in the new system.

As already mentioned, many monks did not know how to write. Zigyab Rinpoche, one of the high-ranking tulkus of the Tashi Lhunpo Monastery, once vividly described how it would take the abbots several minutes to sign their names – taking the fountain pen out from their robes with deliberate movements, passing it from the right hand to the left, unscrewing the cap, screwing it to the back of the pen, passing the pen back to the right hand and finally placing the nib on the paper and forming the letters unsteadily.

Earlier, only some towns in Tibet had schools. Lhasa had schools where people of well-to-do families would send their children, mainly so that they could secure official positions in the government. The students would spend many years practising letters on a wooden slate, till their handwriting became very elegant, and they practically produced calligraphy.

There was a story about a very senior monk-official from the Lhasa government, Khendrung Ngawang Dhondup, nicknamed 'Angula'. He was in Mussoorie and teaching the trainees (senior monks) how to write. Day after day, he made them write the same letters of the alphabet. After several days he remarked to the trainees, 'Now I can almost recognise all the letters.'

Angula took humility to new heights. He addressed even trainees as 'Rinpoche'. Generally, Rinpoche is an honorific term used to refer to tulkus and sometimes abbots. In Lhasa, fellow officials of comparable rank would be addressed as 'Rinpoche' in official letters.

The trainees were taught Tibetan grammar, literature and even some English. The most renowned scholarly saint, Negi Lama, was the main instructor of Tibetan grammar. The daughter of Jigme Namgyal and Rinchen Dolma Taring[3] was the English teacher. I don't know how much English the trainees learnt, but I can imagine they would have found it very hard to pronounce the English letter *f*, which would become either 'ph' or 'ha' when they said it.

When they came back after the training programme, the trainees became lecturers in the new school that functioned at Buxa for a couple of years. The main subject was Buddhist philosophy and some Tibetan grammar and spellings were also taught. Every morning there was a gathering where the *Manjusri stotra*, a prayer in adoration of Manjusri, was chanted, followed by the Tibetan and Indian national anthems. Buxa was a remote place, so it was less embarrassing to hear the words of the Indian anthem mispronounced.

After the morning assembly each teacher went to address his class. There were no classrooms and we had the classes in one of the several houses where the monks were lodged. The teacher who came to our class on the first day was known for his rigidity. The text happened to be a point in a Vinaya text that said, 'Don't keep the company of thieves.' Instead of beginning with auspicious sounds and then moving into the text, he went straight to the point.

Another change was the introduction of democratic practices in our daily matters. The idea of voting on issues was introduced for the first time. I remember there was voting on whether to have future publications in a book form or a pothi form. I voted for the book, which received the majority of votes. But today I would vote for the pothi, because the pothi form has its own charm. The text might be the same but with the pothi we can feel the author speaking to us from the heart, which is not the case with the book form. Maybe this is because I have grown emotionally attached to pothis. I also find it easier to read from a printed copy than on a screen as the physical copy seems more real to me.

Among the first batch of 300 senior monks who were shifted to Varanasi, there were many Buxa lecturers who went either as lecturers or as senior students. The question that then came up was how to continue with the studies of the remaining monks in Buxa. An 'election' was held, and I became one of the first 'elected' lecturers there. I had no experience of teaching but the duration of each period was limited to 40 or 45 minutes, unlike in the traditional system of several hours at a stretch, and so the task of teaching was not that difficult. Of course, there were challenges, especially when the subject matter was difficult as I had been neither a very senior nor a very junior student. I had to continue this stopgap arrangement as a lecturer for nearly a year, after which it was decided that the entire camp would be shifted to Mundgod and Bylakuppe in Karnataka in south India.

22

Entering Academic Life

The turning point in my life came when I joined the Central Institute of Higher Tibetan Studies or CIHTS as it is called, in Sarnath, Varanasi, in 1969. Until then, my outlook and mindset as a whole had been formed by the traditional background of monastic life. It was announced that the Buxa Duar camp would be dispersed to different Tibetan settlement camps in the state of Karnataka, but I was not eager to go to south India. At that time, it looked as if the monks going there would have neither a chance to study Buddhist scriptures in the traditional way nor any opportunity to learn modern subjects. Many of them would become farmers. Looking back, I cannot claim to have learnt Buddhist scriptures in the traditional way nor did I gain exposure to modern subjects by joining CIHTS. Yet, I had the impression that there was no future for monasteries-in-exile or in Tibet.

I left the Buxa camp about a month or two before most of the monks started moving out. I went to Dalhousie, a hill station in north India, on the pretext of having a holiday, though the actual intention was to avoid shifting to the south. I still remember the audience I had with the most Venerable Khen Rinpoche Pema Gyaltshen[4] before my departure. He gave me very kind advice about the importance of being mindful all the time, particularly while travelling. I did not disclose to him my intention of eventually joining CIHTS. I still feel guilty about this. He was an outstanding leader of monks, respected by everyone and renowned for his scholarship and integrity. He never scolded anybody but all of us feared earning his displeasure.

My other guru, the most Venerable Yeshe Thubten, encouraged me to go to Varanasi to study at CIHTS. I followed his advice and went to Varanasi from Dalhousie. It was not difficult to get admission as I had already reached the senior level of Buddhist philosophical studies at Buxa, building on my studies at the Drepung Monastery. I had also been an 'elected' teacher at Buxa when senior teachers left for Varanasi.

A couple of months after I had joined CIHTS, Khen Rinpoche Pema Gyaltshen decided to visit Varanasi. I was very apprehensive about his visit. I had come to Varanasi basically against his wishes, opting out of going to the south with the majority of the Loseling monks. I was not sure how I could face him. I was ready to receive some kind of scolding or at least an expression of unhappiness at my joining the institute. To my utter surprise, he did not show the slightest sign of displeasure. On the contrary, he asked about my well-being and about my studies. He also gave me some thoughtful words of advice.

Khen Rinpoche was taken round to see the hostels and I accompanied him. Monks in old Tibet and in Buxa did not sleep during the day unless they were sick. However, the monk-students at Varanasi had by then developed the habit of taking a siesta after lunch. On seeing everybody asleep under red blankets in a large room, Khen Rinpoche thought it was a hospital and stepped out immediately to avoid disturbing them.

Khen Rinpoche represented the conservative, traditional approach while my other teacher, Gen Yeshe Thubten, was more tolerant of the modern viewpoint. Gen Yeshe Thubten even encouraged me to learn English and to engage in writing articles that could, in the future, form material for a book. It may sound strange but he was also my first English teacher, that too when we were in Tibet. One day I was handling a small knife which had three alphabets inscribed on it. I had no idea what they meant and was curious about them. He told me that they were USA. And that they meant America!

There were eleven monk-students in my class at CIHTS, eight Gelukpas and three Sakyapas, all from Buxa. The curriculum in those days was restricted to the traditional monastic subjects of Buddhist philosophy. We were directly inducted into the first year of the three-year Acharya course, equivalent to the MA of modern universities. Students came from several places for the first four-year course for Madhyama degree and the two-year course for the Shastri degree. Their curriculum included Sanskrit, Hindi and English literature. Other subjects such as economics and history were also taught. We were the third batch of monks from Buxa. The teaching style was more or less the same as in a monastery except that different teachers came for different classes to give lectures on various subjects of the philosophical texts. Some classes were a bit dull but most of them were interesting. When a learned senior Geshe came, he would immediately engage in philosophical debate with some of us and we would all feel that the 40-minute period of the class was too short.

One such senior Geshe was Gen Legden from Sera-Jey Monastery. All of us enjoyed his classes because though his style of teaching was a bit slow, he would gradually get to the point in an unforgettable manner. He concentrated on looking at his book and would not establish much eye contact with the students. One day Kelsang Yeshe, who later became the director of the Norbu Linga Institute of Tibetan Culture, Dharamsala, and I took advantage of this. We started doing mischief in the class and could not stop giggling. Gen Legden caught us in the act and scolded us saying, 'I did not expect either of you would do such a thing.' Perhaps he thought we were mocking him. We did not think it necessary to explain our actions but felt sorry for upsetting him. The next day he acted as if nothing had happened. I began liking him for his behaviour and knowledge. Later, he became the abbot of Sera-Jey. When he retired from abbotship, I made it a point to go and see him whenever I visited Sera in Bylakuppe.

Kelsang Yeshe from Loseling and Tsultrim Kelsang from Sera-Jey, now retired as professors from the Buddhist University at Kyoto, were considered the brightest students in our class. In the annual examinations, these two and I would be the top three each year. Somehow, I would get just a few more marks than the other two.

There was an Amdo monk by the name of Thabkhey, who later became the abbot of Drepung Gomang. He had been a student of Zhungpa Tsultrim, a senior monk-scholar from his college, who was more famous in scholarship than him. In monks' gatherings, an order was followed in seating. According to tradition, the teacher sat on a higher seat. But in this case, I felt many must have found it strange that the teacher, Zhungpa Tsultrim, was seated among the crowd while the student, Thabkhey, occupied a high throne. Later, this kind of thing became quite normal and acceptable. Thabkhey was very fond of food. People normally do not prefer to make their fondness for food obvious. Therefore, he would often tell us that he was going to buy butter. I would wonder how much butter he could consume. I later discovered that butter was his code word for meat!

CIHTS was established according to the ideas of His Holiness, who discussed them with Jawaharlal Nehru. One of the founding members of CIHTS was Professor Jagannath Upadhyaya, who was a rare scholar of Buddhism and a practising Buddhist. His knowledge and understanding of the subject were very profound. I had the opportunity to talk to him about certain points of Buddhist philosophy. He was of old-school appearance, but possessed real foresight and vision. When there was a change in the head of the institute, then called the principal, a few people started playing petty politics. Some even tried to project that he opposed the appointment of the new principal, Samdhong Rinpoche.

In the 1980s, during a trip to Germany, Prof. Upadhyaya and I were together and he explained to me that he was not against the new principal at all. He said that the principal could be whoever His Holiness wanted to appoint. But as the institute was a couple of years old by then, certain procedures of appointment needed to be followed. I took special note of that comment and I still remember the sentence he spoke in Hindi.

What made this Indian scholar unique was that he did not care about money at all. I observed this when I travelled with him in Germany and I was also told this by others who knew him well. He often helped poor students with his own salary. He would ask for a glass of hot milk before going to bed, saying it was a Brahmin's whisky!

23

Compassion and Humility at CIHTS

At that time, CIHTS did not have its own premises. All the classes were held at the Sanskrit University in Varanasi, which was about 10 kilometres from Sarnath. All the lecturers and students stayed at Sarnath in different houses that functioned as temporary hostels. My attendant, Sonam Dhondup, and I shared a room in the Chinese Temple along with Gen Yeshe Thubten. The canteen was close by, in the Tibetan Temple. In the summer heat, fetching the food at midday was quite a difficult exercise. Later we hired a local villager called Bulbul who was an honest and simple person. He did not know anything other than his daily routine and the location of the nearby village. Once during elections, I casually asked him who Indira Gandhi was. He innocently said

Indira Gandhi was the Raja of India. He did not even know that the prime minister of India at that time was a woman! This kind of ignorance did not come in the way of his daily chore of delivering food to us and I was happy with that.

Those were the days when I was quite content with the situation around me. I did not have any particular ambition for my future. I was not a very bright student but not a very dull one either. The daily routine was not an exciting one. The institute had only one bus to transport the lecturers and the students from Sarnath to the city. If my class was in the first shift, I had to get up early to catch the bus. As the driver, called Uncle Wangdak, was known to be a moody person, everyone was worried about being left behind. He did not show even the minimum courtesy of waiting a few minutes for anyone who was slightly late or was not standing at the designated stop. In the evenings, I regularly went to the park around the ruins of the ancient monasteries and temples. I usually walked with Achok Rinpoche who later went abroad, and on returning to India, became the abbot of the Shartse College of Gaden Monastery, a major Tibetan monastery-in-exile, and the director of the Library of Tibetan Works and Archives in Dharamsala. Now he has gone back to Tibet, to his monastery. This walk was the most enjoyable part of the daily routine.

Another pleasurable experience in those days was riding in cycle rickshaws between Sarnath and Varanasi. There were vast empty spaces on both sides of the road and I could see people working in the fields as we passed other travellers on bicycles and bullock carts or those who were walking. When I revisited this place after a few decades, I found the situation dramatically changed. I did not see any empty spaces around and the once peaceful Sarnath had virtually merged with the city.

One everlasting memory of Varanasi which left a strong imprint in my mind is of going to a circus in the city. An elderly monk from Drepung, who became the abbot of Loseling College, was quite amazed after watching the circus show. He said that there could not be a greater show than this on the earth and strongly recommended that I should go and see it. I went to see the show put up by the Gemini Circus Company. The acrobats, the performance of obedient beasts like tigers and lions and so on were extremely astonishing indeed.

That was my first experience of seeing a circus and, of course, afterwards I saw many more, including the famous Moscow Circus. But what did not cross my mind in those days was the amount of suffering undergone by the young performers as well as the animals associated with the show. The suffering was so much that it could not be justified in any way by the enjoyment of the viewers, not to mention the physical violence the performers may have undergone. We should think of the animals, who would otherwise be roaming freely in their natural habitats in vast jungles, being kept confined in a small space, surrounded on all sides by bars and wires. We humans should not have such unlimited authority to do whatever we want just for our fun and enjoyment.

We should also think of the young boys and girls performing seemingly joyful acrobatic acts. In reality, their life was akin to slavery. They did not get much knowledge or education beyond training in physical feats. As they grew older, there was no guarantee that they would be able to continue performing or be able to find a better livelihood. Making other beings suffer for our own living is bad enough, especially from Buddhist religious point of view, but causing others to suffer for our fun cannot be justified from any moral standpoint. I later heard the horrible stories of ancient Roman emperors who made people fight with beasts because they enjoyed watching the sufferings. The site of the sport is still a tourist spot in Rome and is called the Colosseum. The circus show should be categorised as that kind of sport.

The Buddhist religious belief is that I should sacrifice my life for the slightest benefit of others. To do so is deemed as the highest level of spirituality. The next lower level entails that I do not cause trouble to any other sentient being. So, to think of causing suffering to others for the sake of our enjoyment is unthinkable. For instance, in medieval times, kings would hunt animals as a sport. If we are hungry and therefore kill an animal, there is a slight justification, but to do so for amusement cannot be justified. Even though I did not reflect along these lines at that time, today that seems as the most obvious assessment of the circus performance.

The essence of Buddhism came back to me in an interesting manner. His Holiness the Dalai Lama visited Sarnath during my stay there. The prayer and offering session in front of the old stupa left a deep impression on my mind. During the chanting, His Holiness suddenly asked the leader of the group to chant the prayer of 'offering of practice' (*thopa gyatso ma*). The monks were not prepared because that particular chant was not a part of regular prayers, so there was momentary confusion as to what to do. But they managed to perform the chanting with some difficulty. It was the idea and the content of the chanting that led me to think deeply about it. Here is the passage in English which I have translated for readers to reflect on the meaning:

> Brimming with the waters of learning
> Blooming with the flowers of virtues
> Fragrant with the incense of pure conduct
> Illuminating with the lamp of wisdom
> Sprinkling scented waters of devotion
> Nourishing with the ambrosia of meditation
> Praising with the sounds of music

My body as a mansion
Adorned by
the umbrella of compassion, with
the victorious banner of intellectual prowess
and the high-flying flag of fearlessness
I offer this to you
You, who always resides in my heart
Of a hundred-petalled lotus in full bloom
To you Dharma King, I pray
With firm devotion
I pray you may always be pleased.

The idea of this prayer is that the real offering is not flowers and incense; the real offering is the practice, because that is the only way to please Enlightened Beings. The one and only way is through the practice of Dharma. Only that can please the Buddha. Offering water and flowers will not please the Buddha. The purpose of Buddha's teachings is to help others and to help deliver sentient beings from suffering.

Here I would like to relate an incident that happened many years later but is relevant to the subject being discussed. I was living in Defence Colony in Delhi when I found that a small pup had entered a pipe. The pipe was open from one side and closed at the other end. I was drawn by its wails. When I peered into the pipe, I found the pup could not walk backwards and it could not move forward either. I requested some boys to help, but they could not do much. Then I asked the owner of the house if he would let me break the pipe. I offered to pay for the damage. He agreed and the pup was saved. I felt satisfied afterwards but the good thing about these kinds of small deeds is that we do not feel proud thinking we have done something great – they are too small for pride; anyone could have done them. The 'offering of practice' prayer is to remind everyone to do it. It is not a prayer that goes to the Buddha. The Buddha does not gain anything, he does not receive anything. It is only for our own satisfaction, to increase our merit that we follow the path of Dharma. The prayer is a reminder to the person who prays that they should travel along the path of Dharma.

On another occasion, during His Sarnath visit, His Holiness gave a short discourse to a small group seated on cushions on the lawns. Speaking of the concept of omniscience, He mentioned that while travelling to Varanasi by train, He threw away His old toothbrush as it had become quite worn out. He would never come to know what might have happened to it until He reached a certain stage of enlightenment. Some people thought, how lucky was the Indian villager who found His Holiness's toothbrush! Maybe nobody found it. But definitely, all those who listened to him found they understood the idea of omniscience and enlightenment which gives the knowledge of all three times – the trikala of the past, the present and the future.

I have a few other memories of His Holiness's time in Sarnath. A famous and very learned Indian Buddhist monk, Bhadant Anand Kausalayayan, spoke at the seminar on Buddhism and Marxism. He said that Marxism eliminated unemployment in the countries where it prevailed; if it dominated the world, there would be no monks and no prostitutes! For me, raised in the traditional way, it was a bit shocking to hear this from a senior monk. While he was known for his inclination towards Marxism, I did not know whether his statement reflected his positive views of Marxism or otherwise. His Holiness's interest in original Marxism was well known, but I do not remember His response.

At the convocation, among the dignitaries on the dais was the Maharaja of Kashi (the former king of Varanasi), a well-known scholar of Sanskrit literature and well respected by the people in the region. It was interesting to hear His Holiness open His speech addressing the king as 'Gyalpo Rinpoche' (precious king). Non-Tibetans often ask what is the difference between a Rinpoche and a lama – is one higher than the other? 'Rinpoche' is used in spoken Tibetan to address a reincarnate lama while a lama is a teacher or a master, usually in the religious sense. Lamas are not like a cardinal or a bishop in the Roman Catholic Church. In common English usage, 'lama' has become synonymous with a Tibetan monk. But in written text, especially in the Lhasa region, 'Rinpoche', as I have mentioned earlier, is sometimes also used by officials addressing others of equal rank.

In exile, I have noticed an interesting tendency regarding the use of the term 'Rinpoche'. In traditional Tibetan society a person never gave his own name as Rinpoche. But as early as the 1960s, some lamas started giving their name as so-and-so Rinpoche. It seemed to me that they felt proud if a non-Tibetan addressed them as Rinpoche in front of other Tibetans. Nowadays, no eyebrows are raised if anyone calls himself a Rinpoche.

Today, unimaginably important-sounding self-aggrandising titles are used only to attract public attention. The irony is that this seems to be a common and acceptable thing to do. However, I will never be comfortable with such self-glorifying acts. Even now I sometimes think of changing the last part of my name from Tulku to Tulming, the traditional way of addressing oneself, which means nominally a tulku, but the problems of amending all the documents to do so make me hesitate. I suppose my desire for a name change is because traditional values such as humility are firmly rooted in my mind. During His Holiness's visit when I was in Varanasi, my most lasting memory and source of admiration was His utter simplicity and unpretentious nature.

I went to Bodh Gaya probably in 1969 to attend a teaching by Yongzin Ling Rinpoche. He gave the initiation and the discourse on solitary Yamantaka in the upper hall of the Gaden Phelgye Ling Tibetan Monastery. It must have lasted about ten days and many tulkus and senior monks received the teachings.

Ling Rinpoche was quite special. Although he used a commentary text as the base of his discourse, his explanations were all from his inner experiences. When he spoke, his eyes seemed to be fixed straight into the space a little above his eye level. It was very remarkable to observe that as the subject developed into a higher and deeper level his discourse became clearer and more lucid. A fellow participant at the seminar, Dza Thupten Tulku,[5] could not help shaking his head and exclaiming, 'This lama must be Buddha!'

In 1970, Kyabje Trijang Rinpoche gave an initiation of Vajrayogini in the Tibetan Monastery, Sarnath. A gathering of about 200 disciples and senior monks from the institute attended it. The former abbot of Loseling, Gyalrong Khensur Rinpoche, offered a brief long-life prayer. Gyalrong Khensur Rinpoche was well known and a very learned scholar but a bit stubborn. I vividly remember that after the initiation and long-life prayer, he insisted that Kyabje Rinpoche's lunch be served while he was seated on the throne, before the disciples dispersed. That would have been a very unusual scene. Kyabe Rinpoche did not accept this strange suggestion and lunch was served in his room in the Chinese Temple. Since my room was next to his, I was also asked to join him for lunch.

An ever-inspiring and cherished memory of my Varanasi period was during my last vacation in 1971 when I went to Dharamsala to receive the initiations of Guhyasamaja and 13-Deity Yamantaka by Yongzin Ling Rinpoche and the initiation Chakrasamvara of Luipa tradition by Kyabje Trijang Rinpoche. These initiations were attended by a gathering of about 700 disciples and lasted for five days. His Holiness was the main disciple. Naturally, the lama giving the initiation took the central stage, while the main disciple, His Holiness, sat on his left, facing him on a slightly lower seat.

On the preliminary ritual day, there was a lot of bargaining between Ling Rinpoche and His Holiness as to who sat first.

After stepping on their respective seats, the tutor asked His Holiness not to make the prostration while His Holiness insisted on doing so. But from the second day onwards a compromise seemed to have reached. They sat more or less simultaneously and His Holiness did not make the prostration. I thought He must have done that before entering the hall. Anyway, such scenes are becoming very rare now. After the initiations by the two tutors, His Holiness gave the discourse on the four commentaries of Guhyasamaja.

This reminds me of a story from the Kadampa period in Tibet. A lama visiting a different region from his own answered queries about the current situation in his monastery. He said, 'There is a continuous discussion going on as to who will be the head of the monastery. The disagreement is between two top lamas and when I left the monastery, the matter was still not resolved.'

The monks and disciples were shocked to hear this. 'Lamas,' they said, 'are supposed to be a source of inspiration to us and we believe that they have renounced worldly affairs, particularly clinging to positions. What do we hear now? That they are fighting for a position!'

'No! No! No!' The lama hurriedly explained that these two respected lamas were asking each other to take the abbotship, one saying that the other was more learned and the other saying the former was more senior.

24

My Interest in Literature

It was customary for the regent to write the prayer for long-life for His Holiness. The regent was Tagdrag Dorjechang. The verses were beautiful. New arrivals in Drepung Monastery learnt this prayer by heart. When I joined the monastery at the age of twelve,

I was totally enchanted by the prayer. I would hear it morning and evening, every day. In metre and rhyme, it was soothing and whatever meaning I could make of it then was also very calming and comforting. I have no doubt that this sowed an interest in poetry and its appreciation in me. Later, I came to know that this verse was actually penned by Kyabje Trijang Rinpoche. He wrote it for the regent. I could then identify the style of Trijang Rinpoche. This verse contains imagery in which qualities are personified. I have given a simple translation. When translating verses such as these, I feel we should give the meaning rather than get stuck with literal equivalents.

> Across the eternal sky with all the signs
> Of auspiciousness and beauty
> Clouds, immeasurable and full
> Pour down the nectar of immortality
> Please shower upon this upholder
> Of values, material and spiritual,
> All forms of blessings.

My own interest in Tibetan literature grew out of my liking for reading various materials. I was expected by my teachers to exclusively learn philosophical texts like the *Abhisamayalamkara* and its commentaries, but my inclination was to read whatever I could lay my hands on, especially Jatakas, biographies and stories. That helped me expand my areas of interest and also helped me to become familiar with various styles of writing.

The texts I have read were mostly composed by lamas after the old Kadampa period (around the eleventh century CE). If I look at old Kadampa texts, they have a strong influence of the regional language of Phenpo in Central Tibet, located across a pass from Lhasa valley. After this period, I can see that the styles of Sakya

Pandita and Buston of the twelfth, thirteenth and fourteenth centuries are slightly different. The Kadampa style is more native and indigenous. After that, the influence of Sanskrit texts made the literature more stylised.

Around Tsongkhapa's period, which covers the fourteenth and fifteenth centuries, it seems to me that the style had stabilised and acquired a polish. When I read Tsongkhapa's texts, whether it is a commentary on a great Indian pandit's work or his own work like *Lam-rim Chenmo* and *Ngag-rim Chenmo*, I find myself thoroughly enjoying both the content and the language. The subject matter relates exclusively to Buddhist doctrines and practices. It is not written to show off the author's skill in writing, but it flows so well that we can really enjoy the smoothness of the language. The art of writing appears to have reached its zenith in this period. Sometimes I feel Tsongkhapa's texts are more easily assimilated than the more elaborate commentaries of later times. Tsongkhapa's natural style is pleasing to read. The stanza describing Yamantaka's body in the lineage prayer is not meant to be in a flowery style but it is so powerful that we can almost see the image in front of us. The stanza goes something like this:

Where eternal bliss with full emptiness embraces
In a oneness that is a dark blue wrathful whole
Embodying the spectrum of the rasas
To that Yamantaka
The destroyer of inner and outer evil forces
I pray, seeking blessings

The English word often used to translate the Sanskrit word 'rasa' is 'essence'. I prefer to use the original Sanskrit word rather than a translation, because for those who know it, it conveys so much more, a more intense and comprehensive idea of each expression.

Yamantaka is a deity who is considered to be the enemy of Yama or the god of Death. 'Yama' means god of Death and 'antaka' is one who puts an end to it. I have mentioned Yamantaka earlier. There are many deities in Vajrayana Buddhism who are personifications of qualities which symbolise the Buddha's enlightened qualities. Many of the deities are peaceful like Manjusri, Avalokiteswara and Tara. Some are semi-wrathful like Heruka and Chakrasamvara. The third category of deities consists of those who are very wrathful, like Yamantaka. They are not persons but are personifications of inner qualities. There are many forms of Yamantakas, with many mandalas. There are many sadhanas of Yamantaka ranging from Ekvira or single deity Yamantaka sadhana to the 13-deity Yamantaka sadhana, with different appearances. The compositions of each of the mandalas also differ.

Each of the Tibetan Buddhist traditions has its chosen deities. In Gelukpa tradition there are three main deities. One is Yamantaka and the other is the semi-wrathful deity Chakrasamvara, where 'chakra' means 'the whole' and 'samvara' means brought together. This means the merging of all existing phenomena in the one chakra of innate bliss. The third is the peaceful deity Guhyasamaja. Guhyasamaja represents the unison of the rare qualities of enlightenment.

Similarly, Tsongkhapa's invocation of Kshetrapala riding on a wild boar earned the admiration of Gedun Choephel, an early twentieth-century scholar and critic in Tibet. There have been great scholars who produced voluminous works on different subjects, of which I have read very few and that too only in parts. A few lamas whose writings have impressed me more are Gyaltsab Je, Jigme Lingpa, Gungthang, Mipham and Paltrul. Among the direct disciples of Tsongkhapa, the first name that people are likely to pick up in connection with writing is Khedub Je. I do not dispute his fame as a great writer and debater; but for me, Gyaltsab Je's writings are more gentle and smooth flowing. When I read the introductory part of his *Nying-gyen*, the commentary on the *Alankara*, it brings tears to my eyes. Here, I am talking of the great commentators, such as Geshe Sherab Gyatso, Chone Lama Rinpoche and Girteng Lobsang Palden, all from the Amdo region of Tibet.

I have never treated literary style as a separate subject of learning. From my interest in various kinds of literature, a kind of writing pattern seems to have emerged. I can say that it is a more organic growth rather than an attempt to imitate someone else. But much depends on inspiration. Sometimes inspiration comes, for example, from His Holiness and when it does, the writing is much smoother and flows naturally. Sometimes, if something has to be written within a given deadline, the flow of writing does not come naturally.

After Tsongkhapa, Gungthang's writings inspire me the most. I can say that my two collections of maxims, *Earth and Stone* and *Ocean and Moon* are directly inspired by Gungthang's style. I reproduce a few from both the collections:

Of the earth, gold is essence, it is said
Through burning, felling and rubbing it is reached
Of the teachings of the Buddha, it is said
Through the traditions of Nagarjuna and Asanga, it is reached.

With intelligence and courage
One can overcome obstacles
Even as with explosives
Boulders can, into smithereens be shattered.

In the ocean of samsara,
With waves of old age, illness and death,
To cross over to the land of liberation
One has to rely on a true-spiritual captain.

All the travellers in the ship have the same desire,
To reach the shore safe and sound;
One must learn from this; and
Practise ferryman-like Bodhi-mind and the rest.

The lights of the moon and sun as well as the darkness,
Are said to be conditioning causes of the sky
To leave one's mind unconditioned,
Is confirming to the truth in both the sacred and the mundane.

In the 1980s, a great movement in Tibetan writing started for 'free' contemporary writing. Some people became very famous as its leading lights. I think that if we can have modern painting, we can have modern writing as well. Yet I must confess that I could not appreciate these writings. As an art, I think it is fine, even though it is not to my taste. I am able to appreciate modern art, but I am not able to appreciate modern Tibetan poetry.

I am nowhere near being a writer, but from the early part of life, I have had a natural interest in writing. My education in the field of literature is very limited and even basic, as in those days, literature was not included in the monastery curricula. The only opportunity I had of learning something related to literature was when I spent about two months with a well-known grammarian by the name of Sherpa Lama Ngawang Yonten. At that time, he was residing in Payung Basti, a small village near Kalimpong. I went there in 1963 from the Buxa camp with the idea of learning some Tibetan grammar.

Before starting a grammar lesson, Sherpa Lama Ngawang usually made his students memorise Dagyig, a stanza with a formula for remembering spellings of Tibetan words, especially when they were related or close sounding such as Kunkyen, Shakya, Karmapa and so on. This string of words containing the sound 'k' was taught to children to remember that letter of the alphabet. I started memorising the text titled 'Ketaka' that he had composed. Spelling was not a big deal for me because while reading philosophical texts, my attention used to go naturally to spelling. But memorising a Dagyig was, for me, almost like trying to memorise a dictionary from A to Z!

Sherpa Lama had gone to Tibet at a young age and studied under learned lamas in the Kham Derge area. Among other subjects, he also studied Tibetan medicine and his medical treatment combined with reciting of mantra was considered effective in getting rid of illnesses, especially those caused by spirits. An upright man of principles, during our learning sessions he made sure that I sat on a seat which was not lower than his and regularly served me a cup of tea. He did not hesitate to criticise people of higher positions in Tibetan society. Later, he moved to Darjeeling where he took up a job in the editorial office of the Tibetan newspaper *Rangwang Srungkyob* which means 'defending freedom'.

This newspaper was a rival of another Tibetan newspaper called *Rangwang* which means 'freedom'. Both these newspapers came into being after Tibetans moved into exile. Earlier, there was only one Tibetan newspaper called *Melong*, which means 'mirror', that was published in the years before Tibet lost her freedom. This newspaper was published from Kalimpong by Babu Tharchin. Babu Tharchin belonged to Kinnaur. He used to send the newspaper to the regent and some others in Tibet. It was greatly appreciated, for it was only one of its kind at that time.

When *Rangwang* began to be published, Babu Tharchin wrote a couplet '*Rangwang yod-due rangwang med, rangwang med-due rangwang yod*' which means 'When there is freedom, there is no "freedom" and when there is no freedom, there is "freedom".' He was perhaps referring to the political reasons why his newspaper went out of print. It was because a powerful person had tried to influence his policies. When he was not amenable to influence, that person promoted another newspaper. After some time, once again, there were factions within the community and a third newspaper came into being.

25

What after CIHTS?

The question, 'Where do we go from here?' was at the back of our minds in 1971, our graduation year. Until then there had been a general tendency to presume some system or some power would take us to some destination. As the time to leave CIHTS came near, there were more intense discussions among my classmates.

When W.G. Kundeling, the kalon of the Council for Religious Affairs, visited the institute, we approached him en masse, pleading to be advised a way for some further study or occupation. Kundeling was known for his sarcasm and this time, too, he said, 'You people seem to think in the same way as some Apohor (nomadic) groups coming from remote areas of Tibet to Lhasa – afraid of getting lost in the crowd, herding around together, trying to find shelter. There cannot be any arrangement to keep all graduates together. Some individuals may find places of work; others will have to fall back on their own devices.' This induced us to think for ourselves about our future plans.

As I mention this, I recall another remark attributed to Kundeling which became a joke among the monks at Buxa. When the lamas pleaded that he find a suitable place to relocate the camp, neither too hot in the summer nor too cold in the winter, he said that he would try to find a spot near the Dewachen or Sukhavati, the Western Paradise in Buddhism.

Similarly, he was once deputed to Dharamsala from Mussoorie where His Holiness was camping during the initial years of His exile. His job was to ascertain the suitability of the place for His Holiness's residence and administrative headquarters. In order to impress the people concerned about its suitability, he was said to have remarked that the water of Dharamsala was sweeter than the milk of Mussoorie.

It was Kundeling who, along with Dronyer Chenmo Phalha (the grand chamberlain), chartered His Holiness's escape from Norbulingka, with everybody – from cabinet ministers to His Holiness's tutors and family members – following the plan. To take such a huge responsibility requires courage, determination, presence of mind and self-sacrifice, which both these two high ranking monk-officials exhibited.

When His Holiness stayed for about a year in Mussoorie before coming to Dharamsala, the same government system that had worked in Tibet continued to work. Kundeling worked for children's education and in 1960 set up the first Tibetan school for children. When His Holiness moved to Dharamsala, He decided to rearrange the government into five councils – Religious Affairs, Education, Home Affairs, External Affairs and Finance. In this set-up, Kundeling was first in charge of education and later of religious affairs. He served as a minister for many years.

In the late 1960s and early 1970s, he was given the big responsibility of meeting the king of Bhutan to address the political problems of Tibetans residing there. He did not succeed in this mission and people believe this was one reason for his making an exit sooner than expected, though anyway, it was about time for him to retire. After retirement, he settled in Rajpur near Mussoorie.

Some people of that period feel he, as well as Dronyer Chenmo Phalha, did not get the honour and appreciation they deserved for their role during His Holiness's escape and their work in the initial years of exile. I consider him an outstanding person and he was one of the more straightforward and unpretentious members of the Tibetan administration of the time.

When I was about to graduate from CIHTS, I was interested in doing some research on Buddhist scriptures but did not have a clear idea of how to proceed. Anne Klein was an American researcher I had come to know during my stay at Varanasi. She was pursuing studies in Buddhist philosophy. My guru, Yeshe Thubten, encouraged me to help her read *Madhyamakavatara*.

I hardly knew any English philosophical terms. My English was very elementary as I had never studied the language formally. I struggled to read the Tibetan text with Anne, trying to find English equivalents for words and phrases. It gave me great satisfaction when I succeeded in conveying even a little of the meaning of the text to her. The exercise eventually proved useful in two ways. First, it improved my knowledge of English significantly. Second, and interestingly, some of the passages which were difficult to understand in Tibetan became clearer when I read them in English. Anne Klein later became a professor at Rice University in Texas and is now teaching Buddha Dharma to her disciples.

For several reasons, my idea of doing academic research did not lead me anywhere. At the end of my three-year Acharya course, the degree I obtained was called 'Acharya Geshe from the Tibetan Administration'. As I mentioned earlier, monks from Buxa who wanted to pursue their studies further went to Sarnath and the rest went to Tibetan settlements in the south. The feeling was that the monastic system was no longer relevant and that the Geshe title would not be used any longer. The Acharya degree awarded at Sarnath was equivalent to the Geshe degree.

Later, when monasteries were re-emerging and coming up everywhere, the idea of the Geshe degree made a big comeback and became internationally relevant. I was awarded the Geshe Lharampa certificate by the then abbot of Loseling, Yeshe Thubten, in 1975. Now, after the Geshe Lharampa degree has become popular, people asked me about my degree and I half-jokingly say, 'I belong to the period when the Geshe Lharampa degree was abolished.'

Part VI

WORKING LIFE

26

My Work in Two Libraries

In 1972, I was appointed as the Librarian at Tibet House, New Delhi. This was my first experience of working in an office setting and required sitting at the desk whether or not there was any work to do. The job was mainly of a custodian of the manuscripts and books. An additional task given to me was to write the introduction to each volume of the Bodong Panchen's collected works being reprinted by Tibet House under the title *Encyclopedia Tibetica*. I wrote introductions to thirty-eight volumes of this encyclopaedia. The exercise was useful to me because it made me read and study commentaries in Tibetan on tantric texts.

The library was a small room on the top floor of 16 Lodhi Road, Jor Bagh. There were few visitors apart from one or two staff members from the Hungarian Embassy, our next-door neighbour, and a young researcher from Poland. In those days both these were communist countries. I was quite impressed by the discipline of these people. The Hungarians were looking for some material about the pioneer Hungarian Tibetologist Csoma de Koros. The person from Poland, Piotr Klafkoski, was studying Tibetan. Later he went to Dharamsala where he married a Tibetan girl.

Tibet House was then considered a prestigious institution, mainly because it functioned under His Holiness's directions. Rev. Tara, His private secretary, was extremely effective in carrying out His Holiness's orders, in the right spirit. When I joined Tibet House as the librarian, there was no director. The secretary (then called general secretary) functioned as the executive head of the institution. There had been directors earlier. The first was Domo Geshe Rinpoche who later went to USA and settled there till his death. Dagyab Kyabgon Rinpoche was also a director. He moved to Germany to work as an academic at the Department of Mongolian and Tibetan Studies at the University of Bonn. After retiring he established a Tibet House in Germany. This Tibet House was established by a Tibetan, unlike most Tibet Houses which have mushroomed everywhere.

Dr Nirmal Chandra Sinha was appointed the director while I was the librarian at Tibet House. A professor of Tibetology, he was the only non-Tibetan director. I was quite amused because he came in the morning, sat in his office the whole day without having any interaction with the staff, and left in the evening. Once when he wanted the office to buy him a dictionary, I remember the cashier Kungo Ngawang Rigdol complaining about this man who shut himself in the room like a prisoner and demanded expensive books.

The problem, as I now understand, was the lack of a job description for the director. I still don't know what was the thinking behind his appointment. He was a well-known scholar in Buddhist studies, who had worked on the Kalachakra Tantra. He could have compiled a publication of great academic value. But he did not last long in Tibet House. Later, he became the director of the Namgyal Institute of Tibetology in Sikkim for two terms, where he produced some publications on Tibetan iconography.

In those days, the main activity of Tibet House was the emporium. It was a commercial venture which was managed by the general secretary, Mrs Gelek. Jampa Tsultrim, a monk from Gaden Jangtse Monastery, was in charge of the museum. He was quarrelsome and we often heard him shouting at the top of his voice at the secretary for some reason or the other. This was a source of amusement for me.

I recollect His Holiness visiting Tibet House one day and walking into the library. I happened to be reading a commentary by Khedub Je on the Haivajratantra. His Holiness just enquired which scripture it was and seemed to be pleased to know what I was reading. His interest and manner of enquiry left me feeling very fortunate.

Working in the Tibet House was a completely new experience for me. It was also a challenge because my lifestyle shifted from the study of Buddhist teachings to providing service in an establishment. Without noticing, I was being gradually dragged forward on a path which would not be easy to retrace.

I started feeling that the lifestyle of a city was not conducive for someone of my background, which was predominantly monastic. I had the option of going to Karnataka as the Buxa Duar camp was being remodelled once again, this time along the lines of a traditional monastery. All the monasteries had shifted to Karnataka from Buxa Duar. As I had already deviated from monastic study to a different path, at that time it did not seem appropriate to go to south India. I requested His Holiness's office to shift me to another position. The reply was prompt. Rev. Tara asked me to wait until a replacement was found for my current position.

Around that time I came in touch with Prof. Lal Mani Joshi, a very learned scholar with a modern outlook. Among Indian scholars in Buddhism in those days, it was rare to find an English-speaking scholar and Prof. Joshi was one of those rare beings. He was working at the Punjabi University in Patiala near the foothills of the Himalayas. He tried to interest me in some research at his university. An additional advantage, I could see, was the proximity to the German Buddhist monk, Bhikkhu Pasadika, who was doing research with Joshi. Well-versed in Sanskrit, Pali and many European languages, Bhikkhu Pasadika also had a working knowledge of Chinese, Vietnamese and Tibetan. Apart from his scholarship, he was a real Bhikkhu. He never indulged himself in worldly affairs such as craving for name, fame, power or money. At one time he advised me to go to a forest monastery in Thailand and do some research as well as meditation, but I lacked the courage to take the decision. He is a shining example of the combination of scholarship and saintly qualities.

Meanwhile, I wrote to Gyatso Tsering, the director of the Library of Tibetan Works and Archives at Dharamsala, asking if I could get a research position there. He wrote back promptly to say that at the moment there was no vacancy, but I should contact them if I visited Dharamsala.

After some time, a letter from LTWA arrived inviting me to join them. However, I had to remain in Tibet House for some months until Gala Tulku came to take over the work from me. He asked me to stay for some more time to help him become familiar with the nature of the work. I agreed to that. His main worry was about writing the introductions to the Bodong publications. To my utter surprise, after some days he decided to quit the post. So he left before I could leave! I had to remain in Delhi some time longer. Donthog Tulku, who had been in Tibet House earlier, was then appointed to look after the library and it was to him that I handed over my responsibilities.

When I joined the LTWA, I was given a large, empty desk and a chair in a huge room called the 'manuscript room' where many bundles of woodblock print and handwritten Tibetan books were piled up. They included sets of the Kangyur and Tengyur.

The change of job suited me well. The work environment was also very conducive. Every major point of decision was reported to and consulted with the Kuyig, or the Private Office of His Holiness. There was none of the red tape prevalent today in the Tibetan society in exile.

My job was regarding the cataloguing of Tibetan manuscripts. The basic idea was to catalogue in a modern system, all the books which were in the traditional pothi format. But there was no one in Dharamsala who could give me the slightest idea as to how it might be done. Later, it occurred to me that they should have made arrangements for me to visit some of the established libraries in India holding Tibetan collections. One such place was the library attached to the Bihar Research Society in Patna. The rare collection of Tibetan manuscripts brought out of Tibet by Pandit Rahul Sankrityayana were kept there and a cataloguing system was created in which Panchen Otrul[1] and some others were involved. This might not have been the perfect system but it certainly would have given me some idea about how to proceed.

There were also many other *sungbums* (collected works). To invent a system along the lines of the modern system of cataloguing was a big challenge for me. Something inside me made me decide to face this challenge on my own. I brought in two senior monks whom I knew to assist me in my task. One was Sangtshang Rinpoche from Gaden Shartse Monastery, who passed away a few years ago, and the other was Chomze Wangyal from my monastery, Drepung Loseling, who also passed away recently. Both were very sincere and hardworking. I made them sort out the manuscripts. The traditional method of cataloguing was just to list the titles in a particular collection. We tried to make a subject-heading system so that we might find a new way of making divisions. It was, of course, not easy because no model for such a kind of work was available, to my knowledge at least.

On the whole, the work was enjoyable and interesting because when we are facing a challenge or are given a chance to be creative, we feel satisfied with even a small achievement. After many experiments, we were able to come up with a reasonably well-organised system of subject headings. It may not have been the perfect one, but it was definitely a breakthrough in the field. Even though I created the system relying entirely on my knowledge and intuition, it has withstood the test of time and is still being used by LTWA in Dharamsala and has also been adopted by CIHTS in Sarnath, with some modifications.

27

Discourse on Chakrasamvara

I have two very distinct memories of my time in the Library of Tibetan Works and Archives, Dharamsala. These are about visits by the two tutors of His Holiness. Kyabje Trijang Rinpoche gave valuable advice about cataloguing. Naturally, his thinking was on traditional lines. His advice was that since the collection consisted of books belonging to different traditions of Tibetan Buddhism and not just one tradition, an unbiased approach should be adopted. Kyabje Ling Rinpoche came perhaps a year or so after Kyabje Trijang Rinpoche's visit. What I recollect vividly is that Ling Rinpoche's attention fell on a small printed text of long-life prayer lying on my desk, composed just a little earlier by a well-meaning monk for his teacher. He casually picked it up and leafed through it. The author, not being so well-versed in letters, had used the term *drinzang* (*mgrin bzang*) to refer to his teacher, with all good intentions and having in mind the literal meaning 'good-throated'. The trouble was that the word was a synonym for donkey in poetic literature! When he noticed this, Ling Rinpoche just chuckled and said something like, 'Oh gosh!'

Director Gyatso Tsering was very capable and extremely hardworking. I found him dependable and honest. He listened sympathetically to any difficulty or complaint the staff had and made efforts to solve the problem. He was actually from Sikkim, which is now a state of India. He had somehow landed in Dharamsala, I imagine, to be in the service of His Holiness. He worked in the religious office of His Holiness. When the LTWA was established through the religious office, he was made its head. He did not seem to have any regular connection with his native place, except a sister who used to visit him sometimes. In a way we could say that he dedicated his life to the service of His Holiness.

I remember that when I joined the LTWA, the first thing Gyatso-la pointed out to me was that the library was neither above nor below any of the other offices in Dharamsala. I now realise that earlier, there must have been some interference from other offices of the Tibetan establishment.

After some time, I was made a member of the governing body of LTWA. When Gyatso-la resigned from the directorship, I tried to impress upon the other members that Gyatso's continued service might be beneficial for the institution but they remained indifferent. Gyatso went ahead with his resignation and left to settle in the USA. I feel sad that he did not get the recognition that he deserved for his services. I later got a sense there was some kind of pushing by some forces. Such petty politics existed in other Dharamsala establishments also.

During my time in the library, I also had the opportunity to do some academic work and translated a few short pieces, which were later compiled into the book, *The Buddhist Path to Enlightenment*. Edited by Glenn Mullin, it was published in the United States and later reprinted in India.

I had the rare opportunity of receiving an important initiation and discourse on Chakrasamvara Body Mandala by Kyabje Trijang Rinpoche in the statue hall of the LTWA in Dharamsala in April 1975. Many tulkus, geshes and senior monks from outside Dharamsala also gathered to receive this teaching for 12 days. As this discourse was exclusively for those who made a commitment to practice sadhana, it did not attract a huge crowd. We were only 183 practitioners.

Kyabje Rinpoche gave the teachings in a very leisurely and relaxed manner. This sadhana was considered to be an inherited treasure from Trijang Rinpoche's root guru and lineage gurus. People felt fortunate to receive Chakrasamvara teachings from Trijang Rinpoche. Once Trijang Rinpoche told me that people seemed to take it for granted that Yongzin Ling Rinpoche was the treasure house of Yamantaka teachings and anything related to Chakrasamvara could be obtained from him.

These types of Buddhist tantric discourses always consisted of two stages – the generation stage and the completion stage. The generation required generating oneself as the deity and purifying ordinary phenomena, birth, death and the intermediate state. The completion stage was related to inner channels, inner wind and inner drop. The 5-deity Chakrasamvara initiation and white Chakrasamvara long-life practice with the practice of Vajra Japa for longevity were also included in this teaching. One day, during the teaching, one of the disciples sitting behind me made a noise. Some of us knew it was the release of wind from below and we could not control our giggles. Kyapje Rinpoche noticed it and in his dignified style just said, 'I think someone made *Oglung Dorje Deypa* (lower-wind vajra-japa).'

On 9 September 1976, I was walking towards the library after the lunch break when I heard All India Radio's news being broadcast loudly by some construction workers. Suddenly, I heard the announcement that Chairman Mao Zedong was dead. I went numb and could not feel my feet touching the ground. It took a few minutes before my composure returned to normal. Some people started celebrating by distributing sweets in offices. I felt a bit uneasy joining them, not only because rejoicing about somebody's death was not proper according to Buddhism, but also because at the time I did not believe that the death of one leader could result in a dramatic change in the communist regime. On this latter point, I was partially wrong.

One day, His Holiness called a meeting of all the staff of the Tibetan establishments in Dharamsala at His residence. When His Holiness addressed the meeting, it became clear He had been told by someone that the people were losing confidence in the government he was leading. His Holiness showed great concern, as losing confidence in the establishment was a very serious matter, given that we were all working for the legitimate goal of regaining Tibet's lost freedom. He directed everyone to discuss this matter and report the outcome or their thoughts directly to Him. He said that large or small groups or even individuals could come to see Him to tell their feelings. That was the first time I had witnessed His Holiness's passionate speech. The passion was entirely for His people and His country.

By nature, I have never been the kind of the person who loves to speculate on every situation. Instead, I started thinking deeply on the subject of His Holiness's speech and felt strongly that I should avail myself of the opportunity to tell His Holiness what I thought. Of course, I do not remember my exact words now, but the essence of what I submitted to His Holiness was this – Every Tibetan has indestructible faith in Your Holiness's leadership. That is the only strength of the Tibetan people and the only binding force of the three regions of Tibet, without which even if Tibet regained freedom tomorrow, it might not be able to remain a United Tibet of three regions. I do not recall His Holiness's exact reactions, but I felt that my statement did not displease Him.

Another occasion when I had an audience with His Holiness was regarding the idea of attempting the translation of some important Buddhist texts into English. I wanted to request His Holiness's advice on the kind of text it would be good to translate. But I made a stupid mistake. While explaining my idea, I said I intended to work on a basic text such as *Boddhipathapradipam* or *Lamdon* in Tibetan, and because I mentioned a specific text, His Holiness merely said, 'That text is good.' I do not know if His Holiness was really encouraging me to engage in translation and whether I would have accomplished any success or not, but I have not forgiven myself for the stupidity of my way of seeking advice.

On another occasion, I asked His Holiness which deity I should take as *yidam* or my personal deity. Here also I did not receive any explicit reply, all because of a lack of skilfulness in framing my question.

28

More at the Library of Tibetan Works and Archives

The LTWA ran a Dharma class mainly for foreigners. This was taught by Geshe Ngawang Dargye, who was a joyous and happy-looking character and, like me, belonged to the Tashi Dargye Monastery. Sherpa Tulku and Khamlung Tulku were the interpreters. Several times the director, Gyatso-la, indicated that I should be involved in the Dharma classes in one way or an other, but I never pushed the issue enough to make it happen. This was not only because I felt that my English was inadequate, but also because I was not particularly interested in projecting myself as a Dharma guru. Looking back after more than five decades, I suppose I was not shrewd enough to take that path. Today, I see so many self-promoting gurus everywhere, who seem to be quite successful in impressing people and who have become acceptable to many. But I have no regrets. The LTWA was a very peaceful and congenial place for people like me who loved studying in quiet surroundings.

The Western students were very devoted to their teacher and behaved in the same manner as the Tibetan Dharma practitioners. Among them was Vana Jakic, a remarkable lady from the former Yugoslavia, then a communist country. She was very hard-working. She never failed to attend classes and would record every word of the teacher. She was very particular about cleanliness, washing her clothes early in the morning in cold water even in the cold Dharamsala winter.

Vana showed some influence of communist ideology and I asked her to get me a copy of *Das Kapital* in English, which she did. Sometimes I would tease her, 'You are a communist,' and she would shoot back, 'You are a communist,' mentioning instances that according to her showed a communist way of thinking on my part. So once when she offered me a packet of paper napkins, I took one, and then another and so she offered me more and I said, 'No, two is enough.' She said that was the essence of the Communist way of thinking, from each according to his ability, to each according to his needs. She also believed that Tito, the president of her country, was a great person. She is now settled in Seattle in the USA. She had started a movement to have conflict areas declared zones of peace. It seemed to me her project was doing well, but when I saw her later, it had not gone much further and she wanted to do something else for peace. She is full of ideas and energy.

I should not forget to mention two other impressive persons who worked in the LTWA at that time. The first was Khetsun Sangpo, whose task was to compile a biographical dictionary of the lineage gurus of all the Buddhist traditions of Tibet. He held the title of Rinpoche and had been in Japan in the capacity of a learned lama to work in the Thoyobungko Library. He had all the appearance and looks of a university professor. His grey hair were an additional reason for respect. He worked every day in the office late into the night, which was certainly a source of inspiration foreveryone. He completed the project in the time I was there and produced about eight volumes of the biographical dictionary.

The other impressive person was Ngawang Thondup, who was developing methods of teaching the Tibetan language. He produced what was called the 'three study tools' or techniques for learning Tibetan. He designed the Tibetan typewriter. He described himself as a linguist. He loved to discuss certain favourite topics of his whenever a chance arose. One was the Tse Lhobda, the school in Potala Palace in Tibet, where young monks were trained to become monk-officials in the government. He had graduated from there and had become a junior monk-official before the Chinese occupation. He had also gone to China to study at the Central Minorities Institute in Beijing and liked to show off his revolutionary views.

One of the projects I was involved in was the writing of His Holiness's biography. I was a part of the small committee constituted to undertake the task. Ngawang Thondup was very careful in choosing each word of the biography. My job was to compose verses to be placed at the beginning and end of each chapter. The project, however, was not completed as sometime later, it was taken up by another group. They have brought out twenty-four volumes of the biography.

I was at the LTWA until 1977. On the whole, it was a happy period. I learned to work with people of different backgrounds and approaches – until then, I had essentially been enclosed in only one kind of environment all the time.

29

Kuyig 1: At the Private Office of His Holiness (1977–1981)

One day, in 1976, His Holiness summoned me to His office. His instructions were most unexpected. By way of a preface, He told me that there were some very capable people around, but there was a problem of a lack of trustworthiness. People were ambitious and egoistic. He was, in fact, looking to gradually replace the *geytsab* (elders) in the Kuyig.[2] He then said that the work I was doing in the library was fine and asked if I had any plans of pursuing philosophical studies in the monastery. I replied that I had no such plans. His Holiness then said that I should join the Kuyig, not immediately but in the spring of the coming year.

I could hardly believe what I was hearing, for I had neither the experience nor any kind of specialised knowledge to work in such a prestigious office as the Private Office of His Holiness.

Naturally, I accepted the instruction respectfully, as there was no question of going against an order coming directly from His mouth. Looking back, I think if the order had come via some other channel, I might have thought twice before saying 'yes'. When I returned to my quarters in the library, my friends were waiting for me anxiously, curious to know why His Holiness had summoned me. When I told them what had happened, Gyaltsen Ogdong Tsang, one of my senior layman supporters from Tehor who happened to be staying with me, uttered the Tibetan proverb, 'If you keep holding the hot earthen pot your hand gets burned, if you let it go it will break,' and said we were in an awkward position. He agreed there was no choice but to act according to the instructions of His Holiness. It took me a few months to wind up my duties at the LTWA since a replacement had to be found and the catalogue system I had designed had to be implemented and made practically workable.

I joined the Kuyig in February 1977, before the Tibetan new year. At His Holiness's public audience on the Tibetan new year's day, I was one of those who distributed the sacred cords worn a round the neck. On the day of my joining the Kuyig, I decided that during my service to His Holiness, I would not misuse the opportunity and bring up matters which were directly or indirectly linked to my personal interest. It was not like taking a vow in the strict sense of the term, but it was a firm resolve. As I look back now, I believe I can claim that I have stood by that decision.

I was given a seat and a desk in the small room of the principal secretary, Rev. T.C. Tara, under whom I was to work. Rev. Tara was highly respected by everyone because of his dedication, integrity and the firmness of his directions. Under the old regime in Tibet, he had attained the position of a fourth-ranking monk-official, which was a level below Kundeling, with whom he had played a crucial role in arranging His Holiness's escape from Norbulingka. Rev. Tara gave me a task on the first day of my joining – to update the register of monks who had received bhikshu ordination from His Holiness.

I realised very soon that working under Rev. Tara was a great opportunity to learn. His ideas were clear and his working methods very precise. And it was a great source of support to know that he was always there for me since we shared a room. Above all, he was completely selfless. He had a large amount of experience in the government of old Tibet, from which he would occasionally share some interesting episodes. He also quickly developed an understanding of and the ways and methods of working in a new situation, such as dealing with important persons in Indian politics.

Those were the years Jayaprakash Narayan (popularly known as JP) and Acharya Kripalani were at the forefront of the Tibetan cause internationally, and they sought to help Tibetans in India by organising the Central Relief Committee. Rev. Tara had taught himself some English and would glance at newspaper headlines. On finding a word that was unfamiliar, he would ask me what it meant, which I, usually, did not know. He liked to be informed and kept himself updated about major events in the world from the limited sources that were available at the time, mainly newspapers and radio. A telex machine was installed in the Kuyig after a year or so.

Another person with whom I had the opportunity of close interaction was Mr Neushak, the former foreign minister of old Tibet who retired as His Holiness's representative in New York. He was staying next to my room in the same compound. He had been a part of the goodwill delegation sent to greet Mao Zedong in Beijing and present artifacts and other offerings. As a young monk he had joined service by the time of the 13th Dalai Lama. I learned some particulars about the 13th Dalai Lama from him. He told me that the 13th Dalai Lama dressed very well for official ceremonies and gave an appearance of grandeur on the throne. In everyday life, he would dress like an ordinary monk at Norbulingka and walk around by himself. Neushak narrated an incident when, during one such walk, a monk-official at Norbulingka stopped him. Pointing his finger at the Dalai Lama's face, the official said, 'Wait, I think I have seen you somewhere!' The Dalai Lama asked, 'What do you mean?' The official then realised his mistake and ran away.

I had imagined that I would be asked to take notes from scriptures or assigned some work of that kind. I did not foresee that I would be assigned general administrative work. Soon it became clear that no specific task or duty had been assigned to me. I was to try and fill any gaps in administration. The difficult part lay in not knowing the extent to which I should make myself visible. If I became too visible it could be taken as being over-eager to act, and if I were less visible, there was a risk of appearing too indifferent to take any initiative. I needed to perform a kind of balancing act in the Kuyig.

During the initial years I was supposed to follow Rev. Tara's orders. I mostly went through the Tibetan letters and supplications received, brought them to His Holiness's notice and communicated His response, whose formulation had to be clear and direct. Most of the time Rev. Tara would report to His Holiness but sometimes he asked me to draft a reply, which he would improve and send for copying. The requests to His Holiness included appeals to identify the reincarnations of recently deceased lamas. I must say that in those days, His Holiness was quite reluctant to recognise reincarnations because it wasn't His way of thinking. He thought that traditions like this should not be continued without a particular reason. But later he let the tradition take its own course.

Once a group of people sent a supplication to recognise a lama who had passed away a little while earlier. The letter stated that the lama who had passed away had been recognised by the 13th

Dalai Lama. They supported their claim by enclosing the original letter from the 13th Dalai Lama. When I read that letter, I was shocked that people could misunderstand it so grossly, for the letter actually stated the person was *not* the reincarnation of the previous lama. The words of the phrase '*yinngo mashar*' (the possibility of being that is not) had been misread as '*yin ngoma shar*' (appears to be real). Decisions about the appointment of abbots of major Tibetan monasteries-in-exile would also come to the Kuyig, and sometimes my opinion of certain candidates would be sought.

30

Designing a Name Card

As always, even then, there were many people who wished for an audience with His Holiness. It was a tough job to manage. Fortunately, I was not in charge of that. A monk who had been a junior monk-official in the old Tibet government, by the name of Gedhar, popularly known as Gedhar-la, was the person who fixed appointments for Tibetans. He was a jolly sort of a person, with a lot of laughter in him and cracked good jokes. I found him quite a contrast to Rev. Tara who was very reserved and a man of few words. Gedhar-la was a hard-working person. I remember once His Holiness remarked that he was like a real *dang yuan*, a Chinese Communist Party member. And yet, he carried his responsibilities lightly on his shoulders, never dragging them into the realm of power politics, as many people in that position were tempted to. I enjoyed my evening walks with Gedhar-la, which would end at a small restaurant in McLeod Ganj where they served good *then-thug*. Then-thug is a thick broth made with wheat dough and vegetables, with or without meat.

There were visitors from abroad who wished for an audience with His Holiness. Tenzin Geyche, who used to be a monk, headed the section for foreign visitors. He was from the aristocratic family of Tethong. His father had held a high position in the government in Tibet. His job was to deal with international communications and to fix appointments for foreigners with His Holiness. An unexpected situation arose when one day, he was found missing from duty. He could not be traced for several days. After about a month Ngari Rinpoche, His Holiness's youngest brother, received a letter from him marked 'personal'. He said he was with his mother in Darjeeling and intended to remain there for some time, reading up on Tibetan history. When he eventually did return, it was without his monks' robes. He looked like a very respectable gentleman. In his absence I did some of his work.

While at the Kuyig, I had to attend the annual general meeting (which is called 'Assembly' or 'Parliament' today). This meeting took stock of the affairs and was attended by elected representatives and government officials above a certain level. Different settlement camps and monasteries also deputed members to attend the meeting. Each of them would give a report of their activities and achievements. The distinction between legislature, executive and judiciary had not been made at the time, so it was a unique system of combining all these functions, with everybody working together. I call this system an evolution, not copied from any existing sovereign country.

I would like to recall an episode here. A special issue raised a year or two earlier by Ven. Choedar, an abbot of the Kagyupa order, had come up for debate. Ven. Choedar was also a senior lecturer at the Central Institute of Higher Tibetan Studies. The debate was whether the anniversary of Tsongkhapa, the founder of the Gelukpa order, should be observed as a government holiday when the same was not being done for the anniversaries of the founders of other orders. The Kashag (Cabinet) made the statement that it had been decided not to observe Tsongkhapa's anniversary as a holiday any longer. Ven. Choedar, who had raised that issue, responded bluntly saying he was very sorry to hear the statement. He had hoped that the anniversaries of other founders would also be declared holidays. Instead, what was in existence was being dismantled. I thought it was a good point, and he made it very forcefully. His statement comes to my mind quite often. These days, if you have to check the date of Gaden Ngacho, Tsongkhapa's anniversary, you will not find it mentioned in the calendar of Men-Tsee-Khang, because the calendar only mentions office holidays. Ironically, you will find it in the calendars of some Dharma centres abroad.

It is a matter of great satisfaction to me that when I was at the Kuyig, I reported directly to His Holiness. An area of my work that I enjoyed and found fulfilling was the little research I was occasionally called upon to do by His Holiness. Often His Holiness was asked to write a long-life prayer for a reincarnated child or a prayer for the speedy return of a lama who had passed away. It was important to know what such people had been in their last incarnation. I would do this background search. I would make notes for His Holiness after going through the relevant texts, often using His private collection.

Even later, after coming back to Tibet House, I continued to receive such orders directly from Him through handwritten notes on a Delhi hotel notepad, or by summoning me to his hotel room, or sometimes even over the telephone. Very rarely did the instructions come through the Kuyig. This continued until 2008, when some monks from Namgyal Monastery brought a handwritten message from His Holiness to me. I complied with what was asked. However, I am not sure if the material was ever used or whether it was reported to His Holiness properly. What was odd was that the monks wanted the handwritten message of His Holiness back. I refused to part with it because such messages are required to be kept in my safe custody and not meant to be seen by any third person.

In those days His Holiness was not as busy as He is now and would usually honour invitations to events both within India and abroad. One of the first visits on which I accompanied Him was to a small place in Maharashtra to inaugurate a new Buddhist temple. They had sent a photograph that had been taken in such a way that the temple looked a respectable size. It was quite a long drive from the nearest airport and a minister accompanied us, but when we arrived, we found the temple was a very small one and the gathering was also small. His Holiness performed the inauguration and had a meal with the local people, sitting on the floor. I felt that it had not been worth the trouble that His Holiness had been made to take, especially considering it was in hot summer, but His Holiness appeared to enjoy it.

I accompanied His Holiness on a visit to Patna to meet the respected Indian leader Jayaprakash Narayan. There was a gap of half-an-hour between His previous engagement and the meeting. He decided to drop by the library of the Bihar Research Society instead of returning to His accommodation. Picking up at random a bundle of Tibetan folios, He was very pleased while browsing through them to find they belonged to the collected works of Tehor Dagkar Lama who was renowned for his scholarship on all traditional subjects and whose non-sectarian approach had particularly impressed His Holiness. Dagkar was a guru of the previous Doboom. Tashi Tsering of Amnye Machen Institute tells me there are references to Doboom in Dagkar's biography.

This library preserved the manuscripts in Sanskrit and Tibetan brought from Tibet by Pandit Rahul Sankrityayana. When I returned to Tibet House as its director in the 1980s, I tried to get Dagkar's collected works published by Tibet House, but despite the sincere support of Mohsina Kidwai, governor of Bihar and ex-officio president of the Bihar Research Society, nothing happened. It was unfortunate that in spite of such treasures being there, little use was being made of them by studying and preserving them for posterity.

The meeting with JP afterwards was very moving. JP and His Holiness showed their affectionate respect for each other and discussed matters of common concern. It was a memorable experience to witness the meeting of two great leaders of the masses. Later, I had the good fortune of seeing His Holiness meet Acharya Kripalani briefly at the Delhi airport when He was going on one of His visits abroad. I consider JP and Kripalani as two shining examples of great and selfless Indian leaders who never sought any position of power. Such people are an extinct species today.

Lal Bahadur Shastri also comes to my mind as an example of this category of noble people. The story of his tying his clothes and books on his head and swimming across the river Ganga to his school left a deep impression on me. In those days, the Tibetan people believed that if he had not died in Tashkent and been prime minister a little longer, he would have granted official recognition to the Tibetan Government-in-Exile, which would really have made all the difference.

I accompanied His Holiness on His second visit to Japan in 1978 when He expressed a wish to stay at a Zen monastery. We were there for the 12th General Conference of the World Fellowship of Buddhists and the invitation had come from its Japanese chapter. The clearance from the Japanese government took some time to come through, the final papers coming almost at the last minute.

I have a memory of an extraordinary incident from this visit. On the morning of our departure, His Holiness had handed me a tube with a thangka rolled inside to wear around my neck saying, 'Lama, you take this rifle.' This was in fact a historic thangka of Palden Lhamo or Sri Devi Remati that had belonged to the 2nd Dalai Lama. It had become a kind of tradition for Dalai Lamas to carry it wherever they went.

At Hong Kong airport we needed to change aeroplanes and were made to pass through security again, for unlike India, they didn't make an exemption for His Holiness. When the tube went through the scanner, they could not understand what it was and wanted it opened. Two conflicting thoughts were racing through my mind. One, that it was so unfortunate that this sacred object was being treated thus and they were not making a special exception for His Holiness. But in the corner of my heart, I was also aware that I would perhaps get the rarest opportunity – of seeing the thangka, normally unthinkable for ordinary people as it was kept in the innermost chambers of the Dalai Lama's quarters. Somehow, after some argument, they allowed the tube to go through unopened. Afterwards, I have not seen this thangka being carried in the entourage. It may be that the thangka sticks were removed and it was rolled up to carry in the monk's bag His Holiness carries, or He may have decided to bid farewell to the tradition of carrying this thangka.

In Tibet, there exists a tradition of seeking names from a lama for newborn babies. In the Kuyig, an elderly person with beautiful handwriting who used to serve in the old government in Lhasa was called to write down names of boys and girls on a piece of paper. When parents came to seek names, His Holiness would pick up a piece of paper from the lot and give it to them. I felt the small piece of paper was difficult to preserve and the parents would always be worried about losing it. So I introduced a name card, instead. When designing the card, I took inspiration from the small miniature statue of Yamantaka that was distributed during His Holiness's Geshe Lharampa celebration in Tibet which had Vajradhara in gold, handwritten in Tibetan at the back of the statue. I put Vajradhara in Tibetan on the top-middle section of the card and used a green colour border to represent the tree element of His Holiness. I presented the idea of the card to His Holiness and He was happy with it. This name card system is still being used and I rejoice in this small contribution.

31

Travels with His Holiness

I have noticed that when they are excited, often people may do or say things they may not really mean. Here is a small example. It was on one of His Holiness's visits to Kyoto. Because of the Japanese love of ceremony, there was a reception in the hotel foyer even before His Holiness was conducted to His room. At that time a classmate of mine from Varanasi, who was doing research at a Buddhist university in Kyoto, was also present. Just as the reception started, he walked up to His Holiness and said excitedly, 'I am trying to set up a Buddhist temple or centre, please give it a name.' Without thinking much, His Holiness replied, 'All right, Thekchen Choeling.' I was a little startled to hear Him give the name of Dharamsala's main temple to what was then a mere idea. Since then, I have not heard anything about the project.

Another major visit on which I accompanied His Holiness was to Switzerland, Greece and the United States, in 1979. In Switzerland, His Holiness had some days of leisure, staying at the small Tibetan temple at Rikon near Zurich. It was one of the first institutes of Tibetan religion and culture set up in the West. Its architecture appeared to be inspired by a photograph of the Potala Palace. Both tutors of His Holiness were present at its inauguration in 1968. A very learned scholar, Geshe Ogyen Tseten, was appointed as the first abbot and with him were four monks.

His Holiness gave a public teaching to the Tibetans in Switzerland and took a retreat and a holiday. On one occasion, when we were returning to Rikon, He suddenly decided to stop at a small hotel on the way. Since we had not made a booking, we could not get rooms there. We went from one hotel to another, turning back at the 'no vacancy' signs. His Holiness seemed to

Enthronement of Doboom Tulku at Tehor Khangtsen Hall, Drepung Monastery, Lhasa, 1954

(L to R) *Mother Loyak, sister Dolma Lhamo, brother-in-law Nyiga and brothers Ugen, Geleg and Bhuchey, 1984*

Portrait of family members in traditional clothes

Gen Thubten, teacher at Doboom Ritro

In Dharamsala while serving at Kuyig, the Private Office of His Holiness the Dalai Lama

With His Holiness during the installation of the Buddha statue at Buddha Jayanti Park, New Delhi, 1993

Church. Rato Kyongla was somehow involved in coordinating this programme and he read out a welcome speech in English from the pulpit. As his voice was hoarse and pronunciation unclear, it was difficult to make out what he was trying to say. To me, it sounded more like the disciplinarian of Drepung Monastery back in Tibet making his customary proclamations! Again, His Holiness had a hearty laugh.

His Holiness's visit to the Tibetan Buddhist Learning Center in New Jersey was significant. Driving from New York City to this countryside centre was a welcome change. This centre was established by a Khalmuk monk from Drepung Gomang, Geshe Wangyal, who was perhaps the first master of Tibetan Buddhism who started a centre in North America. Many of the present-day well-known Buddhist scholars such as Prof. Robert Thurman and Prof. Jeffrey Hopkins were his direct disciples. Khenchung Thupten Tsephel, a former fourth-ranking officer in the Lhasa government, was a resident there and I remember he had prepared a detailed programme for His Holiness in old-style Tibetan language. His Holiness's programme included teachings to the Buddhists in the area and persons from many Mongol-origin communities settled in nearby places. Younger students of Geshe Wangyal, like Joshua, Diana and Natalie, were in full attendance. All the girls wore a specially designed uniform and took care of the cooking. I noticed that they had acquired the skill of making delicious Mongolian momos from Geshe Wangyal.

After Geshe Wangyal passed away, this centre was run very efficiently by Joshua and Diana Cutler and is still active in promoting the Tibetan style of Buddhism. Joshua and Diana managed to keep the functioning of the centre close to the idea of the original founder despite several attempts to hijack it by people. I make it a point to visit this place whenever I go to the East Coast. For the last several years, I have been visiting the centre almost every year and I feel at home there.

enjoy the experience, which was a departure from the normal routine – from airport to hotel, from hotel to the programme venue and back. His fondness for watches and shoes was well known and we visited several shops just like other visitors as there were no security concerns in those days.

Visiting Greece after Switzerland, I felt the difference in the culture of the people. In Greece, I could see people sitting along street-sides and chatting, almost like in many parts of Asia. In Athens, there was a three-day Dharma lecture organised by Buddhist groups in a hotel named Chandrika. The subject of the lecture was 'Three Learnings', that is, morality, meditation and wisdom. I took notes during the lectures based on which I developed an article which was published in a book brought out by Tibet House, *Atisha and Buddhism in Tibet*, to commemorate the millennial anniversary of Atisha. His Holiness wanted to see a Catholic monastery on an island famous for its discipline and austerity, but for some reason the visit could not be arranged. One evening I went to see a sound-and-light show at the Acropolis. The show was full of wonders for me.

Then we flew to the USA. It was His Holiness's first visit to the country. The year was 1979. Accommodation was arranged in the Waldorf-Astoria. His first public programme was a lecture at Freedom Hall in the Asia Society, New York, which went off very well. In New York, Rato Kyongla Rinpoche offered a lunch for His Holiness. A plate full of momos was sent to His room and whatever was left was distributed to the entourage. Since His Holiness did not have any dinner, His lunch was normally a big one. He emptied the momo plate and asked for more. Rato Kyongla had to confess that nothing was left. His Holiness had a hearty laugh and later would joke with him about the incident.

There was a reception at the Church of St John the Divine in Madison Avenue, where Cardinal Cook received His Holiness. I thought that was good and would be a starting point for contact and interaction with other religions, particularly the Roman Catholic

With President R. Venkataraman during the Global Event of the World Festival of Sacred Music, Bengaluru, 2000

With Nazar Palden Tiwana at Buddha Jayanti Park

With Marina Abramovic, in the performance piece 'The Artist Is Present', 2010

With Alessia Bulgari at the World Festival of Sacred Music, Berlin, 2002

With Thich Nhat Hanh at Buddha Jayanti Park, 2008

With King Charles of the United Kingdom, then the Prince of Wales, 2002

His Holiness then visited the Jefferson Memorial and Capitol Hill in Washington DC. From there, on the way to Madison, He was invited to a meal at the home of a very rich family He has often referred to afterwards, where the daughters became interested in Buddhism and were particularly inspired by His Holiness. His Holiness described how He found sleeping pills in their bathroom and realised that a person may have all the material requirements, but still have more and more worries, and finally have to resort to sleeping pills. In Madison, He visited a small centre which was newly established by Jeffrey Hopkins. It was called UMA (Union of the Modern and the Ancient). His Holiness gave an important talk there, surveying Tibetan Buddhist traditions.

In his welcome speech at Amherst College, Robert Thurman explained each of His Holiness's Tibetan names. 'I welcome Tenzin (*translation*) … I welcome Gyatso (*translation*) … I welcome the simple monk (*explanation*).' He then went on to talk about his idea of translating either the Kangyur or the Tengyur or both. Perhaps His Holiness felt it was a wild idea. He remarked privately that many reincarnations of Bob Thurman would be required to complete the project.

Three decades later, Thurman had made some progress. A conference on 'Translating the Words of the Buddha Conference' was held in March 2009 at Bir in Himachal Pradesh. It brought together many translators, scholars and Dharma gurus, who charted a programme for translating the Kangyur, making plans for the next 100, 25 and 5 years. The conference was led by Dzongsar Khyentse Rinpoche who had the support of scholars, Dharma gurus and lay admirers, including the president of Taiwan, whose special message was read on the occasion. The translators later sought the blessings of His Holiness in Dharamsala. I was told that Robert Thurman went in first and had a word with Him privately. This gave the impression to people who were watching that he emphasised to His Holiness the importance of translating the Tengyur rather than Kangyur.

Though not really a translator or scholar of that standard, I had been invited to the Bir conference at the instance of Gene Smith, because he was aware that in 1990 I had organised an international conference on behalf of Tibet House on 'Buddhist Translation: Problems and Prospects'. I was impressed that Gene Smith, who had not participated in my conference but had come to know of it, had become interested enough to remember it. Bob Thurman became a monk and later gave up his robes, but he continues to be a real practitioner. We were together on the flight back from the Bir conference, and I noticed he was holding some biscuits in his hand and reciting something. It was Vajrayogini Ganachakra Offering Day.

In Seattle, where Sakya Phuntsog Phodrang had settled, there was a reception where many Tibetans staying in that area including Phuntsog Phodrang Rinpoche and his family, came to see His Holiness. As usual, Tibetans were very enthusiastic about bringing khatags and other gifts, but at the end of the programme, all these gifts were left forgotten at the venue. One such gift was a Chinese thermos. When His Holiness asked where the thermos had gone, I felt I was to blame for not remembering to have the gifts collected. It was not easy in those days to get hold of a Chinese thermos.

His Holiness spent a few days at a Zen Buddhist centre in a place called Green Gulch on the West Coast. He participated in a meditation session in the morning where there was a very interesting tradition. A man carrying a flat stick moved among those meditating. If anyone felt a little heaviness in their shoulders, he or she would bend down and ask to be hit. The man would hit rather hard – one, two, three. It made the person feel better. I feel that originally this must have been a disciplinary action for people found dozing and later it was converted into a ceremony.

At Green Gulch I took a day off to visit Lama Anagarika Govinda, who was staying with his wife Lee Watami in a small house a few hours' drive away. His is a name every old foreign Buddhist knows. He is a European who came to India and met a Tibetan lama. His books on Tibetan Buddhism are very popular. They are readable, easy to comprehend and have solid academic grounding. When I asked him, 'Who is your yidam (personal deity)?' he answered 'Demchok'. Demchok is also known as Heruka Chakrasamvara. It was satisfying to meet someone about whom I had heard so much and some of whose books I had read.

All things considered, the tour to the United States was important at many levels. It was natural for Tibetans to feel that His Holiness visiting America meant a lot for the Tibetan cause and the response of the Americans was very enthusiastic and extremely encouraging. Americans are, undoubtedly, very open and straightforward people – different from Asians and Europeans. They are also more receptive to new religions and new cultures and easily influenced by other cultures. Ceremonies and initiations seem to suit their mental make-up. Decades later, I read an interesting article in the news bulletin of a publishing house called 'Snow Line'. This article was written by a lady living in Ithaca describing how overjoyed she had been when approached to play hostess to His Holiness and His entourage for one night. Later, as His Holiness's popularity continued to increase, she had to struggle to get even a glimpse of Him from a distance.

His Holiness always tried to travel with a small entourage. He had two monks as personal assistants – his secretary, Tenzin Geyche, who dealt with English communications (fixing appointments and translating speeches) and I (interacting with Tibetans and arranging audiences). In addition, there were four others – His Holiness's nephew, Khedroob Thondup (son of Gyalo Thondup); a lawyer, Michael von Brück; an American lady, Michele Bohana and a Tibetan from Switzerland. Jeffrey

Hopkins joined us in the USA and was the interpreter for His Holiness's religious discourses.

I do not know how and who decided the composition of the entourage. Khedroob Thondup seemed to regard it his duty to take photographs. I did not understand what role he played apart from that. Michael von Brück became very involved with the Tibetan cause and wrote a book on the legal status of the Tibet issue, but after a few years I did not hear his name in the Tibetan circles and Bohana lost touch with what he was doing. Michele was involved in the founding of the International Campaign for Tibet in Washington DC in 1988. Sometime later I heard that her interest got diverted to Burmese issues. The Swiss-Tibetan was trained as a gardener and had been brought to Dharamsala reportedly to beautify the area around the palace compound. I was always amazed by the different kinds of people in His Holiness's entourage; some with obvious and clearly defined roles, some without.

32

In the Land Far North

We were at the Russian Orthodox Church outside Moscow at the invitation of the Supreme Patriarch, the Metropolitan. They served us an elaborate lunch and the Metropolitan explained to His Holiness that they were pure vegetarians and that was why they served a wide variety of fish. His Holiness asked, 'How do you distinguish between vegetarian and non-vegetarian food?' They answered that they considered fish vegetarian because when a fish was cut, there was no blood. I thought that was not completely correct, but it was true that cutting a fish was not like cutting a goat.

We had this interesting thought to ponder over during our visit in June 1979 to the erstwhile Soviet Union. It was a unique experience in many ways. I also heard people commenting that the visit was politically much more important than His later visit to the USA in September of the same year. It was the height of the Cold War and I understood that the visit to the Soviet Union made many political observers raise their eyebrows. The occasion was an invitation to attend the Asian Buddhist Conference for Peace (ABCP) in Mongolia, the front used by the Soviet Union to extend its influence in Buddhist countries and to counter the influence of the World Fellowship of Buddhists with its headquarters in Bangkok, which was seen as being dominated by the West. I felt that the Soviet Union was trying to balance the growing power of China and the USA and using Tibetans as an instrument in the game. The feeling was strengthened when we made our way from the airport at Tashkent, our first stop, to our place of stay. Everything appeared very quiet and dark.

In Moscow, His Holiness visited a huge, old church where many people, mostly elders, had gathered to pray and I wondered whether it was normally like that or if it had been specially arranged. He also visited the Kremlin and some other institutions. From Moscow, His Holiness was flown to the Republic of Buryatia and visited a small monastery called Ivolginsky Datsan, a Buddhist monastery that had been rebuilt during the height of the Stalinist regime after it was destroyed in the Revolution. His Holiness was received in the temple hall where the monks were chanting in Tibetan. One of the verses was a popular one, chanted by all Tibetans for the longevity of the Dalai Lama. His Holiness was visibly moved by that.

I found it interesting that the monks chanted and recited the text in Tibetan but with a Mongolian accent. They could not speak Tibetan. Some elderly monks, like the abbot, managed to communicate a few words of Tibetan, using them exactly as written in scriptures, just as Tibetans use Sanskrit when they recite mantras whose meaning they mostly do not know except for a few words like vajra. It took me a few moments to figure out what exactly they were chanting because of the different pronunciation, but otherwise I had no problem following and even chanting with them. I noticed that they substituted 'in this land far north' for 'in this land of snow mountain' as we chant in Tibetan in the longevity verse.

There were some regions of the erstwhile Soviet Union – Tuva, Kalmykia and Buryatia – where many people followed Buddhism. That was the northernmost reach of Buddhism. Monks had continued to be ordained in these areas even in the late 1970s, just before the communists took over these areas.

I was very impressed by the Khambo Lama of Buryatia, virtually the head of Buddhists in the Soviet Union, who possesses the basic Buddhist monastic qualifications and knowledge and enjoys the respect of the Buddhist community. I understood that he could not revolt against the State, but he did exercise a certain amount of freedom within the Buddhist community and even resisted some unreasonable orders from government offices or departments, such as singing the praises of the regime. The Buddhists in the region were fearless in honouring Buddhist leaders such as the Dalai Lama, an outsider.

When His Holiness arrived at Ulaanbaatar, the capital of the Mongolian People's Republic (as Mongolia was called then), from the airport onwards, it was a very different scene compared to Russia. The roads, the welcome gates and the entry to the Gaden Monastery, which was the venue of ABCP, bore a festive mood. There were colourful banners with welcome slogans and peace quotations all along the way greeting the delegates. On the day of the inauguration, the main speaker was undoubtedly His Holiness and he was received with devotion and enthusiasm by the participants. From the organisers' side and select delegates, the speeches carried anti-imperialist content, attacking the West as the main obstacle to world peace. One day, His Holiness was requested to address a public rally in the courtyard of the monastery. A large number of people gathered to listen to Him. I felt most people came to see His Holiness rather than to participate in the rally.

Another memorable incident during that visit was when His Holiness visited a museum which displayed, among other things, a model of Kalachakra Mandala, built during Jetsun Dampa's reign. The museum guide, a young woman, earnestly started explaining to His Holiness what a Kalachakra Mandala was, in all detail, and what each part symbolised. His Holiness patiently listened to the explanations for a few minutes, then smiled and said, 'Wait a minute, I am supposed to know all these already.' To me it was like someone explaining elementary principles of science to Albert Einstein.

In another section of the museum, a map displayed the geography of the world. His Holiness noticed something and said, 'Where is Italy?' He had noticed it was missing! This demonstrated His keen interest in geography and the sharpness of His mind. Another painting showed a man struggling with an enormously huge load on his back; it was explained to Him that it depicted how the three lords suppressed people in the old society. He paid close attention to this painting. As this was nothing new to Him after the experience with the Chinese in Tibet, He did not make any comment before he moved on.

A small but interesting episode that showed how people were made to follow government orders to the letter, took place during His Holiness's stay at Ulaanbaatar, where arrangements for Him had been made in a comfortable guest house with a large compound on the outskirts of the city. The motorcade was instructed to have a certain number of vehicles follow one another without fail. One afternoon His Holiness was invited to a cultural performance in the city but He did not feel like going. So He asked me to go instead. I told the liaison officer that I was the only one going so just one car should be arranged. When I was ready to leave, he explained that it was not possible for just one car to go as there were clear orders about it. To my amusement, the entire motorcade followed my vehicle.

Whenever I think of our visit to Mongolia, I cannot but remember one experience that seemed larger than life. His Holiness was shown a simple room, modestly decorated as a chapel. They said it was the 13th Dalai Lama's room during His stay in Mongolia. His Holiness took a seat and glanced through one of the scriptures there. I thought the room might have been renovated and rearranged. And yet I found myself holding my breath. Far away from our homeland, where both had occupied the same palace room in Potala, we were in Ulaanbaatar and the 14th Dalai Lama was sitting in the room that was occupied by His predecessor. If the room was actually the same room used by the 13th Dalai Lama, then the 14th Dalai Lama sitting there was a historic event.

Experiences are of different kinds, but in one way or another they show the beauty of the people and stay in our memory. The hosts had arranged for His Holiness to visit the city's shopping area. As He was walking around, young salespersons watched him intensely. No one had the courage to openly show their religious feelings, but I could feel their devotion. Suddenly I found a woman elbowing her way forward and as though it was accidental, she brushed her hand against His Holiness's robe. Holding the hand that had touched the robe, she went a little distance to a corner and put it to her forehead in prayer.

After the conference in Ulaanbaatar, His Holiness and His entourage were flown by a special chartered plane to visit the grasslands. On this stretch of the tour, we were joined by His Holiness's eldest brother, Taktser Rinpoche, the author of *Tibet Is My Country*. I remember His Holiness and His brother engaged in a traditional folk game called 'apchuk' in Tibetan that was provided on the plane. It was a game played using the cleaned and polished anklebones of sheep. Each of the four sides of an anklebone represents a different animal – horse, sheep, camel and goat.

I later learned that a Mongolian game called 'shagai' was played in a similar manner.

Taktser Rinpoche was a very special person for he was upright, outspoken and had independent thinking. He could speak the Mongolian language, a skill he had acquired from his teacher, who was of Buryatian origin, at the Drepung Monastery in Tibet. He had picked up a working knowledge of Japanese because of which he headed the Tibet Office in Tokyo for some years. He died in 2008 in the USA after a long battle with diabetes.

In the grasslands, His Holiness was invited to a 'gir', a round woollen tent that stayed warm even in cold weather. They offered mare's milk which they called 'airik'. It was supposed to give strength and provide warmth in the winters. This drink was also served every day during the morning gatherings of monk-officials in Lhasa and was called 'chikey' in the official language of the Tibetan government. Chikey was believed to be a Mongolian word.

Just as Tibetans looked at Buddhism from India as pure and genuine Buddhism, Mongolians did the same with Tibetan Buddhism, though there were other elements that had entered the practice. My interest in foreign cultures and habits also included an interest in food and dress. I must admit the most delicious momos I ever ate were in the Ivolginsky Monastery.

In the Gaden Monastery in Ulaanbaatar, I noticed that the jacket worn by the monks was the same as the 'chatru chato', the jacket worn by middle-ranking monk-officials in Lhasa. I realised that it was during the 13th Dalai Lama's visit to Ulaanbaatar that a replica had been made and later it was made the official dress in Lhasa. Many familiar ceremonial objects of the Tibetan government were also from Mongolia, such as the ceremonial teapot. When I visited the museum of Jibcundampa (Jetsun Dampa), the former lama-king of Mongolia, I noticed the interiors could have been of any chamber of the Potala Palace in Lhasa. On the throne of Jibcundampa, I counted twenty-five cushions, each with a border of half an inch of differently coloured brocade. In the Potala and Norbulingka, the throne of His Holiness had five cushions with a width of two and a half inches in five colours. Tibetans took the essence and philosophy of Buddhism from India. They took other cultural ideas such as dress and food from Mongolia and China and added them all to the native culture of Tibet.

33

Bahujana Hitaya, Bahujana Sukhaya

Those were the years when the monasteries of the Tibetan community in exile were in the process of being set up. When I look back, those times were very different from the present, because everybody was content with the resources they had and there were no ambitious plans of creating a sense of grandeur and enigma once associated with Tibetan monks. It was, in fact, the true Buddhist way. And His Holiness also laid emphasis on this. I once saw a photograph from that period that showed abbots and monks receiving His Holiness, carrying incense and wearing chappals, and I felt that it was more like the Buddhist monastic culture, instead of what often happens now – showing off wealth and strength in numbers. And at the monks' gatherings, it was considered a blessing just to be able to have a view of His Holiness. To listen to Him, to hear Him speak, was a pure delight foreveryone without exception. Though the numbers then were much lower than now, monks or non-monks, if they caught a glimpse of His Holiness, they were completely satisfied. No one craved for a picture or a personal conversation with His Holiness. His very vision gave enough spiritual and mental tranquillity.

In those days the monasteries tried to induct new monks from the settlement camps and even Himalayan Buddhist areas, to keep the traditions alive for the future. But the situation, it seems to me, changed in the 1980s, when there were a lot of people coming from Tibet whose parents wanted them to be admitted to monasteries. The reason probably was that the parents felt that the future of their children would be better if they studied in India rather than in Tibet, in Chinese-run schools. So monkhood was a more attractive option. This gradually changed when they started finding alternatives, like sending their children abroad or to regular schools in India.

During my time at the Kuyig, there was a small but significant movement initiated by a few Tibetans who felt that nothing was moving forward for the Tibetan cause. A few of the youth set up something called 'Sungdrel Tsogchung' (coordinating committee), supposedly to push the cause forward. One of the main complaints they had was that the Tibetan establishment only reacted and never acted on its own accord. It did not take the initiative. In those days, such movements were not tolerated by the Tibetan establishment, though appreciating their concerns was another matter. The movement gradually died down. Some of those involved in it remained blacklisted for some time, but they were clever enough to become 'white' in time. Later, some of them even became prominent at the international level.

Sometime in the mid-1970s, it became fashionable in small circles of Tibetan intellectuals to talk in favour of communism, just as today it is to talk of democracy. People made eloquent speeches on the *Communist Manifesto* and *Das Capital* of Karl Max, on the proletarian revolution and so on. They even mocked the earlier Tibetan leaders such as Prime Minister Lukhangpa who fought against the communist system and its totalitarian regime when China started pressuring the Lhasa government.

Around that time, I happened to be in Chandigarh to visit a professor of Panjab University. A gathering of Tibetans, mostly students, took place in the city. I was invited to attend it. I do not remember the occasion. Completely out of the blue, one young man got up and announced that he had established a communist party within the Tibetan community. He read out a document, perhaps the manifesto of the party, and even pulled out a logo, which if I remember correctly, depicted a sickle and a pen instead of a hammer. After that, I heard about this 'Communist Party' once or twice and then it seemed the 'Party' was over. During the peak period of communism, His Holiness visited the Soviet Union and the Mongolian People's Republic. In one of these countries, someone asked His Holiness whether there was a communist movement in the exiled Tibetan community. As usual, He gave a tactful and appropriate answer.

His Holiness has spoken on many international fora about his idea of original communism. My understanding of His Holiness's point is that there is a meeting point between Buddhist social theory and original (not the corrupted) communism. Buddhism is concerned with the welfare and happiness of many (*bahujana hitaya*, *bahujana sukhaya*) as against riches for a privileged few. Communism is also supposed to be concerned with the suffering of the majority. I don't think His Holiness has spoken from the perspective of the active expression of Marxism, for example, class struggle, proletarian revolution and so on.

I cannot claim at all to understand Marxism. But I have read some literature about it, including some in Tibetan language. One thing that struck me was that some people seemed to assert that it does not matter whether 'the highest inspiration of humankind' according to the socialist theory is achievable or not, as long as there is a dialectics. I presume that Marxists believe it is achievable, in the same way we Buddhists assert that nirvana is achievable by all. The word 'dialectic' translated into Tibetan by renowned scholars like Geshe Sherab in mid 1950s is 'tsodub rigpa' which has same meaning as 'yukta' in Sanskrit. Decades later, I learned that in his youth, the prominent Tibetan communist, Bawa Phuntsog Wangyal, before the communist regime took over China, had come to India and made contacts with Jyoti Basu. I have no idea whether he and other young Tibetan people had any support from non-Tibetan or pro-communist groups or individuals. But I realise that most of these modern 'isms' become irrelevant with the passage of time, and thus are forgotten. At a practical level, many of the revolutionary leaders eventually become worse than imperialists. They groom their successors and a dynasty gets established, just like it has happened in North Korea.

I continued to have ample opportunities to interact with Western Buddhist enthusiasts. Many of them were former hippies or were still semi-hippies. In the beginning I got a feeling that they were overdoing their show of enthusiasm. My favourite advice to them always was – it was good to become a Buddhist, but they did not have to be 'Tibetanised'. Some of them remained very stable Buddhist practitioners and remained monks or nuns their whole lives. For others, it was just the experience of a new lifestyle and they soon transformed themselves into something else. Some became scholars, learned in both the Tibetan traditions as well as academic subjects and became university professors, others went in different directions.

The Canadian Glenn Mullin was my first guru to teach me driving. During one of my visits to Canada in the early 1980s, he took me to an empty road and taught me the basics of how to drive. I learnt driving in a few lessons and drove on the highways of Canada while my friends slept at the back. I never attempted to drive in the city because it appeared too dangerous, and in India, I never touched the steering wheel.

Glenn Mullin was popular and friendly with everyone. He specialised in the writings of the Dalai Lamas and got many of the works of the previous Dalai Lamas published in the USA. Later he took Buddhist groups to Tibet and Mongolia to see important Buddhist sites and historical monuments. Now he is a great travelling guru. Around the 1980s, his entry to India was banned, the reason for which was beyond my knowledge, but I knew him to be an outspoken person who would say many things which he did not really mean.

Part VII
TIBET HOUSE

34

Return to Tibet House

Towards the end of 1981, His Holiness called and asked me to go to Delhi as the director of Tibet House. He told me to go there for a year or two and then come back to His Private Office. There were many possibilities for activities there, He said, particularly for establishing contacts with other cultures. There were cultural centres of several countries in Delhi and in some embassies there were cultural attachés, so it would be a good idea to have contact with them.

At that time some changes had taken place in the Private Office of His Holiness. As I have mentioned earlier, there were two sections in the office – one dealing with matters relating to the Tibetan community and the other dealing with international and external matters. Tenzin Geyche, who had disappeared suddenly leaving me to handle some of his tasks, had now returned from his self-imposed exile. He was made the kalon of the Department of Information and International Relations. He also resumed his duties at the Kuyig. In all these changes, my duties too changed.

For some time, communications from the Kashag addressed to me referred to my post in the Kuyig as well as the Tibet House. Kashag was the Council of Ministers. It was an institution that came into existence during the period of the 7th Dalai Lama. Before that, there was no Kashag – there used to be a chief regent who used to rule or look after the administration. This was true for all lamas. The main lama sat aloof, as though he knew nothing of the details of the administration, which may not have been true in all cases. His chief lama managed his administration. All rewards and punishments were meted out by this chief lama. During the period of the 7th Dalai Lama, there was a lot of interference from the ruler of the Ching dynasty. At that time, the ruler himself seems to have suggested a council of ministers instead of one manager. That came to be and was called the Kashag. It generally consisted of one monk and three laypersons.

Prior to my moving, a special meeting was called at Tibet House at my suggestion to discuss the possibilities of expanding its activities. People considered knowledgeable and experienced in culture and academia were invited. This meeting was attended by Jigme Taring, who was the kalon of Education; Prof. Samdhong Rinpoche, director CHITS; Rikha Loten, education secretary; and Mrs Gelek, general secretary of Tibet House. Several ideas came up as everybody expressed their views. During the course of the discussions, I noticed that exhibitions were considered to be very important and impactful. In fact, the original idea with which Tibet House had been set up was to house Tibetan antiques that some people had brought with them from Tibet. So what emerged was an emphasis on the importance of the existing emporium that showcased Tibetan artifacts.

There was another activity of the emporium – to sell Tibetan artefacts. Interestingly, it was Samdhong Rinpoche who went into a graphic explanation, saying that selling a purse of Tibetan style was more relevant and important than displaying the entire Kangyur and Tengyur, for the purse could be taken out into the world and seen by several people. That, he opined, would help present a good impression of Tibet's unique cultural character. The reason I found this interesting was because Samdhong Rinpoche earnestly promoted the cause of the emporium but years later, when he became the kalon tripa (prime minister) of the Tibetan Government-in-Exile, he dissolved all business organs of the Tibetan establishment. Decisions are often not as unbiased or committed to the larger cause as we think they are. Only time clears the picture.

My opinion at the time was that activities for promoting and preserving Tibetan culture should not involve just the physical exhibition of handicrafts and artifacts. There must be ways and means of doing something beyond, but I just wished to be clearer in my mind about how this could be done and so, at that time, I just heard everyone out.

My appointment as the director was basically to fill a vacant post which had not been occupied for many years. At the time I was working in the Kuyig, my rank was sixth level. I was posted at Tibet House on the same level and the general secretary, Mrs Gelek, whom I knew from my days as the librarian at Tibet House, held the same rank at that time. She was considered a tough lady, but I found her extremely cooperative and helpful. I did not have the slightest resentment of being the same rank as my junior. A few of my well-wishers warned me that there was politics afoot and I should play my cards well for there were people who would make sure that I did not climb up the ladder. I did not bother about this at all as I was never conscious of my rank, salary grade and so on. I found it difficult to accept that someone like me, from a monastic background, should care about such mundane matters as rank and salary. Having said that, we must also realise that life is not lived only at the spiritual level. It has many levels. For me, to rise above them was the main focus.

The first question that naturally arose was where to stay. With the help of some people, I had located a place – No. 8, Golf Links, facing Lodhi Road. The owners, the Lalls, agreed to give me half of the first floor, which meant the staircase and the entrance would be shared. The area was considered a posh locality and going to the office was very easy because Tibet House was just across the road. I stayed there for less than a year and then moved to Defence Colony. There I had to deal with typical landlord–tenant problems. The landlord did not care to maintain the premises and did not allow us to maintain them either. So the condition of the house went from bad to worse and turned into a shabby state due to which my health was affected. Perhaps this helped me face odds the Buddhist way, without harbouring any ill will.

Like Mrs Gelek, another known face when I came to Tibet House was Geshe Palden Drakpa, a brilliant scholar from Loseling College (he was senior to me) who was working there as the librarian-cum-religious preceptor. He had a Buddhist monk from New Zealand helping him to interpret in English. In a new situation, finding a friendly face makes all the difference.

My life in Buxa, Sarnath and Dharamsala was more or less close to monastic life. But coming to Tibet House changed my monastic life to a city life where the atmosphere, food, movement and dealing with people were very different from what I was familiar with. I had not foreseen that from a tulku's life, I would enter into a babu's (officer) life. Sometimes I missed the simplicity of life in Tibet. In those days, my food was very simple and my needs were also simple. I started the day with tsampa, Tibet's staple food, and ended the day with tsampa. In this simple life, everyone was happy and contented. Sometimes when I received visitors from Tibet, nostalgic memories of my childhood in Tibet came flooding in – simple things like the satisfaction of quenching my thirst from the cold and fresh water directly from the stream nearby. No need for bottled water or RO water. I still miss the crisp, blue sky and the calm, peaceful environment of those days.

Among the first things I did after taking over as the director of Tibet House in December 1981 was to write letters to the cultural centres of different countries. I clearly remember receiving only two acknowledgements, one from the Soviet Cultural and Information Centre and the other from the cultural attaché of the Nepalese Embassy. I went so far as to call on their offices, but I do not have any particular memory of the visits. The Soviet Cultural and Information Centre kept in touch by sending us their programmes and brochures. Gradually, I developed useful contacts with foreign missions such as the British Council, West German Embassy, Sri Lankan and Indonesian High Commission and a few others. I developed collaborative relationships, from sharing resources to organising programmes, with the Max Müller Bhawan and the Hungarian Cultural and Information Centre.

These interactions had another outcome. I would receive invitations to the programmes of these foreign missions as the head of Tibet House. It was customary to write 'Mr and Mrs' on invitations and I would receive invitations addressed to Mr and Mrs Doboom Tulku. It sounded funny and so I started putting Lama before my name. That helped remove the confusion regarding my marital status in some cases. But very often, in letters, they addressed me as Venerable Mr Lama. This was how I became Lama Doboom Tulku.

In a couple of months' time, I convened the annual governing body meeting of Tibet House, which was chaired by Kamaladevi Chattopadhyaya, who was the seniormost among the members. I remember that this meeting was brief and formal. One of the agenda items was to welcome and formally approve my nomination by His Holiness the Dalai Lama as the director. Kamaladevi was a freedom fighter and active in the promotion of handicrafts. She was mainly responsible for establishing Tibetan handicraft centre in Dalhousie and other Tibetan colonies in the 1970s. She had a unique analytical capacity, even for small details.

Other members of Tibet House at that time were Kushok Bakula Rinpoche, head lama of Ladakh; Pandit Shamnarayan who was the secretary in the Central Tibetan School Administration (CTSA), an Indian government organisation responsible for establishing and running schools for Tibetan children; and

Vijayalakshmi Pandit, the first lady president of the United Nations General Assembly and the sister of Jawaharlal Nehru.

My immediate concern was the preservation of Tibetan culture and tradition. I always tried to help whenever I got the opportunity to do so. A small step in that direction was a project of reviving monastic Cham dances in Tibetan monasteries-in-exile. I chose Drukchen Rinpoche's Sang-Ngag Choeling Monastery situated between Darjeeling and Ghoom. That was the time when every monastery was very poor and for the work at hand we needed ₹30,000–50,000, which was a lot of money at that time. The amount was mainly for Cham costumes and musical instruments. Kamaladevi was the chairperson of Sangeet Natak Akademi and I approached her. She agreed to help the project in principle and also sanctioned travel by air for Mr Dhawan (secretary of the Sangeet Natak Akademi) and me to Darjeeling.

Drukchen Rinpoche, who was very young at that time, received us. I believe that the amount granted by the Akademi was helpful to at least initiate some training. The Rinpoche not only did a remarkable job of promoting religion and culture but also initiated unique outreach programmes such as training nuns in self-protection. His work has been appreciated by many. The monastery is now flourishing.

Though I had no experience of running an institution, with the help and guidance from knowledgeable people, I managed smoothly, taking up issues carefully, one by one. One person from whom I constantly received guidance was Pandit Shamnarayan. He was a father figure to me. I regularly turned to him for advice on many practical matters such as drafting of project proposals, making minutes after meetings and official letters to government departments. He was sincere and transparently honest and did not hesitate to tell me if he disagreed with anything. He was old fashioned in his ways and a strict adherent of rules. Whenever I visited him at his modestly furnished home, he always received me in a formal attire, complete with necktie and turban. He was a spiritual seeker. I remember, during an audience with His Holiness in Dharamsala, he discussed the different levels of subtlety of consciousness. At my request, His Holiness paid a visit to him at his residence when he was sick, not long before his passing away.

Another person from whom I sought guidance in running Tibet House was Ravindra Verma, a senior Indian leader who had been a freedom fighter, parliamentarian and a cabinet minister in Morarji Desai's government. It was during a talk by Zong Rinpoche, which I attended at Tushita Mahayana Meditation Centre in Delhi, that I first met him. This meeting led to an association that was to last for the next quarter century, until his death in October 2006. In the 1980s, he took initiations from His Holiness and regularly practised the Avalokiteswara Sadhana (*Jinasagara*) of *anuttara* yoga. He was a great source of inspiration to me. He was the chairman of Delhi's Vishwa Yuvak Kendra. He was always available to me to consult on matters of work. He later became the chancellor of Gujarat Vidyapith, a position once held by Mahatma Gandhi, Vallabhbhai Patel, Rajendra Prasad and Morarji Desai.

After some time, I observed that most of the workforce as well as the financial resources of Tibet House were used in running the emporium. It did attract visitors, but what happened was that Tibet House meant just the emporium for most people, just the museum to some others, while the library existed for very few. I realised all that was very subjective – it was for people to judge according to their preferences. Since I felt that the emporium took up a lot of time, energy and money, leaving little scope for cultural and academic activities, in April 1984 I decided that it should be discontinued and the space was let out to some business undertakings of the Tibetan establishment for a few years. Eventually, the space was vacated except for the book corner and I turned it into a seminar hall, which was needed very much. Another reason for discontinuing the emporium was that it might have led to Tibet House being counted as a business establishment, so closing it down helped to avoid taxation issues.

My first idea was to apply for grants from the Government of India to initiate cultural and academic programmes. I also realised that to obtain recurring grants would be a dream that would take long to realise. So I applied for a one-time grant of ₹10 lakh from the Ministry of External Affairs as a special case, to be able to get some projects started. As M.K. Rasgotra was the foreign secretary and he was familiar with Tibetan-related problems, the grant was sanctioned. After his retirement, I requested him to become a member of Tibet House governing body, which he did and he continued to be a member till I left Tibet House.

Tibet House had received an interest-free loan of ₹8 lakh when the construction of the building had started, of which about half had been repaid in instalments. I approached the Ministry of External Affairs with a request for waiver of the remaining debt, which was also granted.

Later in the 1980s, we realised that we could not depend on one-time grants from the Indian government and had to arrange regular funding. After much effort and perseverance in dealing with people in the government at different levels, Tibet House started receiving small grants under the scheme of the Assistance to Voluntary Organisations of Tibetan/Buddhist Institutions. But for this, each institute had to apply annually and get papers ready for the next year's grant. I understood the government's policy in creating such a scheme, but the procedure was complicated because genuine institutions that were doing their best were equated with others whose existence was merely nominal – only on paper.

After further persuasion and further contact with people in the government who wished us well, we managed to get recurring grants from the Ministry of Culture. For some years now, we have been receiving ₹50 lakh annually, a small sum compared to what many other organisations receive. At the time I left Tibet House in 2011, we had just submitted a budget of ₹1 crore and received an indication from the government that it would come through from the next financial year.

In 2009, at a farewell Tibet House gave to Karma Dolma, manager, Maintenance and Cash, I told people that she was leaving Tibet House after 14 years of selfless service. At that time, I did not know how long I would be at Tibet House. My one or two years posting at Tibet House never seemed to be ending as there was no order or direction from the Kuyig about my return. Thus, I ended up staying almost 30 years in Tibet House. At any rate, the idea of spending my prime life in a busy city like Delhi was itself something which I would normally not have entertained.

35

Opening Up Conversations

When I joined Tibet House as its director, I did not envisage any of the programmes I initiated to continue for long, certainly not for decades. Yet it might be illuminating to give a brief account of two important and major sets of programmes. The first were the discourses by top Tibetan Buddhist lamas on various subjects of Tibetan Buddhism and the second were the monastic dialogue seminars organised in seven monastic institutions in India.

The first public event I organised was a discourse by Sakya Trizin Rinpoche on an important text of the Sakya tradition, *Parting from Four Clingings*. Among high Tibetan lamas, one tradition of Sakya lineage holders was unique – the title passed from father to son. I read in the first volume of the autobiography of the 5th Dalai Lama that there were two systems of lineage order, the first by inheritance and the second through the recognition of reincarnations or the tulku system. The first had the advantage that the time gap between the previous lama and the appointment of his successor was not large. So both the religious tradition and the material inheritance were handed down smoothly. The 5th Dalai Lama described the disadvantages of the second system, saying that the followers became more concerned about finding a tulku than about the death of their guru, which lead to a number of complicated situations, like wanting to find a tulku from a wealthy and established family.

I had seen Sakya Trizin Rinpoche for the first time in 1960, when he had come to preside over a special prayer session attended by tulkus in Kalimpong. To make the formal request for a teaching at Tibet House in 1982, I went to his establishment, the Dolma Phodrang, at Rajpur and he most graciously agreed to my request. Later, I went to receive him at Cheetal, between Dehradun and Delhi, where he arrived with his small entourage in a Land Rover. We stopped for tea in a small restaurant near the canal.

Arrangements were made for his stay in Tibet House. I was moved by his simplicity and unassuming character, despite his very high position in the long history of Tibetan Buddhism. The teaching he gave lasted several days and was attended by as many Indians as Tibetans; many of them came for the long-life initiation at the end. He spoke good English and used the interpreter only occasionally. His style of teaching was simple, direct, clear and to the point. I also arranged small discussions between the teaching sessions, which were helpful in understanding the teaching.

This programme was an eye-opener for me, because the response was so good. Everything went off very smoothly. I realised it was all easily manageable. The kind of programmes that might be organised in a busy city became clear. It must be remembered that in those years, electronic communications and media were not as strong and aggressive as they are now and social media did not exist. For me, this was the first experience of a teaching from a genuine lama outside my own Gelukpa tradition. There was a striking similarity between Sakya and Gelukpa traditions, not only in the disposition of material, but also in the prayers preceding each session and in the way sessions were structured.

The other public teachings organised at Tibet House in the five years that followed were significant as we covered all the major traditions of Tibetan Buddhism, inviting the most eminent lamas, both in hierarchy and in learning. In 1983, we had the rare privilege of having Kyabje Yongzin Ling Rinpoche, senior tutor of His Holiness, give teachings on the 'four attentions'. The subjects of teachings were mostly chosen by the lamas themselves, and the teachings by Sakya Rinpoche and Ling Rinpoche were both, interestingly, four-fold teachings, which, though not exactly the same, are believed to have come directly from Manjusri. For the leaflet announcing Ling Rinpoche's teaching, I suggested the title, 'A Rare Opportunity', and coincidentally, it turned out to be his last public teaching, for he died in 1983.

Although of different generations (one born in 1903, the other in 1945), Ling Rinpoche and Sakya Rinpoche were alike in many ways – they would receive visitors with due courtesy and depending on the visitor's background, make enquiries about their well-being and have a brief conversation suited to the occasion and the person. They never indulged in discussions of a political or controversial nature. After being served a cup of tea, the visitor was politely encouraged to take his leave.

In 1984, we invited Kyabje Dilgo Khyentse Rinpoche and he gave teachings on the *Heart Treasure of the Wise Ones*, a text by Paltrul Rinpoche, a very famous Nyingmapa master of the nineteenth century (1808–1887). This time we organised the teaching on the lawns of Tibet House under a tent. A special feature of his style of teaching was that his speech was never jerky or rushed but flowed like a great river, natural and effortless. However, his interpreter Matthieu Ricard would very often have to remind him that he needed to give him time to interpret! The text used covered the whole range of the understanding and practice of Dharma, philosophy, mediation and conduct, giving very fundamental and practical instructions regarding its principles, so that it did not become just dry philosophy or an academic exercise with little to do with real life.

The author of the text, whose full name was Paltrul Jigme Choekyi Wangpo, called himself Abu Ralpo. 'Abu' was a pet name for someone who was cherished like a son and 'Ralpo' meant 'the carefree one'. He was very famous for his skill in giving Dharma teachings through writings, mostly in poetry and story form, which appealed not just to lamas and scholars but also to the general public. He also wrote several fables. In the fable 'The Golden Bee and the Turquoise Bee', he described how the bees strayed into a lovely garden of flowers where the turquoise bee got drunk on the nectar of a flower. Suddenly a huge dark cloud hid the sun and, thinking the sun had set, the flower closed its petals, trapping her inside. The bee could not escape and she called out to her friend, the golden bee, saying she had overstepped the Dharma path that both of them had agreed to tread. The golden bee tried frantically to get help but by then the dark cloud started letting all its water pour down as rain. The flower stayed closed firmly. The story ended with the two bees, one inside and one outside, singing to each other about their realisation of impermanence.

This particular writing is very moving because the flow of language is very beautiful. It has both prose and verse. It talks of the love between the two bees. One of them got trapped inside the flower because she was too busy sucking nectar, just like everybody is lost in the pursuit of worldly pleasures. When her friend realised that she could not do anything, there is an exchange of conversation and songs between them, with the main message being that life is impermanent and we cannot go on clinging to worldly pleasures. Paltrul Rinpoche's style of writing is very simple, even a little folkish, with easy-to-sing tunes. It is gentle and not rigid in its construction and so has an enduring charm.

Among others, this teaching was attended by two young tulkus who became great Dharma masters – Zhechen Rinpoche and Dzongsar Khyentse Rinpoche. The first was Dilgo Khyentse Rinpoche's grandson; the second was none other than the internationally famous Khyentse. At that time they were mischievous youths. One evening when the telephone at Tibet House had been locked to prevent unauthorised use and the key taken away by the receptionist, Zhechen Rinpoche taught me how it could still be used by tapping the plunger–prongs in the cradle on which the receiver rested as many times as the number to be dialled.

Lama Kalu Rinpoche gave teachings at Tibet House in 1985 on 'Mental Peace and Enlightenment through Meditation'. He was originally from Tehor and his monastery was very near Dargye Monastery. He was among the first group of Tibetan lamas of the older generation who were exposed to the West. He had established centres at several places in the West during the years of the initial excitement and curiosity about Tibet and Tibetan Buddhism. At that time, there were very few interpreters, and people were, in any case, not expecting too many explanations; they were merely seeking initiations.

These four Dharma discourses, given during 1982–85, were later published by Tibet House as the book, *Essence of Buddhism*, which was later translated and published in Russian.

The fifth Dharma discourse in 1986 was by Drikung Kyabgon Chetsang Rinpoche, a high-ranking Kagyupa lama. The subject he dealt with was mahamudra of Lord Jigden Sumgon tradition and the text he used for reference was *Mahamudra* with five points. The discourse was held in a semi-retreat farm at Asoka Mission located on the outskirts of Delhi. During this discourse, we had specially invited an Indian yoga master from Wardha. In that way and because of the environment, it was a unique event.

Though they were not held every year, the series of Dharma discourses continued up to 2007. Among the twelve discourses held altogether, Namkhai Norbu Rinpoche's Yantra Yoga teaching in 1994 was unique. He spoke in a free-flowing style, without much structure. Recognised early as a tulku by the 16th Karmapa, he was very sharp in his studies and quickly attained the requisite knowledge of both spiritual and academic subjects. He was among the first few people to go to the West, soon after Tibetans started migrating as refugees. He settled in Rome to work with the famous Giuseppe Tucci on his Tibetan collection at the Institute of Middle and Far Eastern Studies.

After retirement he established his Dzogchen communities all over the world. He has a unique concept of Dharma and also of organisational structures. He works with the number nine, so three colours representing three areas – blue for cultural programmes and spiritual practice, red for maintenance and coordination and yellow for financial matters – are found in his logo. Each of the three is taken care of by three people. The yantra-yoga practice is his own invention and he says that the root of this yoga is even older than that of Patanjali's yoga sutras. Based on his vision, he also invented a vajra dance – a systematic and elaborate dance system related to Dzogchen practice. His line of thinking is that Dzogchen practice is independent of Buddhism, though he does not identify with Bon[1]. While acknowledging the greatness of the Buddhism that came from India, he says the root of Tibetan culture is to be found in the Bon tradition. Since people divide

Tibetan Buddhism into four traditions, we have to identify Namkhai Norbu Rinpoche as a Nyingmapa master. However, his line of teaching does not always conform to theirs. In 1997, we organised a Dzogchen Retreat conducted by Namkhai Norbu Rinpoche at Hamdard University, Delhi.

These discourses and teachings helped Tibet House to present not only a variety of traditions but also styles and ways of presenting Dharma-related subjects. They also helped me to appreciate methods of presentations of different traditions and gurus. I can claim with certainty that Tibet House must have been the first of the institutions of this kind to cover such a wide range of traditions and subjects of Tibetan Buddhism. We initiated and continued these kinds of programmes without any kind of bias and made sure they were 'ri-me' or non-sectarian.

I appreciated non-sectarianism within the Buddhist traditions but I did not take that as a banner or the slogan for my work. For me, ri-me does not mean that our approach, our practice and our study is equal to all traditions. The danger of making ri-me as a banner is that we may even make ri-me a separate sect by itself! For me, ri-me means that I don't judge an author by his or her name. If I see a text, I do not see who the author is and which tradition he belongs to. I study the contents first and evaluate whether they are suitable for me and whether the subject matter is relevant to me or to others in today's world. That is my way of looking at different traditions and teachers.

People sometimes asked me why I didn't give some teachings occasionally. As I mentioned earlier, I had no interest in projecting myself as a Dharma guru. My conscience did not allow me to do something that may have been seen as promoting myself in the institution I was heading. In fact, I tried as much as possible to avoid speaking at Tibet House events. At seminars and dialogues, I was compelled to say a few words of welcome and offer an introduction at the beginning. After my tenure at Tibet House, when I was asked to teach in India or abroad, I did more of sharing sessions on Dharma with small groups of people.

What was Tibet House? It never occurred to me to analyse this until several years later when I suddenly found people asking this question. Until then I had assumed it was very clear what Tibet House was. It seemed to me this question came up mainly because some people were trying to stir up some unwarranted controversies regarding what it should be and what it should not be, partly because so many 'Tibet Houses' had mushroomed all over the world. Some among them were playing significant roles; others had adopted the name just because it was catchy.

Indeed, I don't think anybody knew how many places that called themselves 'Tibet House' existed across the world. Some were just shops or restaurants, but they could be called 'Tibet House' because there were no controls about it. Nobody made any systematic attempt to regulate these places. And some clever people found ways of projecting themselves as having the blessings and patronage of His Holiness, without having anything to do with Tibet House in Delhi.

In 2001, the governing body of Tibet House adopted a criteria for recognising the associate status of Tibet Houses that existed anywhere in the world. The first place to be recognised was the Tibet House in New York. There were others who would have liked to get this status, but were rejected outright by the governing body of Tibet House since they had not fulfilled the criteria. The criterial laid down was:

- Similarity in Mission and Mandate with that of the Tibet House
- Proven track record of promoting the cause of Tibetan culture and religion
- Regular, relevant programmes and activities

- Demonstrated capacity (physical assets) and competence (professional skills) to achieve common goals and objectives
- Commitment and capacity (including facilities such as a museum, library, etc.) to provide a visible 'Tibetan image'
- Recognised as an institution of repute in the public domain (similar to Public Charitable Institutions)
- Non-political in the nature of its structure and functioning

---

As I look back now, I am more confused than ever about what Tibet House is. We may say it is a cultural centre, but that leads to the question of what culture is in the real sense. There are tangible and intangible cultures. In practical terms, where these answers lead to is not clear to me. Another popular phrase I find myself using frequently, which I also put on the title of *Tibet House Bulletin*, is 'Tibetan and Buddhist Studies and Culture' which was taken from the letter received from the Ministry of External Affairs. But if I think deeply about this, I wonder if I made any significant contribution towards the study of Tibetan and Buddhist culture. I say this because after all these years, we have not been able to emphasise, bring awareness of, or remind ourselves of the Tibetan value system. We seem to be lost in the preoccupation of how to deal with people who are smart and good at political manoeuvring.

The next chapter will show some initiatives we have taken and the kind of work Tibet House has taken up. But before that, let me give you some pointers to what Tibet House is *not*:

- Tibet House is not a political body, dealing with either international politics or Tibet-related politics.
- It is not an office for looking after the welfare of Tibetan people in Delhi or elsewhere in India.
- It is not the representative of His Holiness the Dalai Lama, because for that there is the Dalai Lama's bureau in Delhi.

- It is not a Dharma centre, similar to those mushrooming all over the world.
- It is not an information centre for those wishing to travel to Tibet.

This has been my understanding. What it should be, will be seen in the fullness of time.

In 2019, there was a Tenshug – long-life prayer ceremony – to be offered for His Holiness by the ex-service personnel of Central Tibetan Administration, Tibetan Government-in-Exile. I did not get a formal invitation but came to know about it through a friend who emailed and asked me to attend. I would have liked to take part in the event, but when I saw the official announcements of the programme, I had to pause and think. The announcement said that only those who were appointed by the particular department managing the service personnel were invited to attend this prayer ceremony. Well, I was directly appointed by His Holiness to serve in both the Kuyig and Tibet House and my appointment letters came from the Kashag. My relieving letter came from the Kuyig in a form of a thank-you letter with a handover order. There was no mention of ex-service personnel's grade or retirement benefits or anything of that sort. I did not bother to find out about them at that time or afterwards. So that was that.

36

Monastic Dialogue Seminars

The monastic dialogue seminars were a part of the new forum I created as a Tibet House programme. There were two objectives of this new forum – one, to acquaint traditional Tibetan scholars with the Indian academic system of studies and two, to acquaint Indian scholars with the Tibetan tradition of studies. Starting in 1986, there were eight such seminars organised until 2008. My idea behind holding these 'dialogue seminars' was also to create occasions for contact between traditional Tibetan monastic scholars and scholars from academic institutions like universities, whose studies dealt solely on the academic aspect of the subject.

As the larger monasteries in Tibet which were once seats of learning were no longer functional after 1959, Tibetans re-established them as monasteries-in-exile. The first seminar on Vijnanavada, or the 'mind-only school' of philosophy, was held at the Sera Monastery, one of the three largest monasteries around Lhasa, which had been re-established in Bylakuppe in Mysuru district. Tibetans started settling in the area in the early 1960s, but by the mid-1980s, they still had only the bare minimum of facilities, for example, electricity connections were just starting to reach the camps. I recall being present the day electricity came to Sera and everybody shouting with joy when it arrived.

The monastic dialogue was held in the main hall of the Sera Monastery. The hall was very simple and basic in its layout. We had academics from Varanasi, Pune, Delhi and many other places. Most of the major Tibetan monasteries were represented. We took special care to arrange the programme for each main speaker, choosing a main respondent who was asked to prepare his points in advance and make them available to other participants before they took part in the discussion. I felt that helped to avoid the irrelevant questions with which discussions sometimes start and which bring down the level of the entire session. It also reduced the chance of an extremely sophisticated question that would discourage other members of the audience to ask their simple but relevant questions. We also made arrangements for the gist of the papers to be translated into Hindi or English if they were in Tibetan, and into Tibetan if they were in Hindi or English, so that all the participants could follow the main points of all the presentations and discussion, at least to some extent. Participants such as Dr Thupten Chogdup and Dr Tsempa Dorje made especially interesting presentations. They were very well-versed not only in the subject, but also in Tibetan, Hindi and Sanskrit.

In the 1980s, we received one or two grants from the Indian Council of Philosophical Research. But our budget remained very tight and the monasteries were still poor, so I remember having detailed negotiations with the monastery authorities in Sera about expenditure. Finally, the arrangement was that Tibet House would pay for the travel of the participants and the monastery would arrange the venue and provide accommodation free of cost for the participants, and also take care of the preparations and the decoration of the hall. The cost of food would be divided equally between the monastery and Tibet House. This pattern of arrangements, especially the sharing of costs, was followed for the first three dialogue seminars in Sera, Gaden and Drepung. In 1996, a seminar on Abhidhamma was held at Sakya College, Dehradun, which offered to bear all local expenses, including the food and some hotel charges.

For the inauguration of the seminar at Sera, I made a special trip to Bengaluru to invite the chief minister, Ramakrishan Hegde. He agreed, in principle, to come, but at the last moment could not make it. However, he made it a point to send, in his place, his minister, R.L. Jalappa. Prof. R.S. Tripathi gave the keynote address and I felt that he may have been disoriented a little as he made a slip-of-the-tongue while addressing the minister, saying '*Is desh key mantri*' (the minister of this country), before correcting himself.

Since this seminar was the first of its kind, I felt it helped both sides tremendously. For the monastic community, it was amazing to see all the laypeople in kurtas and dhotis talking on subjects of high learning with an ease they could not have imagined. Among the academics, when they heard the word 'monastery' they formed a general idea of monks doing meditation and rituals quite well, but did not think they had engaged in such deeper subjects of philosophy as Vijnanavada. The generation of monks involved in this seminar has now mostly passed away or is not there in monasteries anymore. Among the pandits and scholars, some remember events like these with fondness.

The second dialogue seminar in 1988 and the third in 1989 were on Buddhist Logic at the Gaden Monastery and on Madhyamika at the Drepung Monastery, both in Mundgod, Karnataka. A very senior Indian leader, S. Nijalingappa, was invited to inaugurate the seminar at Drepung. This was especially significant because it was during his tenure as the chief minister of Karnataka that Tibetans had been given land for resettlement in large areas spread across the state. He was very pleased to see the fruition of the efforts started during his tenure and the various divisions in action besides the monastery, like the workshop, farming, handicrafts and school.

As at Sera, at both Gaden and Drepung, the monastery compound and halls were neither elaborately decorated nor enormously large at that time, but showed very good taste and represented the Buddhist principles of simplicity while meeting the basic requirements. The authorities and especially monk-volunteers were most cooperative. Their opinion of Indian pandits and professors were also very positive; they were impressed by the knowledge of Buddhist philosophy of the university people. Their only negative remark was about some of the elderly professors being a little particular about being served bed tea, something not known to Tibetans then.

In all the monasteries, we organised the traditional debate sessions (meaning 'tsod dra' in Tibetan, 'vada' in Sanskrit) so that the university delegates could observe them. The audience was particularly impressed by the physical gestures and heights of passion the debate generated, with pushing and pulling and raised voices.

The seminar on Abhidhamma at the Sakya College in 1996 was inaugurated by Sakya Trizin Rinpoche. This was very well organised under the leadership of a dynamic abbot, Migmar Tsering, who unfortunately passed away at a young age. Debate sessions were also demonstrated during the seminar. A few who were monk-students at that time have now become senior, responsible monks and they still appreciate my initiative in bringing traditional and modern institutes together. It was noteworthy that Sakya Rinpoche's two sons were studying in the college at the time. While according to tradition the elder son usually succeeds to the throne and the other becomes a monk, at that time they were intermingling with other students and not given any special treatment. The elder son has now succeeded to the throne.

His Holiness the Dalai Lama inaugurated the seminars on Buddhist Tantra at Gyudmed Tantric University (Hunsur, Karnataka) in 1998 and on Acharya Santarakshita at Namdroling Monastery (Bylakuppe) in 2001. The seminar on Acharya Santarakshita was unique as it was the only seminar on a historical person rather than philosophical theory. In the inaugural speech, His Holiness said that Acharya Santarakshita was much closer to Tibetan thought than the other great Indian Buddhist philosophers, because he was physically present in Tibet and spent a long time there and must have eaten Tibetan barley flour and had Tibetan butter tea. He played an important part in establishing Buddhism in Tibet, along with Guru Padmasambhava and King Songtsen Gampo.

His Holiness mentioned that according to legend, Acharya Santarakshita lived for hundreds of years. He said that it remains to be determined whether biologically a human's physical body can function for so many centuries. His Holiness also said that He was not averse to the idea of getting a DNA test done on some relics of the Acharya (if available). He said that even if he had not lived that many years, his importance in the history of Tibetan Buddhism would not diminish even the slightest bit. In one of the sessions, a participant observed that if Acharya Santarakshita had not lived as long as legend claimed, it would be difficult to piece together the full lineage of Vinaya, but no further discussion on the matter took place.

The seminar on Pramana in Indian philosophical thought was held in the Drepung Monastery in 2003. We repeated the venue for reasons of convenience. At both the seminars held in the Drepung Monastery, I must acknowledge that arrangements were made much easier with the support of my college, Loseling, and the Drete Dhargon monks, who provided numerous facilities and did all the legwork.

We mainly invited experts on non-Buddhist schools of Indian philosophy, like Nyaya-Vaisheshika, Mimamsa and Jaina, as well as the well-known scientist Raja Ramanna. I thought this was important because some of the earlier Indian non-Buddhist philosophical tenets were known to Tibetan scholars only as the *purvapaksha* or the opponent's side, as mentioned in Buddhist texts such as Bhavya's *Tarkajwala* and Santarakshita's *Pramanatattvasangraha*. And the natural tendency was not to do full justice to the strengths of the opponents. I hoped it was useful for at least some Tibetan scholars to learn something more about the tenets of other schools.

The inauguration of the seminar was performed by R.V. Deshpande, a member of the legislative assembly of Karnataka, who was also invited to the inauguration of a new hall at Loseling in 2008. The presentation by Raja Ramanna and the response by a very learned scholar from Drepung Monastery, Gen Namgyal Wangchen, was of special interest. Raja Ramanna's openness to Buddhist theories was well known and Gen Wangchen was basically a traditional scholar who never learned English formally and learned everything by himself. His interactions with Prof. Ramanna were par excellence. As the interaction went on, many of us were left without anything to say.

The last seminar in the series was on the 'real nature of phenomena and its relation with life' at Tashi Lhunpo, Bylakuppe, in 2008. The monastery authorities showed great enthusiasm and went out of their way to support the seminar. The venue had special significance as the original monastery in Tibet had been the seat of successive Panchen Lamas. Although re-established in the 1970s, it did not go into overdrive competing with other monasteries in terms of the external appearance of its buildings and so on. Compared to other monasteries re-established at that time, it is still small, but I must say it conveys a certain dignity of age.

Although there had been only one lama who made a presentation in English at the first seminar in 1986, by 2008 many more were able to follow the language. Apart from a young monk who read his paper in English, there were several other able interpreters. The inauguration was by His Eminence Rizong Rinpoche from Ladakh, who spoke in Tibetan which was translated into Hindi by a scholar from Ladakh, Tsultrim Gyatso. The participation by monks from this monastery was low because this seminar coincided with an annual debate session at another monastery.

This was the first dialogue seminar where we made it a point of addressing modern perspectives in the main theme. Prof. Sundar Sarukkai, a young scientist and philosopher of science, gave an engaging presentation comparing notions of the 'real' in philosophy and science in the context of the development of concepts of matter and space, drawing parallels between, among others, Nagarjuna and Newton. Interesting parallels and divergences emerged, for example, mathematical concepts can be seen as giving access to the truth, whereas the Buddhists regard the ultimate as ineffable. The monks were interested in the scientific evidence for part-less particles and the substance of time, and in the cause of space and whether it had its own nature.[2]

Prof. R.S. Tripathi participated in almost all the conferences and gave the keynote address most of the times. Geshe Yeshe Thabke was also a great supporter of this venture. We received suggestions for many other topics and offers of venues, but we simply could not take all these up. Tibet House came to be recognised as an expert in organising these kinds of dialogue seminars, and there was a good feedback from various people. Since it is not my nature to glorify myself and nor did I think Tibet House had a monopoly over such seminars, we were only happy that it had been an initiative worth taking.

Often, whenever there is a good initiative, there is a tendency to hijack it. In this case also, I noticed similar attempts. During a teaching session, His Holiness emphasised the importance of having dialogues between Tibetan and Theravada sanghas on Vinaya (monastic rules). I came to know that there was some discussion about the holding this seminar on Vinaya and there was a mention that Tibet House had been organising a series of dialogue seminars since many years. The abbot of Tashi Lhunpo Monastery, where we had held the last seminar of the series, approached me and offered to host the seminar in collaboration with Tibet House. In spite of that, I came to know later that CHITS had taken charge of the task and made it appear that His Holiness has personally asked them to carry it out.

I felt that there was need for regular activities on art and culture at Tibet House because the focus of Tibet House at that time was on culture, heritage and arts. To talk about Tibetan arts and culture independent of historical links with Indian art would have been a rather simplistic way of handling these activities that was meant for academic people. Therefore, in 1985, I initiated the Indo Tibetan Art and Culture Study Group lecture series in Tibet House with Prof. Deshpande as its first chairman. The first lecture in this series was delivered by Dr Lokesh Chandra, another well-known scholar of Buddhist history, art and culture. Students of Buddhist art and history in the capital looked forward to this monthly lecture series.

Prof. Deshpande was a doyen of Indian archaeology with deep knowledge of the subject, but more than that, he was an example of a good human being. His humility in learning from various sources was so inspiring that anyone coming in touch with him would quickly rid themselves of any pretensions. His knowledge went much beyond the mere recounting of past facts and took lessons from visible and tangible images, something which is relevant in today's world. I remember he delivered a lecture illustrated with photos of rock carvings. Showing a motif of a flower with a bee on it, he said that from this we should learn that if we have to take something from nature, we must give something back. His knowledge was not a bookish one and he lived with his subject. Once I was with him in Mysuru to attend a meeting on epigraphy where we were put up in a simple hotel. At some point he spontaneously said, 'I am in cave number such and such.' I immediately knew he was referring to his room and remembered that his specialisation was Ajanta cave paintings. I exclaimed, 'Oh yes, you are a cave man,' and we all had a hearty laugh.

Tibet House also held seminars, lectures and conferences on academic subjects. My first experience of organising an academic seminar was in 1984. We held an international seminar on Buddhist Iconography at the India International Centre (IIC),

Delhi. This was organised with the help of the Department of Culture, Government of India, and the Indian Council for Cultural Relations (ICCR). The Department of Culture gave a grant of ₹30,000 while ICCR paid for the travel and lodging of the few international participants. They even sent a car to the airport to pick up the delegates.

I have a small, interesting story to tell here. Dr Kapil Singh, a very learned Buddhist scholar who later became a renunciate and was active in the movement for Buddhist women's rights in sangha affairs, was coming from Bangkok. The person who went to receive her was waiting at the arrival gate with a name board, but somehow they missed each other. After some time, the ICCR office called to report that our guest had not arrived, because the man who went to the airport informed us that there was no sardarji on the flight. He did not know Dr Kapil Singh was a lady.

The idea of the subject of the seminar had just occurred to me instinctively. Later, I felt satisfied with the choice, as I learned that this theme was an important subject in art history and there were several books on the subject, though I had not heard of any other international seminar held exclusively on this subject. I requested D.C. Bhattacharjee, professor at Punjab University, Chandigarh, to be the convener and to edit the papers.

Soon I realised that it was a lot of work to organise a seminar on an academic subject – finding the right kind of participants, organising the programme properly and, finally, getting the papers edited and published to the satisfaction of everyone concerned, especially the participants. It was not simply a matter of arranging the money and then just booking a venue and sending out invitations. I had to struggle a lot in all the aspects, especially with the programme and editing because with collaboration and help, there was also great pressure. And too many cooks can spoil the broth! Dealing with ego was the major problem in organising programmes of this nature. Despite our limited resources and zero experience, the conference attracted good participants and met international standards. The proceedings of the seminar were published as a book titled *Buddhist Iconography* with an introduction by Dr Kapila Vatsyayan.

For someone like me who was brought up in the traditional way, organising this seminar was of special interest because numerous aspects of iconography naturally form part of the subjects of traditional learning, especially in tantric studies. Yet iconography was not treated as a separate branch of study, so to study the subject with a historical perspective was an eye-opener for me. At the same time, I could see the danger of interpreting the art forms and taking the ideas too far. I remember one scholar showing a slide of a Tibetan thangka. At its periphery were the standard depictions of a landscape with mountains, cloud formations, trees, streams and so on. Pointing to one of the mountain shapes he claimed that it was a map of Jambudvipa. Those of us who were familiar with thangkas just smiled.

I became seriously interested in setting up an annual lecture which would be delivered by renowned experts on subjects related to Tibetan and Buddhist studies and culture. I also thought it would be more suitable to have the lecture series titled as a concept rather than making it a memorial lecture in the name of a famous person. In 1989, we instituted the annual Padmapani Lectures series. Padmapani represents the Buddhist principle of universal compassion. The Padmapani figure in the Ajanta caves is the pre-eminent symbol of beauty and serenity in Indian art. Tibetans recognise the Compassionate Padmapani as their patron deity and Dalai Lamas are regarded as the human form of Padmapani. Thus, this series of lectures is a tribute to the institution of the Dalai Lama.

37

Buddha Jayanti Park

A major and a historic event that I saw through to the end was the installation of a Buddha statue at the Buddha Jayanti Park in Delhi. In 1983, His Holiness expressed His wish that a statue of the Buddha should be installed in the Buddha Jayanti Park, the public park in Delhi named after the Buddha in 1956. That was the year when both His Holiness and Panchen Lama visited India on the occasion of Buddha Jayanti to mark 2,500 years of the Buddha's nirvana. His Holiness's idea was to present a statue of the Buddha to India as a token of His and the Tibetan people's appreciation for both the gift of Buddhism as well as for accepting Tibetans in India at a crucial moment in their history.

I was clearly instructed about the project and given the responsibility of managing it. The first two basic decisions were – first, which precise part of the park should be the preferred spot for the statue, and second, the details of material, size, style and whether to install in an open area or in a closed temple-type structure. I did some research and contacted several knowledgeable people and the concerned authorities. Of the three possible spots shown by the authorities, I chose the present site because of the provision of a water body, although there was no water in it at that time. More than that, this spot was in direct alignment with the Rashtrapati Bhawan and India Gate.

For the style of the statue, there were many consultations and different possibilities were explored. Finally, according to the wish of His Holiness the Dalai Lama, it was decided that the statue should be in the Tibetan style of copper gilded with gold. It would be made by a Tibetan master craftsman of Dharamsala. It was also decided that the size would be the same as the statue in the main temple in Dharamsala.

We can see statues installed in temples at many places; but we thought that the Buddha in an open area would have a wider impact on the people and the environment. The idea was to reach out to a vast audience from all walks of life with a message of peace and harmony. His Holiness was very happy with all these ideas. He was particular that the facial expression of the statue should be as close to the one in the Mahabodhi temple at Bodh Gaya.

Discussions with many architects, contacting different government offices followed by letters after letters, meeting people collectively and individually and making countless phone calls were a big drain of energy for me. But it was all for an undoubtedly a good cause.

I received sympathetic consideration from the government authorities and the support from relevant ministries, especially the Department of Urban Development. The site at Buddha Jayanti Park was confirmed and all the procedural formalities were completed. A bhumi puja was performed at the site in May 1990. While these necessary activities were being carried out, the actual work of making the statue had started in Dharamsala by a team of Tibetan craft persons led by the renowned master craftsman, the late Tsedong Uchen Penpa Dorje.

Four different drawings of the Buddha canopy along with their models were prepared by the architects. These models and drawings were presented to Prime Minister Rajiv Gandhi for his selection at a meeting arranged in the PM's office in Parliament House. I was impressed by his gentle manners, soft speech and his respectful bearing towards others.[3] The prime minister went through the models and drawings very carefully and he chose the one designed by a Japanese architect, Nakahara. It had the provision of sixteen columns and the five concentric rings were to spread over flat land rather than on an embankment. Later, the Delhi Urban Arts Commission put certain conditions regarding the scale of the project. Considering the ideal available site, the size of the project had to be curtailed. A Delhi-based architect, Ashish Ganju, worked on the original design of Nakahara to make necessary structural changes by reducing the columns from 16 to 4 and the alignment of the embankments, keeping the basic design plan by Nakahara in place.

The philosophy of the layout was given by His Holiness. He instructed me that the rings must be in the five colours of the Kalachakra Mandala. In this system, His Holiness explained, of the two stages of meditation practice, in the generation stage a person generates or creates. So the order of colours should be from the subtle to the gross, from inside to outside. And in the completion stage, it is the dissolution from gross to the subtle, from outside to inwards. Thus, the colours from the outside should be in the order of the most gross – earth in yellow, water in white, fire in red, wind in black and space in blue.

In the same manner, I used the four colours for the cardinal directions as well. That was unlike the other mandalas – here east was white, south was black (instead of yellow), west was red and north was yellow (instead of green). These colours were represented in the banners carried by the monks in the 'human curtain' during the presentation ceremony and were also the colours of the plants on the four sides of the canopy. The design of the upper reaches of the canopy followed the Gyantse Stupa in the Tsang region of Tibet.

His Holiness continued to take a personal interest in the project and paid visits at the construction site a couple of times when the work was going on. Once He tried His hands on the stone carving instrument used to chisel a beam. At another time His Holiness visited the site and, sitting in front of the upcoming canopy, He opined that there should be a symbol of harmonious existence there. A few ideas were offered, including a swan in a lotus pond (already a symbol of Ramakrishna Mission), by the intellectuals gathered there but nothing was decided on the spot, which was easily understandable. Later, I worked on developing a symbol. We used concept based on a passage from a Buddhist sutra:

> Sequential dependence – of air on space, of water on air, of earth on water, of life on earth, a message of harmonious interdependence.

My late rakhi sister Ashma Singh prepared a design which was approved. His Holiness was very particular about having stone carving with selected verses from Buddhist sutras installed around the Buddha canopy. This, He said, will generate a seed of wisdom in the minds of the visitors, along with the seed of merit planted by seeing the Buddha statue.

There were a lot of discussions whether the Government of India would be willing to openly and officially accept this gift from the Dalai Lama and the Tibetan community in exile. After the completion of physical installation of the Buddha statue with a sandstone canopy, we were looking for a 'representative' from the Indian side to whom His Holiness would symbolically present the statue. A few names were mentioned and it became clear that the Government of India did not want to make it appear as a State function.

At one point I went to the extent of saying that if no official representative was going to be there, I wouldn't mind doing the function with a celebrated artist or a representative of the people. I had in mind the artist B.C. Sanyal or else someone regarded as a really common person, for example, just pick up an auto-rikshaw driver from outside the park. Some people attempted to hijack the show by offering to bring their preferred VIP. Finally, a kind of compromise and good understanding was reached at with the help of M.K. Rasgotra. It was decided that the former president of India, R. Venkataraman, would come and His Holiness would make a symbolic and ritual handing over to him.

The presentation ceremony was very impressive. The ceremony was basically conceived and choreographed by me – the rituals, the processions, opening the 'human walls', the gathering of representatives of all the religions and the gathering of the heads of Tibetan Buddhist traditions. Everything went off perfectly.

Rev. Tara, then principal secretary to His Holiness the Dalai Lama, spent several days helping me visualise the ceremony. Bansi Kaul, a well-known stage manager, helped in the physical choreography of the event. The 'human wall' was formed by seven monks on each of the four sides, carrying banners of different colours (white for the east, black for the south, yellow for the north, red for the west). R. Venkataraman made a very touching speech. He often departed from his prepared text and said that he had never seen such an impressive ceremony in his life. Sonal Mansingh, a renowned classical dance maestro, presented a choreographed dance piece. The whole exercise from discussions with people to the actual presentation ceremony took a decade, from 1983 to 1993. The majestic statue is now a constant reminder of the Buddha's message of harmony and interdependence.

In conjunction with the installation of the Buddha statue, a conference titled 'Ecological Responsibility: A Dialogue with Buddhism' was organised as His Holiness the Dalai Lama had suggested that gathering people for this occasion should not be just for the sake of celebration but ought to address the pressing problems facing the world. The ecological problem was identified by His Holiness as a major problem. The conference was organised on a large scale. At the inaugural session held at Delhi's prestigious Siri Fort Auditorium, Radha Burnier, international president of the Theosophical Society, gave the keynote address. Other speakers were Jose A. Lutzenberger from Brazil and the late Ramachandra Gandhi. The point of emphasis was that everyone should respect nature's rules and not allow humans' aggressive and limitless desires to take over the earth.

I invited monks from Tashi Jong in Himachal to chant and play monastic music at this session and His Holiness took special note when they played a rare musical instrument, the Tibetan long horn which was called 'buhag'. In the buhag, the horn was compressed to form a kind of a flat ring. The academic sessions were held at IIC. We had speakers like Ramachandra Guha address the audience. The consecration and presentation ceremony of the statue as well as the conference were preserved for posterity in a film directed by Amar Kanwar, *Earth as Witness*.

This project inspired me to install similar statues of the Buddha in other continents. I started exploring and soon my contact in Germany identified Bremen as a possible site for a statue. I went there specially to see the suitability before discussing the project. The city authorities were very eager to have the statue installed in a public park, where there were already some statues installed of the Buddha in the reclining pose and of mani stones (carved with 'Om Mani Padme Hum'), prayer flags and so on, representing Himalayan religious culture. There was a Japanese style of canopy, with a Japanese Zen Garden nearby. I found this site suitable for the installation of a Buddha statue and confirmed the site.

We raised funds and an eight-foot Buddha statue was commissioned, to be made by a Nepali craftsperson stationed in Bylakuppe. In consultation with the Kuyig, it was decided to use the phrase, 'Inspired by the installation of the Buddha statue in the Buddha Jayanti Park, New Delhi, by His Holiness' as inscription and this was communicated to the Bremen authorities. The statue's canopy was the responsibility of Bremen city authority and they sent the architectural drawings and design plan of the canopy which was both artistic and had relevant symbolism of simplicity. At the time of my exit from Tibet House, the statue was waiting in Bylakuppe for shipment to Bremen. I heard later that the statue did reach Bremen safely.

I also tried to find a possible site in Canada through a Tibetan contact, T.C. Tethong (TC-la). Correspondence went on for a while with University of British Colombia, Canada, through him. I visited the university campus and a spot was identified but then there was a change of person in the university who was dealing with the project. The communications started sounding unworkable because they said that the statue could be installed but the responsibility for maintenance would have to be ours. TC-la suggested that the Tibetan community in Canada could be involved for funding and maintenance. He also said that the place of the installation of the statue could become a place of gathering for the Tibetan community. I felt that would defeat the whole purpose as I was against making these sites places of worship or sites of gathering for a particular community. Finally, it did not work out as I had anticipated.

I tried to find a suitable site in South Africa through a contact but it did not go any further than mere correspondence.

Speaking of the installation of Buddha statues and their maintenance, it may not be out of place to point out certain things with regard to the statue in the Buddha Jayanti Park in Delhi. It was meant to be a gift to India, the birthplace of the Buddha. It was assumed that the concerned departments would take care of the gift. It is true that there was hesitancy in accepting it officially and the same attitude led to its poor maintenance. Tibet House's responsibility should have ended with the installation ceremony. However, I felt it was important to make sure that there was no vandalism or deterioration of the statue by weathering or by birds. Hence, in consultation with and encouragement by CPWD, we appointed a Tibetan person to maintain cleanliness and make the daily offering of water bowl in front of the statue. This went on quite well for many years and we changed several persons during this period. In fact, the first two people served there many years before their deaths (indeed, the second died in front of the statue, from heat stroke). Both these men were Tibetans who had retired from the security forces in India and their sense of duty and dedication should be remembered. After this it became extremely difficult to find a dedicated person, because the generation which values dedicated service is almost extinct. In the gaps between caretakers appointed by us, there was a watchman appointed by the park authorities.

At some point this watchman, with a view of collecting money from visitors, started putting sindoor on visitor's foreheads as was done in Hindu temples in India. I immediately sensed the danger of the place being misused for self-gain with the watchman setting himself up as the pujari or priest. I put an end to it. During one of the gaps between caretakers, pigeons started sitting on the Buddha's head, there was dust around and the gold gilded metallic petals of the statue base began to disappear one by one. We tried our best to prevent such things from happening. Later, we replaced the missing petals.

During this time, a 'dignitary' from Dharamsala visited me and exclaimed that somebody had seen how dirty the place was and they had taken a bucket of water to clean it, as if we had been failing in our duty. But what people forget is that washing the area once is one thing, keeping it clean all through the years is quite another.

Rev. Tara had received some suggestions about a mechanism for protecting the statue from dust and vandalism. I was not in favour of putting the statue in any kind of an enclosure. However, considering the dust, pollution and vandalism, it became necessary to install some kind of protection. The idea of mounting a protective shield of thickened glass around the statue was proposed to the concerned authority in the Indian government and after many visits and exchange of letters with concerned officials, politicians and those whose words count, we received the approval from the CPWD. A detailed architectural drawing and proposed plan was submitted to them some months before I left Tibet House. The execution of the work by CPWD had not been done by the time I left.

Years later, I paid a visit to the park and was greatly saddened to see the area around the statue in a pathetic state. There seemed to have been a lapse in the upkeep and maintenance. The execution of the thickened glass protective shield around the statue was different from the plan I had submitted. The breathing space and provision of air passage was not sufficient. The glass shield was covered with dirt and grease and so the visibility of the statue was reduced. The initial idea of openness and harmony was gone.

A series of events called 'Ceremony of Remembrance' were organised at Buddha Jayanti Park yearly since the installation of the Buddha statue in 1983. We conceived this series as a regular programme with His Holiness's presence and teaching on alternate years. This has become an event which is much looked forward by the people of Delhi, both Tibetan and Indian.

In 2005, we held a conference on Mahayana Buddhism. We considered this important because an average person only knows of Mahayana and Hinayana as two sects of Buddhism, like the Shias and Sunnis or Shaivites and Vaishnavites or Catholics and Protestants. The fact is, however, that with both Mahayana and what is sometimes termed 'Hinayana', there is a history of the development of their philosophies, art and culture. Both speak of 'sila' as the basis, 'samadhi' as meditation and 'prajna' as the real path to salvation. The issue of whether Mahayana is the Buddha's original teachings or not had been brought up as early as Nagarjuna's time, but the subject of the commonality between both traditions as well as their distinctive aspects are not talked about much. The idea underlying the conference was to raise such questions to increase the understanding about the philosophies of the two sects.

The conference was inaugurated by His Holiness the Dalai Lama and the keynote address was given by Bhikku Pasadika, an eminent scholar and Buddhist practitioner I had known since my days at Sarnath, who had been working in Buddhist studies for over five decades. José Cabezón discussed the primacy of showing what an entity was *not* when conceiving of philosophical truths in Buddhist logic, Linnart Mäll's presentation was on the *Astasahasrika Prajnaparamita*, Shunzo Onoda spoke about Mongolian edition of Kangyur, Michelle Sorensen highlighted Chod. There were other speakers including Jampa Samten who presented an interesting paper on the study of Pali and Tibetan versions of the *Mahaparinirvana Sutra*. Papers from the conference were edited by Darrol and Susan Bryant and Tibet House brought out a publication under the title *Mahayana Buddhism: History and Culture* (Sambhota Series XV).

38

Larger Concerns of Tibet House

We held several workshops among the Tibetan community on ecology. The first was in June 1995 and was held at the Youth Hostel of the Tibetan Children's Village in Rohini, Delhi. The late Ravindra Varma was the guiding light in this whole exercise. The workshop was aimed at generating awareness on the issues of ecology, especially among the Tibetan community. The participants were teachers drawn from Tibetan schools in India. There were over forty participants and the workshop lasted for a week. There were talks by experts, discussion sessions and performances by artists. After the workshop, the participants were given the task of organising a painting competition in their respective schools on the same theme. We received many creative works by children who participated in these competitions. These paintings underwent a selection process and the best ones formed a mobile exhibition that went to different schools in turn.

In 2004, again under Ravindra Varma's guidance, we collaborated with the NGO Inner Challenges and invited Tibetan school teachers and members of the Tibetan Women's Association from the Tibetan settlements in Mundgod, Karnataka, to participate in a workshop on ecology at Shreyas, Bengaluru. The group analysed the causes responsible for the present state of the environment, like the influence of modernisation and changes in attitudes and value systems due to a materialistic lifestyle. They pointed at the lack of awareness of the effects of such a lifestyle as the main cause of environmental degradation. The participants called for collective responsibility, need-based consumption, water harvesting, use of solar energy and a simpler lifestyle. Among the resource persons were L.C. Jain, Ramachandra Guha, R.V.G. Menon and other well-known specialists in this field.

In 2007, with the help from the Ministry of Environment and Forests, Government of India, we organised a week-long workshop on 'Community and Environment Issues' at Rewalsar, Himachal Pradesh. In this camp we had participants from Tibetan schools and monasteries in northern India.

A group of twenty participants from Mundgod Tibetan Settlement was taken to Tarun Bharat Sangh Ashram, Rajasthan, to engage in a week-long training workshop towards a sustainable world in February 2010. The entire training programme was guided by Dr Rajendra Singh Sisodia, the 2001 Ramon Magsaysay awardee for community leadership, who was popularly known as 'Water Gandhi'. The training proceeded through planned steps of practical ecological programmes for water conservation and waste management through a judicious mix of lectures, discussions, interactive games and field visits. As a result of this workshop, the enthusiastic trainees pledged to work for the cause of ecological harmony under the banner of Green Volunteers. A follow-up workshop of one day was also organised in February 2011 in Mundgod Tibetan Settlement where specially designed Green Volunteers jackets were distributed to the participants, with funding from Joshua and Diana Cutler from the Tibetan Buddhist Learning Center in New Jersey.

Another pioneering initiative of Tibet House was the seminar on 'Compassionate Economy' in September 2002. This came up after discussion with some intellectuals, primarily the well-known Russian economist now settled in Amsterdam, Prof. Stanislav Menshikov. Prof. Menshikov had been close to Gorbachev in his final years as the general secretary of the Communist Party of the Soviet Union and was said to have helped to frame the policies of glasnost and perestroika. At His Holiness's request, in 1992 Prof. Menshikov compiled a book on compassionate economy in Russian.

I first met Prof. Menshikov in 1990 when he presented his ideas at a conference on 'Art Meets Science and Spirituality in a Changing Economy' in Amsterdam, wonderfully organised by Louwrien Wijers. I liked the professor's frank and straightforward style of presentation and sense of humour. He had left the country before the dissolution of the Soviet Union and was already making fun of the Soviet system. He told a story about an American dog asking a Soviet dog how the situation was back home. The Soviet dog replied, 'I am tied on a tight leash and the plate of food is only half-full.' The next time the two dogs met, the Soviet's answer was, 'Okay, now the leash is much longer, and the plate is full, but the plate is placed far away and I cannot reach it. The only consolation is that I can bark as much as I want!'

I saw the seminar on compassionate economy as a part of the frank and meaningful dialogue between disciplines, emphasised by His Holiness. This led Tibet House to go beyond the preservation of Tibetan culture and Buddhist studies and attempt intercultural and interdisciplinary activities, carrying messages for the betterment of all human beings. Graciously accepting our invitation, Prof. Menshikov came with his wife, also an economist, and delivered the 14th Padmapani Lecture on the topic 'Compassionate Economy Has a Future'. This was followed by a day-long seminar, with presentations by economists, politicians and Gandhians.

Giving priority to strengthening welfare systems by decreasing consumption and increasing taxes, Prof. Menshikov said it was important to study how compassion and market motivations combine in individual economic behaviour. Religious and educational institutions should work towards making guidelines of conduct foreveryone, whatever their position in the economy or the political system. This would be a step towards providing all humans a decent existence and also move towards the best use of resources. In all these systems, a compassionate economy would actually be the most efficient. The seminar developed some of these ideas further.

In 2010, we thought of having a second conference on the subject the following year and some steps were taken and contacts made. There was some response, but we could not take the idea further and I left it there.

Several exhibitions were organised by Tibet House, mostly of thangkas. One worth mentioning was on 'Compassion and Reincarnation in Tibetan Buddhist Art'. Conceived in 1995 after a lot of thought, it was an endeavour to show how Avalokiteswara was conceived and represented in the Tibetan tradition. It included images of divinities such as Amitabha (Avalokiteswara's spiritual patron), deities regarded as emanations of Avalokiteswara, King Songtsen Gampo of Tibet, lineage gurus starting with Guru

Padmasambhava, Dromtonpa (Atisha's chief disciple), the Grand Lama of Sakyapa, the Karmapa and, of course, the Dalai Lama series. The Bon tradition was also represented through images of the deity called Chamma which was regarded as the emanation of love and compassion.

What took time was the obtaining of permission to borrow thangkas from various institutions – Dharamsala, a Bonpo monastery in Solan and Rumtek Monastery in Gangtok. The exhibition travelled to three German-speaking countries – Germany, Austria and Switzerland – and a publication of a very high quality, both in terms of content and printing, was produced by Roland Steffan of the Historical and Ethnographical Museum in St. Gallen, Switzerland. Roland was a very accomplished scholar of Sanskrit and Tibetan. I knew him from my Varanasi days as a virtuous Buddhist monk. He has a good sense of history, especially of Buddhism in India, Tibet and China. I believe he became a Buddhist in Germany after taking refuge with a master from the Mongol region, who had fled from the Soviet Union.

Between 1997 and 2007, we organised about a dozen exhibitions, some small, some on a larger scale. One of the exhibitions, 'Buddhist Tales of Kashmir in Tibetan Woodcuts', was inaugurated by Narasimha Rao when he was the minister of Human Resource Development. Later, he became the prime minister of India. Every utterance of his showed a deep knowledge of Indian culture and also Buddhist literature, especially when we discussed the *Avadhanakalpalata* thangkas based on a work by the Kashmiri poet, Ksemendra.

For another thangka exhibition, I sought the help of Ranesh Roy, who can conceive the whole design of a space and the material at the first sight itself. I knew him earlier, from his exhibition on Rajiv Gandhi at 1, Safdarjung Road, the late Indira Gandhi's residence. The whole exhibition was designed using newspaper clippings on Rajiv Gandhi, around which photographs were interlinked. I remember he had mentioned that he had told

Sonia Gandhi, 'If you want a full exhibition on Rajiv Gandhi, you cannot ignore Sanjay Gandhi.' So Sanjay Gandhi was also shown on the side. Ranesh gets things done on time, not a minute before, not a minute later – he is right on the dot.

The exhibition that he helped me organise was to be inaugurated at Tibet House Museum by Arjun Singh, the minister of Human Resources Development. On the appointed day, I went to check the arrangements 15 minutes before the arrival of the chief guest. I saw wrapping papers and other material all strewn on the floor and it did not look as though the exhibition was going to be ready on time. I was a bit worried and to add to the worry, the minister arrived 10 minutes early. That was a great surprise, because in India VIPs always arrive late and keep the organisers waiting and troubled. But Arjun Singh had arrived early and I could not take him to the venue. The only place to sit was my office, so he sat in front of my desk. That was quite an experience for me, because we need to make a lot of effort just to be able to sit in front of a cabinet minister in his office, but at that time, a senior cabinet minister was sitting across my desk!

One exhibition that was conceived by His Holiness was, 'Living Tibetan Buddhism: A Photographic Journey'. Once when I was consulting Him about having a large exhibition of thangkas, His immediate reaction was that these ideas of thangka exhibitions were all fine, but it would be really good if we could get a professional photographer of real talent and organise a thematic exhibition. He went into great details, as I noted down what he said, outlining sub-themes, such as monastic traditions, the religious life of laypersons, the relationship between monks and laypeople, pilgrimages, and Tibetan medicine, astrology and sacred art.

I made great efforts to implement that idea, formulating a good concept, selecting a photographer and even travelling to places in India to conduct research on the material we needed to put together to depict each of the aspects suggested by His

Holiness. Finally, we chose Bruno Baumann, the well-known German photographer who had visited Tibet many times. We arranged for him to visit several Tibetan places in India to shoot especially for the exhibition. We also used some of his earlier works. The exhibition was inaugurated by His Holiness the Dalai Lama in Graz, Austria, during the Kalachakra initiation in 2002.

As always at Kalachakra events, it was a big crowd. On the day of the opening of the exhibition, many other things were happening at the venue and some local dignitaries had also arrived. There was far too much pulling and pushing, and I felt it was a bit of a pity that His Holiness was not given enough time by people around him to appreciate the exhibition. The following year, we took the same exhibition to Bengaluru and in 2005 showcased it at Tibet House.

39

Interfaith Activities

That morning when I left Tibet House to meet P.P. Srivastav, the municipal commissioner, to discuss some matter regarding property tax of Tibet House, I did not know that the day would go down in Indian history as a memorable day for many reasons. I also did not know that the same day would give the impetus to Tibet House to start involving itself in inter-religious seminars, prayers and dialogues.

When I met P.P. Srivastav, he gave me news that made me forget why I had gone to see him. It was the morning of 31 October 1984. He said that the prime minister of India, Indira Gandhi, had been assassinated. The news was still not out in the public domain. What gave the news a disturbing edge was that the killing had been done by her security personnel, against a backdrop of hatred with a religious dimension.

By noon the news had spread everywhere. His Holiness was returning from a visit abroad that evening. In those days, it was something of a tradition to inform me of His arrivals and departures and I would go to receive him. On the way to the airport, I saw a long line of white ambassador cars on Aurobindo Marg, near 1, Safdarjung Road, and realised her body was being brought back from AIIMS to her residence.

I had first heard of Indira Gandhi in my teens in Tibet. In 1957, the book *Letters from a Father to His Daughter* was translated into Tibetan and was available in Lhasa. Out of pure interest and curiosity, I also read some biographical accounts of Indira Gandhi later. I was in Buxa when she became the prime minister, and the monks were very happy because they knew Nehru as the man who respected His Holiness. Nehru had received Him during the Buddha Jayanti celebrations and later offered shelter to Him and to Tibetan refugees. I was told Indira Gandhi also was very respectful and courteous when His Holiness visited her. She would greet Him at the car and personally see Him off as He took leave. I had felt sorry when I heard of the Congress splitting into two groups headed by Morarji Desai and her.

The aftermath of the assassination created very depressing scenes on the streets of Delhi. I did not actually see people being killed, but I heard of mass killings, looting and burning, that continued for many days. When people started wondering what might be done to contain the problem, some of us felt that though it might not pacify the situation, it was nonetheless important to have people of religion express concern. Generally, from the 1990s onwards, people increasingly felt the need to organise interfaith gatherings at various levels, but in our case, it started in 1984, when the Sikh community became the target of attacks in Delhi after the tragic assassination of Indira Gandhi.

I hurriedly arranged a gathering of religious representatives, including my friend Gyalsey Rinpoche, the abbot of Tawang Monastery, as well as those like Prof. Sondhi, who were very concerned about the situation. We did not have even a small hall in Tibet House and there was no time to book a venue in nearby places like the IIC, but we managed to get a hall in the building of our immediate neighbour, the Institution of Electronic and Telecommunication Engineers (IETE). Invitees were requested to talk of the importance of understanding and not allowing the situation to worsen.

I cannot claim this gathering helped to calm the situation but those who were present at the event and those who were informed through them appreciated our initiative and felt that this was just what needed to be done. It was a response from our side to what the situation called for. This was my first experience of organising an inter-religious gathering and from then on, I was drawn into the flow of inter-religious activities on different scales and of different kinds, sometimes as an initiator, sometimes as a participant, both in India and abroad.

In one such inter-faith meeting in Delhi, organised by TOUCH (The Organisation for Communal Harmony) in the 1990s at IIC, I met Nazar Tiwana who had founded this organisation in 1993. Nazar was the son of the premier of undivided Punjab under British rule. He was a pious and soft-spoken person. I got to know him better and one day he requested to be initiated into the Triple Jewels. I took him to the Buddha statue in Buddha Jayanti Park and gave him the vow to take refuge into the Triple Jewels. I even added 'Palden' to his name. From then on, he started signing his name as Nazar Palden. Palden is the Tibetan equivalent of 'Shri'.

Nazar and his wife Sita, daughter Yasmin and son Omar, were settled in Chicago. I went to Chicago several times and stayed with them twice. Some people said I must have had some karmic relationship with him. In 2015, when I was touring in the USA, I heard Nazar was critically ill and admitted in a nursing home. From the airport, I went straight to see him. He did not even open his eyes and I was told that he was not able to eat or drink anything for quite some time. I sat at his bedside for a while. He looked lifeless. I gave him a sip of water and did some prayers. Then I returned to my place of stay.

The next day morning I heard he was gone. His wife requested that I go with them to the funeral. I did and as a special gesture the crematorium staff opened the coffin so I could say a few prayers. In fact, he was my travel companion for the rest of my USA visit as his family asked me to carry his ashes back to India to immerse in the Ganga. On my return to India, I went to Varanasi to immerse his ashes. His family continues to stay in touch with me.

Inter-religious meetings became a regular activity at Tibet House. Every year we organised two functions in front of the Buddha statue at Buddha Jayanti Park. One was held on Buddha Purnima and the other on 2 October, as a 'Ceremony of Remembrance' of the statue's installation. I thought it was appropriate to make the first an occasion for prayers and sutra reading, representing different Buddhist traditions, and the second an occasion for inter-religious prayers and cultural performances involving well-known musicians.

On 6 July, the birthday of His Holiness, we would have a gathering of representatives of different religions and have a programme of tree planting at different venues. This was my own small way of addressing the two issues dear to His Holiness – inter-religious contact and ecology. In 1987, I organised a seminar, 'Inter-religious Forum for Communal Harmony' at

Teen Murti Bhawan, which was addressed by His Holiness and Dr Karan Singh, besides representatives of other religions. On this occasion we organised visits to several places of worship in Delhi by His Holiness and other delegates. We started with chanting from the holy texts of different religions at Rajghat, which was very pleasant. His Holiness and the others proceeded to visit a Gurudwara, a Hindu temple, the Jama Masjid and the Sacred Heart Cathedral. The idea at that time was to maintain a forum for communal harmony after the seminar. However, it was difficult to sustain the participants' interest without assuring them of a prominent role. Somehow, we managed to carry on with the mission without giving it an obvious organisational structure. I was particular not to let these events become a forum for speeches, because speeches have a tendency to go on too long. So we requested people to recite from a scripture, with a brief message.

I realised that many inter-religious bodies existed at the international level. When such bodies grow, they take the form of large organisations with a hierarchy of positions, which mostly leads to disharmony rather than harmony. After several years of the visit that took place after the 1987 seminar, another institution in Delhi, associated with the name of His Holiness, organised a visit to different places of worship. The organisers conveyed the impression that it was the first time such an event was being organised in Delhi. I just smiled.

I have attended many inter-religious gatherings abroad, some large in size, some moderate. What I have found is that people speak eloquently and find good things to say about other religions, some going into the areas commonly agreed on and views that are shared. All these are very good, but what I feel is that areas where there are different concepts should also be talked about, because they are there, and we cannot succeed in bringing people together by just pretending these differences do not exist. I feel that to recognise differences is also important. It is absurd, for example, to say that atman and shunyata are the same, while they are exactly the opposite. The point is that theological and philosophical differences should not come in the way of working together for larger human or ecological concerns.

I cannot claim to have a profound knowledge and understanding of other religions, but I respect all religions, their founders, as well as their main principles. The benefit to their true followers should be admired, such as, to take instances I have personally encountered, the concern for truth among Muslims, education among Christians, generosity among Sikhs, all-inclusive theory among Hindus and supple thinking among Buddhists. People who are born into a particular religious tradition must have a karmic relationship with it. Changing a person's religion or tradition should not be encouraged generally, because not everybody is a philosopher nor can everybody be made a philosopher. The majority of the people will remain simple followers. Changing religions without acquiring a firm foundation in the new religion can create much confusion, especially at the time of one's death.

Tolerance is a frequently used word at such gatherings. I don't deny it is important, but more important is understanding. To give an example, when the Bamiyan Buddhas were destroyed, of course, I also joined the condemnation; in fact, I organised a meeting to talk about the culture of destruction. But if we realise that these people are not against Buddhism or the Buddha statue in particular, our response may be different. To consider any statue as holy is alien to them, and thus, we can, so to speak, understand their understanding.

I talk of understanding and tolerance, but not too loudly, knowing my own limitations.

40

Festivals

While we encourage and organise interfaith meetings without tiring, what is neglected is the coming together of a religious group and the dynamics within it, for example, in an intra-Buddhist gathering.

A group of about 121 monks and nuns from different traditions of Tibetan Buddhism were rehearsing for the World Festival of Sacred Music (WFSM) at Namdroling Monastery in Bylakuppe. As I watched them, I found that when one monastery was reciting a prayer, other monasteries did not join in even if they knew the chant. For example, when the monks of Sera-Jey Monastery were chanting the Heart Sutra, monks from other monasteries of Tibetan Buddhist tradition chose to remain mere spectators. The Heart Sutra was something everyone knew but no one joined in. On the other hand, when the Thai monks chanted a sutra, Sri Lankan monks joined in, though not very loudly as the rhythm and pronunciation were not exactly the same.

I often felt that we ought to do something meaningful for the northern and southern (Sanskrit and Pali) traditions of Buddhism to help them work together. Earlier, there was a good working relationship between Tibet House and the Mahabodhi Society of India at Birla House, New Delhi. When somebody asked for suggestions for a representative of Buddhism in Delhi, I often recommended some monks of the Theravada tradition living in Delhi. There is a great scope for remarkable work if Tibetans and Theravada practitioners join hands.

It was with such happy thoughts that I visited Sri Lanka in 1984 to attend the General Conference of the World Fellowship of Buddhists (WFB) in Colombo as a part of the delegation of Council for Religious Affairs of Dharamsala. It was normally difficult to get a visa to Sri Lanka, especially for Tibetans living in India, but at that time the Government of Sri Lanka decided to give blanket clearance to all invitees to the conference. Two other members of our delegation were Pema Chinjor and the Council's General Secretary Garje Khamtul Rinpoche.

Sri Lankan president J.R. Jayewardene inaugurated the conference. I had met him earlier in Kolkata at a function in the headquarters of the Mahabodhi Society of India. At the inaugural ceremony in Colombo, we had some difficulties regarding the sitting arrangements. From my understanding, we were there to represent Buddhism from Tibet. The seating arrangement was made country-wise or within a country, state-wise. The organisers clubbed us with the participants from Himachal Pradesh, India. I resisted this arrangement and said we would sit on the floor if due recognition was not given. But, for the sake of not creating a scene, my colleagues suggested that we do not take the matter further.

I remember that in one of the sessions of the conference, a senior monk, who was the leader of one of the Nikayas (sect), commented on the reference of Buddhism being scientific. He said that Buddhism should not be compared with science. Buddhism did not require any certificate from science to validate it. The monk was right. His Holiness the Dalai Lama took this reasoning one step further. He felt that science and Buddhism could work together. His Holiness said that we should find ways to make the wonderful developments of science into something that offered altruistic and compassionate service for the needs of the humanity and other sentient beings with whom we share the earth.

There was another occasion earlier when His Holiness encouraged the use of science. The delegates who had gone to the Colombo conference also went to Anuradhapura, a place where the Buddha's tooth relic was preserved. I could not join them because I had to rush to Seoul to attend another conference. But this reminded me of the remark His Holiness had made in 2001 when I had organised a monastic dialogue seminar on Acharya Shantarakshita. He had said that Acharya Shantarakshita was supposed to have lived hundreds of years. His Holiness was not averse to DNA testing if any relic of Acharya existed, but He said that would not in any way reduce or change our reverence for the Acharya. In that context, I wondered about the tooth relic.

Getting back to the activities of Tibet House, in 2003 we held a three-day festival of 'Sacred Chanting and Singing'. On the morning of the first day, people gathered at Buddha Jayanti Park where His Holiness the Dalai Lama gave a discourse on the 'Four Seals of Buddhist Doctrine' followed by short performances by eighteen different groups and individuals representing five continents and many of the world's spiritual traditions. His Holiness expressed his appreciation to all the participants. He remarked that the chanting of the mantra 'Om Mani Padme Hum' by the women from the Tehor region of Tibet was very soothing. He said this chanting was normally done when they were fasting. Over the three evenings, the participating groups and individual performers gave full-length performances at the Rose Garden of IIC.

In 2006, we had planned a three-day festival of Buddhist Music and Ritual to mark 2,550 years of the Buddha's Parinirvana. I wanted this event to be inaugurated by the prime minister since this programme was jointly organised by Tibet House and Ministry of Culture, Government of India. I sought an appointment and Prime Minister Dr Manmohan Singh received me at his South Block office. I was accompanied by Ms Chungkey, Tibet House secretary, and Ms Pelmo, daughter of His Holiness's nephew, Khedroob Thondup. Ms Pelmo was an intern at Tibet House at that time. This meeting was to invite the prime minister to inaugurate the festival and to request him to increase the government grant for Tibet House.

I was astonished to find National Security Advisor M.K. Narayanan also present at the meeting since in the normal course, as the head of a small cultural institution, I would not be expected to bring up any national or international topics in front of the prime minister. The prime minister gave a patient hearing and said that he didn't know where he would be on the day of the function. As for my second request, he agreed to pass it on to the concerned department. M.K. Narayanan walked with me to the door as I was leaving. It just slipped from my mouth that I did not expect him to be there. His reply was more astonishing. He said, 'Of course, you are a famous man!' This led me to think – I knew that I was definitely not a famous man. Should I be wary of contacting VIPs? Was I being watched? But why?

On the first day of the festival at Buddha Jayanti Park, there was a special event in which there was a procession similar to the Golden Procession that used to take place in Lhasa during the Tsogchod festival commemorating the 5th Dalai Lama's anniversary. Participants in the Golden Procession were from selected monasteries representing the four major traditions of Tibetan Buddhism. I had earlier travelled to appraise the heads of these monasteries of the idea and organised rehearsals. The audience that morning enjoyed the painstakingly choreographed and rehearsed procession. To His Holiness it must have been a reminder of the scene He had witnessed many a time from the upper storeys of the Potala Palace, when the procession started from the main temple at Lhasa, proceeded to the front of Potala Palace, and moved clockwise around it.

An event was organised in the main hall of the India Habitat Centre later that day for the participants from Sri Lanka, Japan, Korea, Nepal, Mongolia and Tibet to have exclusive contact with His Holiness. His Holiness released the book *Tibet House: Mission and Activities* at the event. He then gave a talk on the 'Importance of Inter-Cultural Activities for a Deeper International Understanding'. As I reached the podium to make the short speech I had prepared, I searched frantically in my bag but could not find it. I then said whatever I could remember rather haphazardly. His Holiness's spontaneous comment was, 'Everything was so well organised, but this is strange.'

His Holiness made a brief speech on the importance of inter-cultural activities for a deeper international understanding. He appreciated the performances at the inaugural ceremony, making a special mention of the Gongkar Choede drum dance. Afterwards, everybody filed past to receive His Holiness's blessings. When the programme finished, there were about 15 minutes left according to His Holiness's schedule. He was eager to spend more time there, but those around him whispered something and whisked Him away, which I found improper. It made me wonder why they should have done so. Another strange experience!

Among the public performances in the evenings, the deep-voiced chanting by a vocalist from Tuva Republic of Russia was most impressive. A very professional troupe from Korea performed a spectacular sacred dance that was much appreciated by everyone. A young singer from Mongolia chanted Tibetan shlokas and the mantra of Vajrapani, their patron deity. Music, dance and festivities filled the minds of all those around.

41

Sacred Music

To mark the beginning of the third millennium, we thought that a prominent event ought to be organised in the name of His Holiness to highlight the Buddha's message of peace and harmony. WFSM was conceived in 1996 as a single event to take place in India, but by 1998 the idea had gathered momentum, inspiring the larger public to arrange local, regional as well as national festivals in thirteen different cities across the world, from Vancouver to Hiroshima, from Berlin to Cape Town. We believed that the event would enhance the image of His Holiness beyond Tibetan supporters and Buddhist enthusiasts. At these festivals, people of all faiths and cultures came together to share their sacred music. Music was chosen as the most meaningful way to express the deepest hopes of humankind.

His Holiness appealed to all like-minded people to join in this endeavour. He said that music symbolised the yearning for harmony with ourselves and with others, with nature and with the spiritual and the sacred within and around us. An announcement of the event was made by His Holiness at a press conference in Brandeis University where He made a special effort to present me as the person responsible for the worldwide event.

Over the span of two years, this festival took me to many cities around the world, starting from Delhi, to Vancouver, Los Angeles, Chicago, Waterloo, New York, Attleboro in Massachusetts, Cape Town, Bengaluru, Bangkok, Chiang Mai, Hiroshima and finally, Berlin. I travelled to Los Angeles (LA) to discuss the concept of the festival with Judy Mitoma of the Center for Inter-Cultural Performance in UCLA. Finding tremendous enthusiasm among the people involved, we decided to hold the first festival in LA itself. His Holiness was present in the opening ceremony which was held in the stadium called Hollywood Bowl, a huge open area for events. This was followed by events at different venues over nine days. I know that this festival initiated a series of events which the UCLA conducted under the same name and they hold this festival on a regular basis.

The LA event was followed by a three-day festival in Chicago with an impressive evening show at the Old Saint Patrick's Church. The next even took place at Waterloo in Canada.

The South African leg of the WFSM was scheduled in December 1998. A few months before the event, I had an audience with His Holiness in His hotel suite in Delhi and reported the progress of the WFSM in different parts of the world. He was very appreciative of the good progress. He then called His secretary Tenzin Geyche, whom I have mentioned earlier, and instructed him to include me in His entourage for the visit to South Africa in December that year. Tenzin Geyche murmured something but reluctantly obeyed. As the Bureau of His Holiness in Delhi was responsible for coordinating His Holiness's visits abroad, I expected to receive a word from them regarding my travel documents. I did not hear from them even when the date of the visit was very near. I was obliged to call and check with Tenzin Geyche and was shocked to hear that he had completely forgotten about it. I wondered how he could forget a direct order from His Holiness, but I left it there. Sometime later, I was informed by the Bureau that I was to travel with His Holiness to South Africa. I joined the entourage, but it was not a happy tour for me. I must say that during the visit, I felt humiliated and there was an atmosphere of coldness.

The festival was held in Cape Town from 9 to 11 December and His Holiness graciously inaugurated it in an open public park. The chief of the native Zulu band of musicians escorted His Holiness from the entrance to the seat and from the seat to the podium from where He was to speak. His Holiness said that the chief reminded Him of the great chamberlain in Tibet whose role was to escort Him in ceremonies.

The evening programme was full of great joy and grace. The Zulu band's performances were lively and demonstrated the pure native culture. After His Holiness's departure from South Africa, I stayed back for a few days at the house of a South African family to familiarise myself with the culture of that land. From the window of my room, I could enjoy a breathtaking view of the Table Mountain every morning as the clouds slowly fell below the edges of the mountain like a tablecloth.

Attleboro in Massachusetts also hosted the festival, though not on a very large scale. A well-known Buddhist leader and a festival patron, Ajarn Sulak Sivaraksa, was responsible for the festival in Bangkok and Chiang Mai in Thailand. A five-day programme in Miyajima island in Hiroshima – a befitting setting – was managed by the well-known rock musician Toshinori Kondo with his inexhaustible energy and will-power. The three-day Berlin event at the House of World Culture marked the final event of the festival. It was considered that the festivals in Hiroshima and Berlin were of special significance as they represented two places where humankind went through extreme suffering – the bomb and the wall created by humans.

During my visit to London in January 1999 in connection with the preparations for the global event of the WFSM, I had the unforgettable experience of calling on Lord Yehudi Menuhin. I had first encountered his name in the 1970s in his foreword to B.K.S. Iyengar's *Light on Pranayama*. He received me graciously, was extremely kind and gave all encouragement. He agreed to be a patron of the event and gave me advice on the organisation of the festival. Accepting my invitation to grace the inauguration in India, he noted the year and date in his diary but most unfortunately, he passed away in March of that year. We marked our tribute to him at the launch of the main event of the WFSM in May 1999 in Delhi, where Ustad Amjad Ali Khan and his sons performed in the presence of His Holiness. I have preserved the advice for the festival that he had written by his own hand and given me.

The global event of the WFSM took place in Bengaluru, India, from 9 to 16 April 2000. A total of 650 artists gathered from 15 countries all over the world – Benedictine monks and nuns from the Netherlands, Gamelan players from Indonesia, Baul minstrels from Bengal, organists from Germany and qawwali singers in the South Asian Sufi tradition, not to forget the Tibetan artists like the flutist Nawang Khechog and a choir of 121 Tibetan monks and nuns. We heard trumpets from Japan, the Zulu band, Spear of Shaka from South Africa, the Israeli shofar as well as jazz, spirituals and Mongolian shamanic drums and south Indian Yakshagana. Indian classical music on the veena and on the santoor represented the host culture.

Besides the music, the event brought together eminent personalities from different traditions and faiths that represent the finest thoughts and the minds of humankind. On the morning after the inauguration, a programme called the 'Meeting of Minds' was arranged to reflect on the common inspirations and goals where His Holiness the Dalai Lama, R. Venkataraman, Dr A.T. Ariyaratne, Ravindra Varma, Ajarn Sulak Sivaraksa, Father Maximillian Mizzi, Swami Balagangadharanatha, Samani Kusum Pragya, Dr Ausaf Ali, Dr Homi B. Dhalla, Sister Karin Lelyveld, Dr Raja Ramanna and Khambo Lama spoke eloquently. On this occasion a compilation of sacred music was brought out titled *The Song of the Spirit*.[4]

When the national organising committee was being formed for the WFSM, the former president of India, R. Venkataraman, was kind enough to agree to my request to be the chairman. Not only did he lend his name to the committee, he also played an active role, showing concern about the arrangements, especially funding. I had many meetings with him at his residence to discuss the nature of the programmes over a cup of specially prepared south Indian coffee. During one such meeting, the topic of Indian elections came up and he said that instead of having coalition governments which normally led to complications and prevented smooth functioning, there should be a system of holding a second election between the two groups with the maximum number of seats. I am sure others have also talked about this as well, but I mention this here since I heard it directly from him and thought it was a very good idea.

R. Venkataraman participated in the Indian independence movement. He was member of the Indian Parliament, held important portfolios in the government and, above all, was a wise man. Even after his tenure as president, he continued to carry the image of the 'president of India'. At one of the preparatory meetings for the festival, the mayor of Cape Town, South Africa, was present and I remember Venkataraman addressing her as 'Your Worship'. During the main event held at the J.N. Tata Auditorium at the Indian Institute of Science in Bengaluru, Venkataraman did not know that Chief Minister S.M. Krishna would be coming to the inaugural ceremony. Venkataraman arrived ten minutes before the starting time and I had a hard time holding him at the porch. In terms of protocol, I could not ask a former president of India to wait for the chief minister, so I had to engage him in conversation. Luckily, the delegate from Israel played his shofar till the chief minister arrived. Venkataraman's speech was carefully thought out and well received.

Other prominent figures like the Lord Yehudi Menuhin, Pandit Ravi Shankar, Prince Sadruddin Aga Khan, Vaclav Havel, Archbishop Desmond Tutu, Swami Chidananda Saraswati and Madame Danielle Mitterrand were gracious enough to consent to my request to be patrons of the festival. One person I would have liked to be a patron was Mikhail Gorbachev. I had met him earlier at an international conference in Kyoto in 1992, where he was launching the Green Cross Movement on Ecological Issues. We tried very hard to contact him, but in vain.

One year later, I met Bishop Desmond Tutu at the Bengaluru residence of Dr M.C. Jain. The Jain couple was hosting Desmond Tutu and his wife, who had come to India to spend some quiet time in the beautiful area in the outskirts of Bengaluru. Dr Jain was a friend and had briefly participated in the seminar on Compassionate Economy I had organised in New Delhi. Desmond Tutu was extremely warm and affectionate towards me. Despite the fact that I was just a humble Tibetan monk, he showed all the courtesy of treating me as a Buddhist representative and a friend. He showed grave concern about democracy and social justice in Tibet. He expressed great respect for His Holiness. Both His Holiness and Desmond Tutu remained best of friends and continued to engage in a very important dialogue concerning the future of humanity. When I started writing this memoir, Desmond Tutu had retired from his public life as Bishop. But today, when I am finishing my story, he has bid adieu to the world, a world to whom he remains the iconic Desmond Tutu.

Likewise, His Holiness, who has also retired as the head of Tibetan establishment, will always remain the Dalai Lama of Tibet to the world; to the Tibetans he is Chenrezig. He can never be the ex-Dalai Lama.

For a project of the size of the global event of WFSM, raising resources was critical and that was one of the major tasks for me. It was tough but we managed to get some financial support from institutions, individuals and business houses in India and abroad. The major expenses on local hospitality and transportation for over 700 artists and organisers for nearly ten days was undertaken by the House of Khodays in Bengaluru. I had many meetings with Mr Hari Khoday and in one of the meetings, I told him that I would not hesitate to go door-to-door for help for hosting artists, if I had to. Mr Khoday did not respond to this comment. Initially, the meetings did not lead to any commitment from him. However, he finally agreed to take care of the local expenses and provided a special team to help oversee the operation in the local areas of Bengaluru. Other workforce for the event came in the form of volunteers from Mumbai, Delhi and Bengaluru.

The festival was a great success and I give credit to everyone who helped, especially to all the wonderful artists who were committed to the ideas that the festival was seeking to promote. My friend Kiran Ganguli was the key person behind this event and he helped me from the conception stage of the idea. Kiran

Ganguli, or 'Gang' as he was known to his close associates, is someone whose ideas are very clear and fresh. He possesses the ability to efficiently execute the work in hand. As a person he is very simple and unpretentious. He has a remarkably thick moustache. I remember an instance when we were at the construction site of the Buddha canopy at Buddha Jayanti Park. Ling Rinpoche, then a young child, kept asking me whether his moustache was real. In this age when no one, from ministers to beggars, can function without mobile phones, he manages everything quite well with just a landline, which he uses only when it is absolutely necessary. He normally travels on a bicycle in the city and hires a car only when he knows the work will require him to go to different locations and take most of the day otherwise. I believe this is his way of contributing to environment conservation and it keeps him fit and healthy. I draw inspiration from him, mainly from his simplicity and practicality.

I noticed an interesting tendency of people during my work on this event. When some success was achieved, people came up with suggestions of 'follow up actions' and 'should be a regular event' and so on. While it was a good sign and indicated full marks from the audience, it led me to think what kind of 'follow up actions' people might be thinking of. Commitment to have regular events or institutionalisation of such occasions may not be always desirable. Institutionalisation has its drawbacks. As I have observed throughout my public life, right from the time when Tibet House was wondering whether or not to continue the emporium, decisions are not made only to further a cause but also to sensitise the people towards the cause. Sensitisation may happen better if an event or an idea is presented in a short but effective manner.

42

The Art of Administration

Administration, I feel, was best done and was most effective when the basic processes were respected and followed. Of course, the processes could and should be changed periodically to keep up with the changing times, but that should be done with deliberation and a detailed consideration of all consequences, in full knowledge of all the stakeholders.

Now I must tell you a story. Around 2005, I wrote an article for the *Tibetan Review* which was published on the front-page with the headline, 'Tibet House Has Its Own Governance', where I referred to the status of Tibet House as it had come down from the early stages of its existence. Although nobody got back to me with comments, it may have provided some food for thought to some people.

In 2007, the Kuyig sent a circular to Tibet House, Tibetan Homes Foundation (Mussoorie), Library of Tibetan Works and Archives (LTWA), the Norbulingka Institute and Foundation for Universal Responsibility (FUR), saying that the annual meetings of these institutions would, in future, be chaired by the Kalon Tripa, the chairman of the Council of the Ministers of Tibetan Administration in Dharamsala.[5] Another letter from the Kuyig said that the present Kalon Tripa had already been chairing the meetings of LTWA. This I had known as I was also a member of that governing body. The same letter also reminded me that the present Kalon Tripa was a member of the governing body of FUR. This was also known to me, as at that time I was also a member of the governing body of FUR and, in fact, one of its founding members.

But the circular was alarming to me because I could not implement a major change like that without taking the Tibet

House governing body into confidence. Earlier, on several occasions, His Holiness, who was the chairman of Tibet House governing body, made it very clear that He would not be able to chair the meetings. He said that going through technicalities like checking annual budgets and so on were not his cup of tea. My feeling at the time and even now is that His leadership and patronage are the main thing, the details anyone can take care of. Thus, at my request, His Holiness had appointed M.K. Rasgotra as the vice chairman of the Tibet House Society.

In the absence of His Holiness, M.K. Rasgotra chaired the meetings. When appointed as the Indian High Commissioner to the UK, M.K. Rasgotra had expressed the wish to retire from vice chairmanship, but other governing body members of Tibet House unanimously requested him to continue. He had been very helpful to Tibetan refugees during the difficult period in the beginning when he was posted at the Indian Embassy in Kathmandu. To just push him aside, without due procedure and honourable recognition, and appoint another person to chair the meetings, would not be appropriate.

I discussed this matter with a few active governing body members, both Indian and Tibetan, including the vice chairman. In November, when Jetsun Pema, one of the important members of Tibet House, called me to talk about the future status of Tibet House, one of the points she suggested was that M.K. Rasgotra should be requested to chair the governing body meetings for life. I also discussed this with a senior legal expert to get a legal opinion on this matter. The outcome of these discussions clearly suggested that it would not be appropriate to make the Kalon Tripa, who was the head of a political body, chair the meetings. Besides, the Kuyig circular did not specify the status of His Holiness with regard to the Tibet House Society. This lack of clarity created a predicament.

A background paper was prepared giving the opinion of Tibet House. This was sent along with the reply to the circular, which put forward the suggestions that had arisen during consultations. These were that His Holiness should continue as the chairman, with the request that He appoint one or more vice-chairperson(s), which would not require amendments to the rules and regulations of the Society. However, if His Holiness had made up His mind about not holding the chairmanship, He should be requested to accept title of 'Patron of the Society' and to make the joint secretary in the Department of Culture, Ministry of Tourism and Culture, Government of India, the (ex-officio) chairperson (as it was in CIHTS), while His Holiness's representative in Delhi would be the ex-officio vice chairman. This would entail amending the Rules and Regulations. Such an arrangement would also reinforce the Indian government's long-term commitment to the institution and maintain a balance in the governance.

I also felt it was my duty to state in the letter my opinion that M.K. Rasgotra's skilful way of guiding Tibet House was admirable and that at this juncture Tibet House and the Tibetan affairs at large would not gain anything by pushing him out, except gain the reputation for inelegant behaviour. After some time, I was informed verbally that it would be fine to have M.K. Rasgotra chairing the meetings. But basically, it became clear that all my efforts of putting ideas together was a waste of time and energy on my part. All these descriptions are based on the situation prevailing in those days.

On 16 July 2006, there was a meeting of the heads of three institutions – LTWA, CIHTS and Tibet House – called by the director of CIHTS, Prof. Ngawang Samten, purportedly at the direction of His Holiness. I found it a bit strange that I did not receive any communication from the Kuyig in this regard because normally, in that kind of a situation, all the stakeholders should be informed. The purpose stated for the meeting was to discuss how the three institutions might collaborate more closely.

Before the meeting, Prof. Samten remarked that out of the Buddhist–Tibetan institutions recognised by the Government of India, two were just sleeping – Central Institute of Buddhist Studies (CIBS) at Leh and the Namgyal Institute, Gangtok. I felt this was a rather strong statement. The Leh Institute had been making remarkable contributions in the area of Buddhist learning, not only in the institute's campus, but also through programmes initiated in the monasteries of the region. Similarly, the Namgyal Institute had also done some outstanding work, especially in the area of Tibetan language publications. So I failed to understand why such remarks were being made. One strong word of caution was that academic progress cannot be measured on a day-to-day basis. Such institutions were working steadily and with inspiration. They needed to be supported.

Anyway, the day of the meeting dawned. The meeting was also attended by the Representative of His Holiness in Delhi. We prepared the minutes, which said that connecting with universities in India for Buddhist studies could best be done by CIHTS, while the LTWA could strengthen its various programmes, especially in the area of oral traditions, particularly Tibetan. As far as Tibet House was concerned, we agreed that its strength was the collection of artifacts, exhibitions of which could be arranged more regularly. The minutes said that CIHTS, because of its workforce, should co-ordinate these efforts. As the meeting was chaired by the director of CIHTS, we would naturally expect CIHTS to function as the nodal agency. That was the impression given without clearly saying so. Unfortunately, there was no follow up, and that was the last time I heard about this idea. Since Tibet House had been the venue, we prepared the minutes and circulated them among those who had attended but surprisingly, there was no response or comment.

Earlier, when CIHTS, under Samdhong Rinpoche became a deemed university, Dr Kapila Vatsyayan, who was the patron of the institute from the government side as well as in her personal capacity, suggested to me that it would be good if Tibet House became the city centre of CIHTS. My spontaneous reaction was a firm 'no'. Tibet House functioned with great sensitivity. It dealt with a wide variety of people. I told her that Tibet House, though small in size, because of its prime location in the centre of the Indian capital, made some ambitious people eye it as a space to spread their wings. That would be detrimental to Tibet House and to the image of Tibetan Buddhists in India as a whole.

Much later, on 19 December 2008, Rinchen Khandro Choegyal from Dharamsala visited me. She said she had come specifically to discuss matters related to Tibet House. The gist of what she had to say was that a 'group of important persons' had come up with the idea that Tibet House, though doing well was, architecturally speaking, not Tibetan and also a lot of space was wasted in the present structure. The suggestion was doing the rounds among 'important persons' that the present building should be demolished and rebuilt. The new structure should have a Tibetan look and should serve multiple purposes. There should be provisions for space to accommodate the Foundation for Universal Responsibility, the Bureau of the Dalai Lama, perhaps a Tibetan medical centre and also a place for His Holiness to make brief stopover between programmes in central Delhi.

I was, naturally, shocked to hear this. Although I knew that the Tibet House building did not have any features of Tibetan architecture, yet it was one of the few structures that were considered architecturally significant. It belonged to the school of the famous French architect, Le Corbusier. Many students of architecture came to study the building. The interesting part in that conversation with Rinchen Khandro Choegyal was that she carefully avoided mentioning any person's name in the so-called 'group of important persons' who stood behind this idea of demolishing the Tibet House building. Nor did she mention that the idea came from His Holiness. If it had been His Holiness's idea, He would have called and instructed me and that would have been the final word. But she did not say so and refused to mention any names. After that, till today, I have not heard anything about dismantling Tibet House.

I tried to respond calmly to the lady, but I was firm that the idea of demolishing was not acceptable to me. As far as space for His Holiness was concerned, we had already thought of that and had even got a complete architectural blueprint ready for a light structure on top of the Tibet House building. We could have taken up this project, but the atmosphere generated by this sort of a situation did not encourage me to build something which later someone else might suggest be demolished.

43

Tibetan Institutes

In Varanasi and also earlier when I was in Buxa, I had been associated with CIHTS. In the earlier part of this book, I have described how we would all huddle around a tape recorder that played and replayed His Holiness's message of turning the transit camp for lamas in Buxa into a proper academic school. The specific idea was that in this changing world, monastic style of institutions may not be relevant to the people for long. This new idea was not easy to digest for many monks, especially those of the older generation. But this was a specific instruction from His Holiness through a tape-recorded message and was played to the monks over-and-over again.

So the Buxa lama camp was changed into a school where the main subject was Buddhist philosophy. Tibetan grammar and literature were also taught. When the first batch of 300 monks was sent to Varanasi, I was selected, again as you may remember, as one of the teachers to teach the remaining monks in the lama camp, which continued to function as a school. The first principal of the Tibetan Institute in Varanasi was Zong Rinpoche, who was also expected to supervise, from time to time, the remaining monks at Buxa. I went to Varanasi as the third batch of students to fill up the slot of the Acharya degree course. Later, I was involved with the institute in different ways – as a member of the governing body, as a member of expert committees and so on.

In the 1980s, the idea came up of changing the name of CIHTS at Sarnath, Varanasi, to a university for Buddhist studies, 'sacrificing' the word 'Tibetan' from it and making it a Buddhist University. By that time I had already come to Tibet House. His Holiness instructed me to coordinate this move to change the name with the director of the Sarnath Institute, Samdhong Rinpoche. So I approached him and he showed willingness to cooperate. He tactfully said that he would prepare a blueprint for the proposal at the earliest. I eagerly waited for it as in those days everybody trusted everyone else. Sure enough, he prepared a plan for the university. The plan looked clear and proposed turning the entire Sarnath area into a university campus.

According to the plan, while the existing Tibetan institute would become the nodal point for examinations and administration, the Chinese Temple, the Burmese Temple and the upcoming Thai Temple would become departments of Chinese–Buddhist Studies, Burmese–Buddhist Studies and so on. I must say that it was an impressive and ambitious plan. I submitted it to the Kuyig. Some meetings were held to receive inputs on this plan, but these were no more than consultations or brainstorming sessions. I have no knowledge of any follow up or decision after that.

When the director, Samdhong Rinpoche, was preparing to leave the institute, a search committee was constituted to look for suitable candidates to take up his position. According to the procedure, the search committee would present the list of shortlisted candidates at the board meeting of the institute. The board meeting would further cut down the shortlist and make a recommendation to the Ministry of Culture, Government of India, which had the final say. I understand some meetings, of which I was not a part, regarding this issue were held at the institute.

Prof. G.C. Pande, the chairman of the institute, a very renowned and revered scholar on Indological subjects including Buddhism, informally told me that I would be the successor to Samdhong Rinpoche. Many of the senior Indian scholars I knew, both in Varanasi and elsewhere, asked me not to refuse in case such a situation came up. I am habitually slow to react to sudden news and was totally unmoved at the prospect. I did not pay any attention and did not try to follow up what exactly was happening at CIHTS.

One day as usual, after office hours, I went to the IIC and there, in the lounge, I saw Samdhong Rinpoche sitting alone in a corner. I went up to him and we sat together. He broke the news to me that he had left CIHTS two days earlier. 'Oh?' I exclaimed. He said he had handed over charge to Prof. Geshe Ngawang Samten in the evening and left the institute early next morning. I was surprised. Had he bypassed all the procedures of selection and handing over? Did that mean that the procedures worked only if they served the purpose of a particular person or a group?

Much later, I heard from a senior staff member of CIHTS that the selection committee had chosen me as the top candidate from the list and their decision was presented at the board meeting and was approved. Then a magic wand had been waved and one evening Samdhong Rinpoche had handed over the position to Prof. Ngawang Samten. The swift action gave the whole thing a sense of urgency in Samdhong Rinpoche's context and also closed all possibilities of examining how to rationalise the decision taken against the decision of the board.

Another institute with which I had been involved was the Namgyal Institute. It was an old institute of Buddhist studies in Sikkim. I had heard and seen photographs of this place even when I was in Tibet, in the Tibetan language magazine that used to be published by the Sikkim government, *Yargye Gongphel* (Development and Progress). The murals depicting Indian pandits were imprinted in my mind ever since seeing the photographs in the magazine. Each time I go to the institute, I see a very familiar scene. The paintings are in the *karma gadri* style of Tibetan painting, which I have not seen on the walls, but only in thangkas. It was during the Chogyal of Sikkim's visit to Tibet that His Holiness presented a set of many Tibetan texts, which formed the basis of the library.

The institute was named after a dynasty of Sikkim rulers, the Namgyal. For a brief period, soon after Sikkim became a state of India, the name was changed to 'Sikkim Institute of Tibetology', but after some years I was glad to see the original name back in use. I thought it was a wise decision because, while we should always go ahead, occasionally we should turn back to take stock of our background, too. The main strength of the institute was the collection of books, which were catalogued in the traditional way, without it being very difficult to find texts.

From the time of its inception, this institute had the unique feature of having a resident monk scholar from each of the four Tibetan Buddhist traditions – Geluk, Nyingma, Kagyu and Sakya. They had the freedom to engage in writing, teaching, guiding researchers and so on. With the passage of time, these resident monks have gradually passed away or moved elsewhere. At several governing body meetings of the institute I, as a member, brought up the importance of renewing this practice but no concrete steps were taken.

I once received a phone call from Tenzin Geyche of the Kuyig, asking if I would be interested in going to the institute as its director. It was apparent that the governor at that time, who was the chairman of the institute, had asked His Holiness to send a Tibetan. I knew that the institute was well funded because the Centre and State (Sikkim government) funded it in equal measure. I was, on the contrary, struggling to get funding at Tibet House. I said I would not be interested in going there because I felt that in a learning institute, the head of the institute should be someone who was well acquainted with the history and culture of that region, not someone imported from outside. I am glad I took that decision on the spot.

When Tibet was free, many Ladakhi monks would go to study in Tibetan monasteries and many of them returned to their homes as learned lamas. Among them was Bakula Rinpoche, who was one of the most respected lamas in the Ladakh region. After the drastic changes in 1959, it was no longer possible to go to Tibet for religious studies, so Bakula came up with the idea of establishing a centre for the study of Buddhism in Ladakh. He invited my guru, Yeshe Thubten, and a few others to be the first teachers there. As with most institutions, it had a humble beginning, with simple infrastructure. Later, it was named the Central Institute of Buddhist Studies, Leh. Today it is a full-fledged university. Many of the early students of that time became well-known scholars. Most of them are now retired. I was associated with this institute as member of its governing body. Since then, the infrastructure has grown, especially the library facilities.

The learned Ladakhis who were brought up in the traditional Tibetan way are still upholding the scholarship traditions. One such Ladakhi, Gen Jamspal, is my friend. He studied at Tashi Lhunpo in Tibet. He is very particular that the traditional way of using the language, writing, spelling and composition should be preserved. He goes one step further, saying that like Ladakh, in Tibet too, originally all the letters written would have been pronounced. Therefore, he insists that everyone should pronounce like that. His American students are taught the same method. Once he and one of his American students participated in a conference I organised in Delhi. His student demonstrated how he learned Tibetan before reading out his seminar paper. Afterwards, my playful response to his demonstration was, 'Your Greek is very good, how about your Tibetan?'

Those Ladakhis who have studied with Tibetan lamas in India also speak like Tibetans. But there is a section of people, mainly from the younger generation, who feel that since now Ladakh is not a part of Tibet politically, they should have a distinct language. Some of them argue to the extent that their language was not Tibetan and even change the spellings of several words. I feel it is very narrow minded to call that modified language something else and not Tibetan. For example, if we meet people from North America or Australia or New Zealand, none of them would say their language was not English, though what they speak and write may be somewhat different from British English.

There was a big debate between these two ways of thinking at a seminar I attended in Leh. The subject was raised by Ladakhi linguistic enthusiasts. Their way of pronouncing is also followed by Western scholars, because it is much easier to write down the spelling. The present way of pronouncing Tibetan words by Tibetans, especially the system followed in the Lhasa area where many people from many parts mingle, does not follow any logic. In some parts of Amdo and Kham, it has always been possible to discern the spelling to some extent, but not as clearly as it is with Ladakhis.

A significant venture needs to be mentioned. We were sitting in His Holiness's suite in Ashoka Hotel. His Holiness got up, went to His bedroom and returned with His religious robes (*namjar*, one of the three Dharma robes) and a small Buddha statue which He carries during His travels. Then He carefully folded the cloth on the table and placed the statue on it. It was clear that His Holiness had something important to announce. We waited with reverence and anticipation.

His Holiness gave a gist of His philosophy of the issues of universal concern. By using a part of His Nobel Peace Prize money, He desired to have an organisation to work specifically on these issues. The draft of the trust deed and other relevant papers had already been prepared and were circulated. Those present were Kapila Vatsyayan, Ngari Rinpoche, Lobsang Dargye, Rajiv Mehrotra, one of His Holiness's attendants and I. The organisation would be called the Foundation for Universal Responsibility (FUR) and we would be its founder members. His Holiness would be the chairman of the Foundation and Rajiv Mehrotra the member secretary.

After the meeting at Ashoka Hotel, I attended the meetings of the foundation several times. The meetings would be formal when His Holiness was present, but otherwise informal. I was given the title 'alternate chairman'. When I expressed discomfort with that, I was called the 'vice chairman' instead. No formal meetings were ever held without His Holiness's presence, so my title was never used. Soon the title underwent another change – from vice chairman, I became a 'marg darshak' and so did Kapila Vatsyayan. I was told this title meant 'the one who shows the way'. Somehow, my eye glasses read it as 'redundant'. The foundation promoted some awareness about the Tibetan style of Buddhism. In my understanding, FUR was conceived to spread His Holiness's idea of universalism. That was never emphasised.

There are people who behave as if they are the keepers of His Holiness's thoughts and ideals. But on the whole, few people have been able to understand His idea of universal nature. It needs a much larger vision of humanity than most people have. Just as an example, when we organised workshops or camps on ecological issues with the hope of creating awareness among Tibetans on basic issues – mainly the relationship between humans, between humans and other creatures, between sentient and non-sentient beings and between the elements. I felt somewhat satisfied feeling they had understood the points stressed during such gatherings.

When it comes to the practical implementation of His ideas, it always remains confined to the Tibetan community, without involving the Indians in the neighbourhood or from the villages around. Thus it becomes a limited activity or exercise, like clearing discarded plastic bags and planting trees. This is not to suggest that these acts are not useful, but ecological principles must go beyond hygiene and healthcare of the community. Essentially, what I am saying is that, while His Holiness's thoughts and ideas are universal in nature, we Tibetans end up projecting His Holiness as a community leader, or at best, a Buddhist leader. By involving others while addressing even small problems, we might generate real and organic relations and friendship between people of different cultures and languages. What happens, unfortunately, is that when somebody from our community refers to contacts and friendship among communities, the effort ends up in a public meeting, setting up an organisation or maybe an Indo-Tibetan friendship group, making a few speeches that provide a stage for a few people to promote themselves as the champions of something, and does not go further.

Typically, people present fantastic ideas and attractive proposals to His Holiness. His Holiness listens in all earnestness and then suggests that it would be good to explore all possibilities to put the idea into practice. Then we will hear the person saying His Holiness liked the proposal very much and that they were selected to carry it out and so on. Some mileage, some publicity, some appreciation or some such thing will be gained and then the project will be forgotten. The hard work and perseverance required will not come forth for they will fail to put their heart into areas that actually matter. And good ideas will just vanish into thin air!

In the mid-1960s, an office called Tsomgyur Khang (office of composing and translation) was created. This office was headed by a young high lama from Kham Dagyab. The office started bringing out some useful booklets on health care, letter writing and so on. This lama was well versed in Tibetan literature and other subjects such as astrology and religious texts. I don't know the exact story but the lama was not one who would bow down easily to dignitaries. He was sent to Tibet House as its director in the mid-1960s. He eventually went to Germany where he has been flourishing. The Tsomgyur Khang was later merged with LTWA. The merger tactic used to be adopted by the then Dharamsala authorities for shunting people they didn't want to see around. Creating an institution and then changing its role or nature and placing it under another agency had become the habitual behaviour of some people in Dharamsala in the 1960s. Good work and momentum was often adversely affected by such rash acts.

From my experience in running institutions, I feel that creating institutions and making changes to their role and nature needs careful thinking in terms of pros and cons. As a member of the governing body of the Tibetan Children's Village (TCV), when I received information about the idea of moving the academic faculty of the Dalai Lama Institute of Higher Education in Bengaluru, a project of TCV, to the Central Institute of Higher Tibetan Studies, Varanasi, I asked Jetsun Pema, the director of TCV about the desirability of the move. I received a big frown and a flashy answer saying, 'Rinpoche, for the interest of general concern, we should be ready to do anything!'

Within a year or so, I started hearing complaints from her that the authorities in the institute in Varanasi had begun issuing orders asking for the submission of this documents and that report and so on. Soon it became clear to her that it was not a workable idea and the proposal was abandoned.

When I was working in LTWA in the manuscript room, I came across some old files. Among the files was one containing the proposal of the drawings and art works for the logo of the Gaden Phodrang government (in exile). The Gaden Phodrang government period (1642–2011) has ended and the words 'Gaden Phodrang' in the logo of the Central Tibetan Administration (CTA) have been replaced by the Tibetan translation of Satyameva Jayate (truth alone triumphs). Today however, Gaden Phodrang represents the Private Office of His Holiness while the government is separate (and the government has a logo with 'Satyameva Jayate' written on it).

This brings me to the question of the Gaden Phodrang logo on the letterhead of Tibet House. I had been trying to protect and preserve this logo and protested against its removal from the letterhead of Tibet House. In the meetings of the governing body of the Tibet House Society, the question of appropriateness of using this logo on Tibet House letterhead was brought up several times by members, pointing out that Tibet House, being a cultural centre, could not represent the government of exiled Tibetans. And each time I convinced the members that the logo was used as the logo of the chairman, His Holiness the Dalai Lama. Tibet House, to me, was not subordinate to any another institution. Similarly, inspired by His Holiness's specific directions to me when I was sent to Tibet House as the director, to have good interactions and develop good relationships with foreign cultural centres in Delhi, I decided to put the sub-heading, 'Cultural Centre of His

Holiness the Dalai Lama' on the letterhead of Tibet House. This initiative was questioned during one governing body meeting, as to how such a decision had come about. My explanation was that although the decision was made without the mandate of the governing body, it was a purely administrative decision made by me because His Holiness was the founding chairman of the Tibet House Society. It was decided then to maintain the status quo.

Ironically, some people tried to educate me that 'the Cultural Centre of His Holiness' was a phrase I had coined. This sort of behaviour made me laugh. And why would I go to the extent of coining such a phrase and fight for its existence and the logo with other members of Tibet House governing body? Did I have any personal interest in Tibet House as some people might think? My intentions have been pure from the very beginning.

Now that the Dalai Lama has de-linked Himself from the 'administrative and political responsibilities', the term 'government', which the Tibetans were once proud of using on every occasion, has also been abandoned. It has been replaced by a more acceptable name for others – Central Tibetan Administration (CTA). But I strongly feel that somebody must think of some ways of honouring the name of His Holiness the Dalai Lama in the names of institutions He was directly involved in establishing.

In 2010, at an informal meeting with Vice Chairman M.K. Rasgotra and Dr Kapila Vatsyayan, the two most active and senior members of the Tibet House governing body, it was agreed that the museum was the heart-and-soul of Tibet House from its very inception. Though the library had a fine collection including a rare Narthang edition of the Kangyur and the unique Bodong collection, it was smaller than the LTWA or the libraries of CIHTS and the Namgyal Institute. It was agreed that while the name of the institute as 'Tibet House' should not be changed, the description on the letterhead could be along the lines of 'Dalai

Lama Museum of Tibetan Arts and Culture'. Doing so would not only distinguish Tibet House from the cultural centres attached to foreign missions in the capital, it would also distinguish the institute from the many Tibet Houses that have sprung up everywhere over the years.

This would also avoid the confusion sometimes created by the phrase 'Cultural Centre of His Holiness the Dalai Lama', which leads people to imagine that they may approach Tibet House for appointments with His Holiness or that Tibet House was the office representing His Holiness in Delhi. Even worse, some people tried to apply pressure on Tibet House using His Holiness's name. Others liked to interfere in the institution's functioning and passed orders in the name of collaboration. That may be the case with similar institutions elsewhere, but with regard to Tibet House, I could see that three things were happening – there were orders coming from many quarters, but there was no single person or office to approach for guidance; people were trying to apply pressure but no one took any responsibility; there were expectations from many but helping hands from none.

In all the instances I have mentioned, the failure to build institutions has been because of a lack of good administration. It is important to follow procedures and be transparent. Then only can we build lasting and strong institutions.

Part VIII

PEOPLE AND PLACES

44

People Who Left an Impression

Tibetans lovingly call him 'Gene-la'. I have a feeling that he was born for Tibet. He evolved into a genuine Buddhist in the real sense of the word. He was not only a treasure house of knowledge, but also a sea of wisdom. A person of compassionate nature, truly humble and deeply dedicated to the cause or goal he has once set, his humility was exemplary. He always gave credit for his achievements to others, and recognised even small qualities in others. He was never heard talking ill of anybody. Who was he?

Let me introduce you to him. His name was E. Gene Smith. He founded the Tibetan Buddhist Resource Center (TBRC) in USA. TBRC does admirable work for the preservation of Tibetan literary traditions. They have succeeded in collecting a huge amount of Tibetan literary treasures, which they have made available to everyone in digital form. I knew him since the early 1970s. He was born in Ogden, Utah, in 1936 to a Mormon family. His life's mission commenced in 1965, the year he came to India and incidentally, the year in which Tibet House was established by His Holiness the Dalai Lama.

Gene was a diabetic patient like me. He died on 16 December 2010, soon after a visit to India. I organised a memorial ceremony for him on behalf of Tibet House, where Dzongsar Khyentse Rinpoche also spoke. He had many more qualities than just scholarship. I salute him more for his humility than his vast knowledge.

About two years before his death, he made the decision to step down from the position of the director of TBRC and identified a young and energetic man, Jeff Wallman, as his successor. Not long after Gene-la's passing, Jeff came to see me at Tibet House.

I gave him some advice based on my experience. I told him teamwork was very important but, at the same time, it was vital to retain the focus of the institution. In the name of cooperation, we should not let someone suddenly appear on the scene, take us for a ride and try to hijack Gene-la's lifelong work.

I hope this team led by Jeff will carry on what Gene-la had built, with renewed determination and energy. New vision and ideas in this fast-changing world are certainly welcome and necessary. But what is more important for the preservation of Tibetan culture is to see that the values set in the Tibetan Buddhist tradition are recognised and taken forward with a modern approach. It is crucial for the TBRC, and for that matter the Tibetan society, that modernisation does not become radicalisation.

Later, in 2015, when I was visiting the USA, Jeff came to see me in New York. He told me that my advice proved very useful as he had to face many situations of the kind I had mentioned. When I visited the TBRC in July 2018, they had moved to Boston and a new director had taken over just two days earlier. The team, some Tibetans and some Americans, arranged an enjoyable lunch and after that we had a small conversation. I realised that Jann Ronis, the new director, was very familiar with Tibetan affairs. It was then that they told me that the name of the institute had undergone a slight change. It had been changed to Buddhist Digital Resource Center (BDRC), dropping the word Tibetan. The reason, they said, was to soften the stand and widen their scope. I did not say anything, just shrugged my shoulders.

Another person I met and had treasured interactions with was Krishnanath-ji. He was a follower of Jiddu Krishnamurti. Krishnamurti is a universally accepted world teacher. The Krishnamurti Foundation is engaged in discussing and keeping his thoughts and philosophy alive. It has centres in India and abroad. I was fortunate to have a good association with the study centre in the outskirts of Bengaluru and the centres in Chennai and Hyderabad. I spent weeks at a stretch in the Bengaluru study centre and participated in their discussions and workshops. I also had the pleasure of staying in the Chennai and Hyderabad centres. The common features I appreciated in all these centres were the way they were set up – simple yet comfortable, disciplined yet non-regimented and a peaceful yet not secluded atmosphere. People were friendly, helpful and considerate.

Krishnanath-ji was loved and respected by all in the Krishnamurti Foundation. I have known him since my Varanasi days, in the early 1970s. He took part in the Independence Movement of India. At that time, he was already associated with the socialist movement in India. I remember attending a meeting at Kashi Vidyapith, Varanasi, for felicitating him on becoming the general secretary of the All India Movement for Banning English for Official Purposes.

It was at the study centre in Bengaluru that I got to spend most time with him. We spoke on a large number of subjects. He had a profound knowledge of both traditional and modern subjects, and was a true disseminator of wisdom. His public speeches were a treat to listen to, reflecting his wisdom without being loud. If his speech was in English, his principles made him speak few words in Hindi in the beginning such as '*Mein angreji nahin janta hoon*,' meaning 'I do not know English'. But his English was more than perfect. For me, any conversation with him was an opening to a fresh understanding of the subject. Whatever little knowledge I gained of Krishnamurti's philosophy was mainly through him. It was easy to understand his explanations, perhaps due to his Buddhist approach to subjects and goals.

Very often my conversation with Krishnanath-ji helped me to understand my own culture one layer deeper. I fondly remember a short conversation with him on *Dekhne ki Kala* (Art of Looking), one of J. Krishnamurti's Parisamvad booklet series.

The conversation drifted to the subject of the difference between 'avalokan karna' and 'dekhna', that is, observing intently and looking. *Chenrezik* (*spyan ras gzigs*) in Tibetan is the translation of the word 'Avalokiteswara', the name almost every Tibetan chants. But if you do not understand the real meaning, you may get the idea that the meaning is 'somebody is just looking from above'. Looking is a more detached action whereas observing intently is more participative.

Similarly, the reference to the distinction between 'vigyan' and 'kala', that is, science and art according to the ancient Indian classical book called *Sukraniti* was also an eye opener for me. Krishnanath-ji was a special friend and a mentor for me till he passed away at Bengaluru in 2015. I can say that the Tibetan Buddhist thinking-circle became poorer and the void felt by innumerable individuals and institutions that he was associated with, is difficult to fill.

In India, there is a Hindu festival called Raksha Bandhan or Rakhi. It celebrates a brother and sister's loving and protective relationship. This sometimes gets extended to men and women who may not be relatives but have a close bond like a brother–sister. I had a rakhi sister and her name was Ashma Singh. She was from a Sikh family. I knew her through her sister, Renuka Singh, an academic scholar. I was acquainted with Renuka through Indo-Tibetan and inter-religious activities. Ashma was a graphic designer. I found her graphic designs very appealing. She did the cover design for *The Sheltering Tree*, a book of verses that talks of taking care of trees and other elements. The design was a spreading canopy of the bodhi tree. She designed a simple but tasteful museum ticket for Tibet House using some figures from woodcut blocks. This ticket was liked very much and appreciated by visitors. Many of them preserved it as a souvenir. The logo of

Padmapani lecture series of Tibet House depicting a hand holding a lotus of the Ajanta painting was also her creation.

As a person, Ashma was very gentle and kind with a great sense of humour. Every year on my birthday, she would bring me a bottle of buttermilk as she knew I liked it. After marrying a Mongolian doctor, she moved to Mongolia where she suffered an illness that ultimately took her life. She breathed her last in an Indian hospital. I did chants of some Buddhist sutras at her home, sitting beside her body. I felt sad at losing a very special person. I commissioned a thangka of Tara in her memory and gifted it to her family on her first death anniversary. Also, in her memory, I compiled a Tara stotra text in Tibetan, Sanskrit and English and got it published as a small booklet. The Sanskrit version of this stotra text was edited by Prof. Angrup, who was temporarily working in Tibet House library.

Prof. Angrup wrote Tibetan perfectly and had studied at Sanskrit University in Varanasi and at Delhi University. He stayed in a simple room at Tibet House. His needs were minimal and he was either studying or chanting or meditating at any time. He literally lived on black tea and tsampa (roasted barley flour). Once I asked him, 'What about some milk in your tea?' He said, 'No, no.' When I asked him, 'Why? Don't you like milk?' He said, 'It is not that I don't like it, but if I keep adding to the things I like, there will be no end to it.' He was humble and a yogi in the real sense of the word. I heard that a few years after he returned to his home village in Lahul, he passed away.

Tibetans living in India should have closer contacts with Indians, especially in cultural matters. For instance, Tibetans living in Indian towns and cities should connect their life with locals and take part in the local festivities. Diwali is a beautiful event to join in and connect with the neighbourhood. When the whole area is lit up, our not bothering about the occasion is like observing a boycott with a blackout. To the locals, it would underscore our alien status, and it will be bad behaviour on our part. Tibetans should also join in certain issues with Indians when there are genuine humanity-related problems or secular issues. Otherwise, our Indo–Tibetan relationship talks will remain limited to a few people sitting on a stage and giving some rhetorical speeches.

The tendency in recent times to observe 'Thank You, India' or events based on such sentiments may be with good intentions, but I don't agree with them because Tibetans have been living in this country for more than 60 years and that is a long time. Tibetans should identify themselves with, as much as possible in terms of human feelings, the needs and social problems of the local people because they have been living here for so long. One fine morning we cannot just wake up to say 'thank you'. That sounds to me like we are ready to pack and leave – that is not a good idea at all. Saying thank you is different from expressing appreciation.

Nurturing gratitude and installing the Buddha statue in the Buddha Jayanti Park was a symbol of appreciating Tibetan relationship with Indians. I was surprised when the events planned by the Government-in-Exile did not allude to it. For some reason, they forgot to mention the spot in the Buddha Jayanti Park. I was sad that nobody reminded anybody.

45

India International Centre and Some Interesting People I Met

My interest in inter-religious and cross-cultural contacts brought me in touch with interesting institutions and individuals. One such institution was Swami Veda Bharati's ashram in Rishikesh. In the Indian tradition of swamis or sadhus, only a select few are honoured with the title of 'Mahamandaleshwar'. Swami Veda Bharati was one of the thirty or so swamis who were conferred with that title.

It was not just the name and fame of Swami Veda Bharati that attracted me. He combined the best of ancient and modern, scholarship and experience of spirituality. I met him at his public discourses, but came in touch more closely after visiting his ashram in February 2007. He invited me along with the late Jampa Rinpoche, accompanied by a group of monks from Loseling Monastery, Mundgod, Karnataka, to perform the consecration ceremony of the newly installed statues of the Buddha, Guru Padmasambhava and Bodhi Dharma at the main entrance of the ashram hall. In my mind, this represented Swamiji's inter-religious and cross-cultural approach.

I was invited to visit his ashram again for a longer period, in March 2011, soon after my abrupt exit from Tibet House. I spent more than a month there. This period proved to be very enjoyable as I drew inspiration from being in close proximity every day in a very congenial atmosphere. It was during this time that this book began to take shape. I also conducted Buddha Purnima celebrations during this period at his ashram, reciting Jayamangala Gatha in Pali with the ashramites. I was also happy that on this occasion, I offered a community meal or 'bhandara', as it is called.

It is noteworthy that Swami Veda's name does not figure in the official name of the ashram. Instead, he dedicated the ashram to his guru, Swami Rama, who had a worldwide fame. So the ashram was called 'Swami Rama Sadhaka Grama', literally, the 'Seeker's village of Swami Rama'. The ashram was in an ideal location – near the banks of river Ganga at Rishikesh, a very peaceful and pleasant place. It was an ideal place for the practice of yoga and meditation. Everything moved smoothly there, without any kind of pull or twist. Sessions of yoga and meditation, meals, tea times and so on, were as per schedule, in the right spirit. People carried out their duties devotedly and devotionally. The place was a model for such spiritual institutions. One day, Swamiji said to me, 'Don't try to establish an ashram, it is not easy to run.' I took the essence of that advice but I could not help saying that the ashram was very inspiring.

My favourite haunt for three decades in Delhi has been the IIC. When I was working as the librarian at old Tibet House which was functioning in a rented house at Jorbagh, I attended an international conference of librarians in or around 1972, at IIC. This was my first acquaintance with IIC and my first-ever experience of attending an international conference. Later, when I was posted as the director of Tibet House in 1981 located in the present building, I started organising conferences on different subjects related to Tibetan and Buddhist studies and culture in this reputed centre.

Apart from national and international conferences and seminars, I had the pleasure of organising festivals, exhibitions, cultural shows, special lectures, workshops and so on in IIC. Members' dinners were occasionally organised in collaboration with foreign missions. I thought I could introduce Tibetan cuisine in these dinners as it would enhance the appreciation of Tibetan culture by people worldwide. So, I initiated such dinners several times which members used to look forward to. Thus, on the whole, I can say that I introduced Tibetan Culture to IIC, and IIC to the Tibetan world.

Soon after I was posted at Tibet House as its director, I became a member of IIC, in around 1982. The librarian of the centre, Dr H.K. Kaul, facilitated my membership in the category of associate member. After one year, I applied for the full membership and to my pleasant surprise, I was granted life membership straightaway, which had its own advantages.

IIC is a place where we can meet everybody who counts in matters of intellectual interest. Artists, journalists, retired civil servants and ex-army officials love to gather at the centre. Politicians make appearances to get a chance to impress others without having to make an appointment. Some self-styled intellectuals hang around to gossip about world affairs. They earned the nickname 'jholawalas' from *India Today* magazine in the 1980s when many of them moved around with a cotton bag slung on their shoulders. Some of my IIC acquaintances treated the lounge as their sitting room and could be found there from breakfast to dinner. For me, it was a suitable option after hectic office hours, to cool off while meeting interesting people over a cup of tea and my favourite cheese straws. It was here that I made good contacts, useful for running Tibet House. I can say that this place was virtually my second office, where I got many things done for Tibet House. I am grateful to IIC for that.

Among the interesting people I met at IIC was the late Prof. Ramachandra Gandhi, lovingly called 'Ramu-ji'. He was a truly unique person. I always found him sitting outside, alone, in contemplation, looking up to the sky. I would occasionally disturb him with questions and seek his suggestions and advice on a concept or some scholarly matters. He would close his eyes for a while and then come up with a clearly worded reply. I invited him couple of times as a resource person for Tibet House programmes. Once he gave the Padmapani lecture where he displayed three modern art paintings and based on them, he gave his speech on a philosophical topic. For me, it was a first experience that philosophical points may be expressed using paintings.

I was involved in the compilation of His Holiness's biography in Tibetan at that time and I remember discussing and exploring the book title with Ramu-ji. For the Hindi version he suggested

'Karunasagara' and for the English he suggested 'Joy of Compassion: A Biography of His Holiness Tenzin Gyatso, the XIV Dalai Lama of Tibet'. These gave me the idea for the Tibetan title '*rgya-chen snying-rjei rol-mtso*' which went very well with the verses of the long-life prayer of His Holiness the Dalai Lama composed by Regent Tagdrag Rinpoche. I gave this Tibetan title to Ngawang Thondup Narkyid who was handling the project in the Kuyig, Dharamsala. This title is now being used as the series title of the multivolume biography. I mention this here because I would like Ramu-ji's significant contribution be acknowledged.

Ramu Gandhi had a special way of looking at things, philosophically and also visually. Once he gave me a black-and-white photo postcard of the Tiananmen Square uprising. He had made many copies and was distributing them at IIC. The photo had Tiananmen Square full of tanks, military personnel and a small innocent-looking child with hands folded in namaskar, an image capturing the tragic event with a powerful message of compassion. As a person, Ramu-ji was very simple, a bit moody at times and straightforward. He was not very social and did not indulge in small talk with people. But his philosophical understanding was very profound.

In the course of our conversations, I tried to get some understanding of Vedanta from him. One thing he said which struck me was that the atman was not an entity, so we cannot talk about it in terms of whether it was there or not there. Everybody said that the atman was beyond everything, but he had a different way of explaining it that made more sense to someone like me, though I cannot claim to have completely understood the finer points he made. At my request, he recommended some good books on Indian darshana systems. I tried to read some of them but could not do justice to them.

At times I found Ramu Gandhi very happy, even making jokes – 'mast'. Once I had gone away for a few days and when I came back, he asked, 'Where have you been and for what? For masti?' I said 'No.' And he said, 'Oh, I am disappointed.' He had a special arrangement with IIC as far as his food was concerned. He would take channa bhatura with tomato for lunch and rice and dal with some tomatoes for dinner after most people had left the dining hall. He was not in favour of electronic gadgets, but one day he said, 'I may keep a very simple cell phone so that I can make an emergency call to the doctor when needed.' And eventually, he did get one.

Just a few days before he passed away, when I met him he complained of the heat because his place in Bengali Market did not have air conditioning. I suggested that he should move to IIC or Vishwa Yuvak Kendra or Gandhi Peace Foundation until the heat relented. He accepted my suggestion and took a room in IIC. Before long, I believe, the end came in the night in his room. It was sad that he was not able to make use of his cell phone to call the doctor as he had intended.

Ramu-ji had a lot of praise for Amit Jairam, a young poet. I knew him well, too. In fact, Amit and I had translated some Tibetan verses on ecology that I had composed with substantive points from His Holiness. It was very easy to make him understand what I wanted to convey and he would immediately write down the translation by pen on paper. We decided to call it a transcreation and not a translation because it was not a literal conversion but a re-creation in English. It was published later, under the title *The Sheltering Tree*, and was specially released by His Holiness at the inauguration of the conference 'Ecological Responsibility' that I organised in 1993 in conjunction with the presentation of the Buddha statue at the Buddha Jayanti Park, New Delhi. I later sat with Amit to translate some verses into Hindi in praise of Mount Kailash, composed by His Holiness, as his Hindi was also very good. The piece was published with an introduction by Ambassador Bhandari in an illustrated book on Mount Kailash.

Amit was a joyful person. His visiting cards interplayed with the sounds of his name – 'omit', 'a myth' and a few others. I visited him in hospital when he was unwell. Unfortunately, he died young. It was a pity to lose such a talented young person.

At IIC I also met Rajinder Puri regularly. I enjoyed his cartoons in the magazine *Illustrated Weekly of India* during my days in Dharamsala in the 1970s. I used to think that he was really fearless. The magazine later folded up. After that his cartoons became less regular. I found his analytical articles very thought-provoking. One such article was about who really ruled China. He said there were wealthy people in China who remained hidden but controlled the Communist Party from behind the screen. That was how, he said, the Cultural Revolution was carried out. This was a very new thought because normally people believed that in a communist country, it was the party that ruled. In China, some said, it was the army (People's Liberation Army or PLA) that ruled. But Rajinder Puri's view was totally different. So, if he was right, it was interesting that in a communist country there could be so many power centres. He is no more now.

I have mentioned but a few of the interesting people I met at the IIC and elsewhere. Many more do not find mention here, but they know and I know that we have had good meetings and conversations over tea and coffee on many days. If I were to mention all the nice and interesting people I have met, it may become a very long list.

46

Travelling in and around Asia

I have always enjoyed travelling. I like to see new places, meet new people and observe new customs and ways of thinking. I think that has contributed greatly to my education. I love travelling by road for then I can stop wherever I want. My luggage is light. I have a few changes of clothes and generally books related to the purpose of my visit. I always carry with me the small Buddha that His Holiness gave me. My travels have generally been smooth, though once I missed a flight when I fell asleep at the airport at Singapore, en route to Indonesia.

In August 1992, I was a part of a delegation that attended the 6th General Conference of Asian Buddhist Conference for Peace (ABCP) at Ulaanbaatar. We participated as Tibetan Buddhists from India. Our group was headed by Garje Khamtrul Rinpoche, the secretary of the Council of Religious Affairs, Dharamsala. We carried with us a message from His Holiness the Dalai Lama to be read out at the inauguration. During this conference the delegates were divided into smaller groups and each group was given a theme related to the general subject of the conference. The group which I was in was given 'Panchsheel'.

At the official reception given by the mayor of Ulaanbaatar I consumed, as I realised later, horse meat, and that too raw. I felt a bit of uneasiness as in Tibet we do not eat horse meat. In Ulaanbaatar, at official banquets they also serve sheep's tail, which is actually a large chunk of meat placed in front of the chief guest, who in ancient times must have taken what he preferred before others were served. These days, however, the chief guest merely makes a symbolic gesture and then the meat is cut into pieces that are distributed to all guests. This gesture of the chief guest distributing pieces of food was copied in Tibet with items other than sheep's tail; at large functions, the food is served symbolically to His Holiness before being distributed to others.

So far, I have visited this part of the world four times, including participating in the ABCP conference in 1990 when Kushok Bakula Rinpoche became president of ABCP. Venerable Erdenev Jinpa Gyatso, who was the Deputy Khambo Lama earlier, had become Khambo Lama of Buryatia. It was thanks to Khambo

Lama's kindness that I managed to bring some rare Tibetan Buddhist texts from there and got them published by Tibet House.

Indonesia is another country I found culturally interesting. I visited it in 1983 with Geshe Palden Drakpa. Readers may remember him as being the learned monk who was working in Tibet House library as Dharma Preceptor when I came to Tibet House. We were fortunate to visit Borobudur, a UNESCO heritage site 45 kilometres from Yogyakarta. It was a very striking experience. There was a stupa built in the design of a mandala; art historians have different theories regarding this unique structure.

What I know is that a Tibetan lama by the name of Manlung Guru visited this place around the thirteenth century. He sailed from a place in eastern India with an intention of visiting Sri Dhanyakataka, which was in the south Indian state of Andhra Pradesh. Instead, he reached Yogyakarta on the island of Java and mistook the Borobudur stupa to be Sri Dhanyakataka. He made sketches of it with a description of the Vajradhatu Mandala. Whatever the origin of this stupa might have been, to see this world famous monument was like a dream come true. I noticed that Buddhism in that country was a blend of the original Buddhism and Taoism, along with local traditions. One significant development in Indonesia during my few days stay was that the Indonesian government formally recognised Buddhism to be one of the religions in Indonesia. This was a good coincidence!

I must also add that Dhanyakataka, the old name for Amaravati, was a direct translation of Drepung, where I had studied in Tibet. Both mean 'grain town'. The Buddha is said to have visited Dhanyakataka.

I wish I had the opportunity to visit some other places in Indonesia, particularly Svarnadvipa (the island of gold) where Atisha Dipankara visited to receive teachings from his guru, Suvarnadvipi Dharmakirti. Atisha Dipankara was a very important teacher who promoted the Indian tradition of Buddhism in Tibet.

In March 1984, His Holiness asked me to be a part of the entourage that was to visit Japan where He was to consecrate a new pagoda at the Narita-san temple complex. A famous temple in Japan that attracted a lot of patronage, Narita-san housed the complete set of the original Narthang Kangyur donated by His Holiness. They had invited around twenty monks from Namgyal Monastery and the arrangements were perfect according to Japanese tradition, where the consecration and homa are performed according to the Guhyasamaja Tantra over three days. For some years Narita-san had been very generous in supporting a number of Tibet-related projects in India and sponsoring Tibetan students in Japan. I requested His Holiness to put a word to Narita-san authorities to support Tibet House, which He agreed to do.

On this visit, there were some events that would affect the relationship between Narita-san and the Tibetan establishments in India. In the middle of His Holiness's busy programme sponsored entirely by Narita-san, Pema Gyalpo, the representative of His Holiness in Japan, arranged a separate programme in an indoor stadium to showcase a lesser-known head of another Japanese temple. It was a fire puja performed by His Holiness and the head of that temple separately, in parallel, not jointly, on the same stage. This looked very odd to me and the stage setting was also most inappropriate. The ceremony was arranged like a circus show where the audience watched while seated around in the dark, while bright lights were focused on the stage. It was obvious that the Narita-san authorities were not informed of this extra programme. I observed they were very upset by this incident, which was like hijacking His Holiness from them. After the programme, when we returned to the hotel, the deputy abbot of Narita-san, in his limited English, kept asking in frustration, 'Why, why, why?'

The Japanese are very sensitive in such matters and this incident must have angered Narita-san a lot. Subsequently, the relationship between Narita-san and Tibetans in exile became more and more distant. Evidently, Narita-san authorities thought their contacts with Tibetan Buddhism were best developed inside Tibet and China as I heard later that they tried to invite the late Panchen Lama from China (as far as I know the visit did not materialise). And the other temple afterwards also distanced itself from Tibetans, or perhaps it was the other way round.

Korea has a long history of Buddhism, both for its study and its practice. Wentshek, a famous commentator born in 613 ce, whom most people took to be Chinese, was in fact from Korea. He had visited China and studied Asanga's works with Hiuen Tsang. According to Buston, he was a disciple of Vasubandhu, which means he must have visited India. The dominant Buddhist tradition in Korea is the Chogye order, which is the sangha order with a huge hierarchical structure. The second Buddhist order Taego is the laypeople's order, where music and dance are more significant. Jingak, the third, though much smaller, is interesting. They regularly chant 'Om Mani Padme Hum' but they do not know much about Avalokiteswara. The main figure in their temple is Amitabha.

During my first visit to Korea in August 1984 to attend the 'God Conference' in Seoul, I visited the headquarters of the Jingak order. They showed interest in knowing the link between the mantra they chanted and Amitabha, so they wanted to have a translation of *Manikkabum* in English. I commissioned a translation on their behalf and though work started on it, nothing came of it.

Attempts were made to restart, but unfortunately the people I had given the task either did not live long enough or became busy with other things.

I also visited an ancient site outside Seoul. This was the wooden temple, Kyonju. It was very impressive. I learnt that they had a long tradition of carving woodblocks for printing. In Tibet this tradition of carving wood came much later, perhaps in the fourteenth century.

The tantra practice of Buddhism was very evident in the arts, especially in architecture. When I entered any large temple in Korea, I noticed the presence of the four guardian kings, represented either in painting or sculpture, which was the same in Tibetan tradition and originated from Chinese mythology.

Another Buddhist practice I noticed in Korea was repeating full physical prostrations hundreds of times at one go while chanting prayers, which was also done in the Tibetan tradition. The difference, I observed, was in the way it was done and I must say that the Korean way was slightly more tiring physically.

One of my visits to Korea was in 1997 at the invitation of the Korean Institute of Buddhist Studies. They sponsored my visit, paid my airfare and put me up in a hotel. The purpose was supposed to be the establishment of sustained contacts between Korean Buddhists and Tibetans in India. The head of the institute, who was familiar with India, insisted on signing an agreement to this effect. On the second or third day after my arrival, he arranged my visit to his office. When I arrived there, he lit incense and brought the agreement written in English in an attractive folder. The terms were simple – they would bring Korean groups to India; we would receive them in Tibet House, show them around and coordinate their visits to Buddhist sites. In return, they would support some of Tibet House's projects. When I looked at the text of the agreement, the English language was very poor, with many spelling mistakes. I suggested redrafting it. He said the moment was auspicious and we must sign the document. He promised to correct the errors later. So, I went ahead and signed the document. After my return to India, I reminded him about re-doing the text of the agreement and followed up on this a couple of times. There was no response and that was the end of the agreement.

Separately, I also met the president of Dongguk University, which already had some contact with Tibetans in India. I wanted to present the new edition of a set of Kangyur to the university. I intended to establish a relationship involving exchange and collaboration in cultural matters with them. I made a symbolic presentation of the Kangyur index volume and the president graciously and ceremoniously accepted the gift. However, this initiative was not taken further due to difficulties in communication.

Another of my visit to Korea was to find participants for the WFSM that I was planning to organise in India, to usher in the new millennium. Though there were many who appeared keen, it was not easy to establish a reliable contact.

I visited Korea again in June 2001 and I stayed in the Jungto Society at the invitation of their head monk, Ven. Pomnyun Snim ('snim' means monk in Korean). He was different from the other snims I had come across – he was neither business-minded nor driven by any political motivation. He kept a low profile and was actively involved in social service. He had established a place for destitute children in the city of Gaya in India.

I observed during my short stay there that members maintained a strict discipline and made sure that everyone staying there attended the early morning service, which included breakfast with an elaborate ceremony. While it was still dark, the person who was on duty to wake everyone up would go to the door of each room, sound a hand-held wooden gong near the door and would not leave until the resident switched on the light. He made sure everyone was up for the day. When everyone assembled for breakfast, the service started with chanting and unwrapping a package containing a set of three bowls of different sizes nestled in one another and a pair of steel chopsticks wrapped in a big cloth napkin. From receiving this package, unwrapping it, setting out the bowls and being served the first items of breakfast, up to washing the food down with light tea, rinsing the bowl and drinking the water so as not to waste even a grain of rice, and then re-packing everything, it was all done systematically while chanting, by everyone at the same time.

I found Korean food habits worth observing. They liked eating and they ate a lot. Their food consisted of items such as noodles, many meat items and seafood. They were very hospitable and liked to feed their guests. I travelled from Seoul to Busan (formerly Pusan) by car. On the roadside, if a person was a good eater, they could stop anywhere and enjoy a variety of seafood, including dried octopus. Some of the food items were repulsive to look at, but probably very tasty. I didn't try any of them.

At Busan, I stayed in a temple. All of us, the monks of the temple and I, ate just before sunset. After eating, the monks left the temple to go to their houses or wherever they were staying. At night I woke up shivering. Due to my diabetes perhaps my sugar levels were dipping. I explored room after room but found them all locked. Finally, I managed to find the kitchen and opened the refrigerator to find something to appease my hunger. The next day when I reported the adventures of the night to my hosts, they filled my room with all sorts of eatables!

In December 1984, I received an invitation from the Soviet Union for a goodwill visit. There was no special agenda beyond understanding their culture. The visit covered Moscow, Leningrad (now St. Petersburg), Kiev and the Buddhist Republics of Buryatia and Kalymyk. The trip was then extended to Ulaanbaatar in Mongolia. It was extremely cold, the peak of winter in fact, but the reception was warm. I was offered a big fur coat, a fur hat and gloves. One morning I was taken to visit the

Lenin Mausoleum where there was a very long queue as usual, but I was taken inside as a special guest. Without consciousness of any gesture on my part, I found myself standing before Lenin's body with my fur hat off. I then asked myself, what was I doing standing like that there? I consoled myself with the thought that Lenin also had Buddha nature.

I also visited the Academy of Sciences in Leningrad where a staff member of the academy showed me around. Early next morning there was a knock on my hotel room door. When I opened the door, one of the scientists I had met earlier was standing there. He came in quickly and was careful to make sure the door was firmly bolted. He then started making prostrations before me. I was taken aback and was not sure what was happening. He then took out his rosary, and said, 'I am a Buddhist but I cannot show my faith in public. Please bless this.' I was moved. I did not have anything with me to give to him because I had left all my small Buddha statues for distribution in Moscow. All I had with me was the small Buddha statue given to me by His Holiness at the time of my ordination. I carried it with me everywhere ever since and, of course, it was dear and precious to me. Instinctively, I put it in his hands and he gratefully placed it on his head and then quickly in his pocket. I could see how happy he was. He made a quick exit because he did not want himself to be seen by my guide who was put up in a room nearby. As I saw him leave, I felt happy for him. But with the Buddha gone, I felt a sense of emptiness, a void within me that lingered for quite a long time. When I narrated this incident to His Holiness the next time I met Him in India, He said it had been a good sacrifice and gave me another Buddha statue and blessed it with prayer verses. This small statue is my most precious possession and companion wherever I go.

On the train journey to Kiev I noticed that my guide, who was a Buddhist from Buryatia and had received modern education in Moscow, was talking more freely with me. He talked about the actual degree of freedom in their country, a topic he would not bring up in hotel rooms and other places where he appeared reserved and careful in his conversations. Later, when I visited a city in Germany that had once been part of East Germany, a staff member in the hotel I was staying in, who had worked there during the previous regime, told me that they used to plant listening devices in the hotel rooms to listen to conversations. Before I left Moscow, a courtesy call was arranged for me to meet the head of the Religious Department. I knew the function of that department would not be to promote religious activities but mainly to regulate them. I was told my visit to Soviet Union was reported in the *Pravda* newspaper, which was a communist mouthpiece.

In Ulan-Ude, I was received by the Buryatia Republic's president. I noticed a miniature tank placed as a piece of decoration on his table and I said casually, 'You people like tanks very much.' I noticed he seemed uneasy and he made it a point of telling me quickly that it was not that they were very fond of tanks, but taking a defensive stand was also important. My guide, who I believed was an important person from their side, was very careful not to give me any wrong impression of their policy and way of functioning.

One of my dearest memories of the goodwill visit in Ulan-Ude was when I had the rare opportunity to see the historic Sandalwood Jowo (the idol of the standing Buddha which has been mentioned in Tibetan literature that talks about Buddhism going from China to Mongolian areas). I had read about this most precious work of art many times in my life. To be able to finally see it and appreciate its beauty with my own eyes was indeed very moving. The statue is life-size and its fair substance gracefully reflected the artificial light of the storage room where it was kept, together with many other art works, as if in captivity. I felt immense pleasure just gazing at it. Later, I heard it was moved to a monastery, and I was very pleased.

Another country of great Buddhist cultural and historical interest is Bhutan. The customs of Bhutan were not completely new to me, after about the nine years that I had spent on its border at Buxa Duar. The Bhutanese in that region used the route through Buxa to reach the Indian plains. Bhutan is a small landlocked kingdom, enclosed and protected by high mountains. This particular position has ensured the preservation of cultural and religious traditions and prevented them from getting polluted. The wise ruler, being aware of the inevitability of change, is judicious in letting new ideas and ways take place in gradual steps, so as not to make them too drastic.

In May 2005, I received a kind invitation from Mynak Tulku, the director of the National Library of Bhutan, to take part in a conference on Bhutan's literary and scriptural heritage as a 'mirror of the past and bridge to the future'. I presented a paper on Serkong Dorjee Chang, a great lama of Tibet who was sent by the 13th Dalai Lama to Bhutan and who became one of the rajgurus, or royal preceptors. I was pleasantly surprised by the impressive standard of scholarship among the younger people. There were a number of papers presented by older scholars whose standard and knowledge of literary sources was admirable.

The Bhutanese start all important functions with the *marchang* ceremony ('mar' is butter and 'chang' is beer), where a bowl of *chang* decorated with butter is offered to the guardian of the state, Mahakala. I observed this at the inauguration of the conference as well at the opening of the National Assembly in the Tashichho Dzong, which I attended thanks to a special invitation through Mynak Tulku. The King was present in the Assembly and seated on an altar-like structure in the middle of the stage, but he did not make any speech. The Crown Prince (who later became the king) was seated on his right, on a simpler throne. The prime minister, who is the first among equals among the seven ministers, made the opening speech. I could follow most of the speeches made in Bhutanese. I noticed one of the topics was the King's bravery in confronting and defeating infiltrators from outside the border.

The discipline during such events, in terms of the movement of the people serving tea, khapse and so on, was very well choreographed and of a high level, like the Japanese. There was a great discipline in the society as well. I liked the fact that adults were expected to wear traditional dress in public as a way of expressing their culture. Among Tibetans and Indians, by contrast, there was a difference – on formal occasions it was the women rather than the men who were seen in traditional dresses.

Later, reforms were carried out and a new constitution was adopted in which the King was still above the law but he was not a part of the government, which was elected through a multi-party system of democratic elections.

The most memorable was my visit to the Kyichu Lhakhang, one of the temples the 33rd King of Tibet Songtsen Gampo, built at eight sites in different directions from Lhasa, before building Jokhang, the main temple, in order to subdue the hostile forces in the area. While entering this relatively small chapel, I had exactly the same feeling as if I was entering one of the chapels in the Jokhang temple – the iconography, the feel of the place, the low doorway, even the smell of butter lamps, everything was the same as in Tibet. Every Tibetan visiting Thimpu area must not miss the opportunity of going to this chapel.

There were two temples of this category in Bhutan, the other being the Jampa Lhakhang, a Maitreya temple in Bumthang, eastern Bhutan. I also visited some dzongs. They were both administrative centres and monastic institutions, of which Tashichho Dzong was the chief. I did not have the energy to make the steep climb to Taktsang, the Tiger's Nest Temple, a cave where Guru Padmasambhava meditated, and I regret that. Later, Taktsang started being promoted by the Bhutanese government, unlike the earlier two which were built by Tibetan kings.

The Theravada tradition prevails in Sri Lanka, Thailand and other South East Asian countries. During my visits to Sri Lanka and Thailand, I was impressed by the tradition that the sangha was highly respected by the public. On formal occasions in Sri Lanka, monks were seated before the VIPs, including Prime Minister Jayawardene, and would not have to get up to greet a politician. In Thailand too, the supreme patriarch of the sangha, the Sangharaja, and the king were equal in rank, but in public the king knelt before the senior monks. I was later informed that this tradition was slowly disappearing. Unfortunately, I hear that, as is true all over the world, the lure of power has made monks behave subservient to politicians.

47

Europe: The Danger of Being Left Behind

We were waiting at the crossing point from West Berlin to East Berlin for our papers to be cleared, when our bus driver thought that it was the opportune moment to give us a briefing. 'Ladies and gentlemen,' he drawled in his American accent, 'Be careful. Please stay together as a group while visiting museums etc. Any moment, if the authorities tell me to leave, I will just drive away for I will have to comply and you,' he said turning back to look at some of us in the front seats, 'may be left behind illegally.' If that threat was not enough, he told us it was very dangerous to carry Western literature, even newspapers, into that part of Germany.

When Prof. Jagannath Upadhyaya and I had travelled together by train to Frankfurt, we had remarked on the striking contrast between East and West Germany. While the buildings in the eastern part wore a grey and grim look, as soon as we entered West Berlin, everything suddenly became bright and elegant.

We had later joined this conducted tour to East Berlin. The contrast between strict control under the communist regime and the liberal atmosphere of the west was marked. Many years later, in 1989, when I saw on television the sight of the Berlin Wall coming down, I could hardly believe my eyes. I re-lived my visit there.

I visited Germany many times. On a trip to Berlin, I visited the Buddhistische Haus, a Theravada temple built in 1924. This was probably the oldest Buddhist temple in Europe after the St. Petersburg Buddhist temple in the European part of USSR and has been the seat of the German Dhammaduta Society from 1957. Subsequent to the founding of this temple, different Buddhist traditions entered Europe, including Zen Buddhism and Tibetan Buddhism. Since 1975, there exists a European Buddhist Union, a federation of Buddhist communities and organisations, some of which are also active in the society and engaged in admirable social work.

In 1986, I was invited to attend a conference organised by the Council for World's Religions, which was held near Frankfurt. After attending it I went to Hamburg to attend the International Congress for Asia and North Africa Studies. In Hamburg, I stayed at the Tibetan Centre established by my friend, the late Geshe Thubten Ngawang. Ven. Gen Ogyen Tseten happened to be staying there at that time.

In the quiet aftermath of the conference, I spent some time with Ven. Gen Ogyen Tseten. Although I knew him from Tibet, it was in Hamburg that I developed more reverence towards him by noticing his humility and deep knowledge of Buddhist philosophy. In the afternoons, he would take me to a nearby Chinese restaurant for an early dinner and talk about the fundamental teachings of the Buddha. The later years of his life were spent at Sera Monastery in south India. I once travelled there to receive from him the initiation of the Goddess with White Umbrella. He passed away in 2007 when I was in Bengaluru on a visit and I was able to attend his funeral at Sera Monastery.

Another beautiful experience I had in Germany was when I visited Stuttgart in 1996. I was accompanying a group of Tibetan monks from Sera and Drepung monasteries of south India, who were taking part in a special concert of music and chanting on the theme of death, called the 'Ritual of Transformation'. The programme included a unique fusion of Tibetan Buddhist rituals and Western classical and sacred music. The monks performed the traditional Yamantaka ritual. It was interspersed with Mozart's *Requiem*, performed by the Stuttgart Philharmonic Orchestra, and *Gregorian Chants* by Benedictines (Catholic monks). That was an amazing combination. As far as I know, this was the first time in the world that something like that took place.

This wonderful event was organised by the city government and very well received by the public and the media. By then I was already working on the WFSM and thought that this city would be a good place to hold a major event of the festival. And so a foundation was established for this purpose and formal meetings were held. I also developed good contacts with the House of World Culture at Berlin and other places like Dresden and Munich. Eventually, I learned that there was rivalry between the key persons in Stuttgart and Berlin and it became more practical for me to deal with the latter.

In 1990, I had gone to Arcidosso in Italy. Namkhai Norbu Rinpoche, whom I had earlier met in Amsterdam, invited me to the opening ceremony of the gonpa[1] at Merigar. His Holiness was giving a teaching on Dzogchen using the text called *Tshigsum Nedeg* to mark the inauguration of the new gonpa. Merigar was near Arcidosso. From the institute one could enjoy the view of Monte Amiata since Arcidosso was on a hill. His Holiness expressed his desire to climb the hill, but His schedule did not permit it.

I found Namkhai Norbu's approach to teaching Dharma very interesting. His scholarly knowledge of Tibet's ancient culture and the practice of Dzogchen teachings that came to him from his gurus were blended in a practical way. We had invited him to Tibet House in 1994 to give teachings. Namkhai Norbu Rinpoche passed away in a hospital on 27 September 2018.

When I visited Rome in 1996, my friend, Father George Kovalcal from India, was in the city. He was posted at the Vatican and took me to places I would never have seen otherwise. I visited St. Peter's Church for the first time. I saw parts of the Church and the Vatican which are normally not accessible to the public. I visited Italy again several times and saw places such as Florence, Pisa, Venice and Rome.

I must tell you something interesting. For a full ten years my face gazed at Amsterdam through a photo. It was almost as if I was doing avalokan, as Krishnanath-ji described it! In 1990, I went to attend the conference 'Art Meets Science and Spirituality in a Changing Economy' that was held in Amsterdam. His Holiness graced the occasion. One evening, our convener Louwrien Wijers, arranged to take His Holiness and the rest of us for a boat ride in the canals for sightseeing.

Some pictures of ours were naturally taken while we were in the boat. We did not just look around and enjoy Amsterdam along the canal, we also saw the photographs of famous people, like the Shah of Persia, King Albert of Belgium, French president Jacques Chirac and others. Some years after the event, Louwrien wrote me an email telling me that a five-metre-tall photograph of me was set up in the centre of Amsterdam with a caption 'Dalai Lama 1990'. I immediately wrote to the concerned authority, pointing out the mistake and requesting them to make the necessary corrections. When I checked again after some time, I came to know that they had changed the caption but not the photo. They probably didn't want to spend money on it and did the easier thing. I did not know how much I could go on protesting. So I left it at that. To my relief, in 2011 I was informed that all the photos had been removed after being there for over a decade.

Once on a flight, I met a nun, Sister Karin. In those days my mind was full of ideas for the Festival of Sacred Music. So as we greeted each other and got talking, I asked her if she would participate in the festival. She said 'Yes' and participated with a choir composed of nuns and monks. She even gave a beautiful speech at the 'Meeting of Minds' event, in the presence of His Holiness, that was held during the festival.

On a visit to the Netherlands, I went to the Christian monastic establishment led by her and Emmanuele. The institute was active in peace work. Their latest activity, I heard, was the establishment of a school for peace education. I visited her nunnery again when I stopped over in Amsterdam, flying in from North America as I felt I needed some rest. She invited me to stay for a few days. At that time I had some food restrictions, so they kept plenty of brown bread and sausages stocked in my room. Since I was not a vegetarian at the time, I practically lived on bread and sausages for about a week.

I went back to the lovely city of Amsterdam when I participated in an international event called 'Spirit of Peace and Love' in 1995. It was attended by well-known people like Namkhai Norbu Rinpoche and E.F. Schumacher, the author of *Small Is Beautiful*. I received the invitation through the artist Louwrien Wijers who had organised the earlier conference at Amsterdam.

Louwrien was a devout Buddhist and a good friend. Let me tell you something interesting about her, which will show how she was full of fun and seriousness at the same time. I was staying at her house in a room painted all in green. One fine morning I peeped into the room upstairs and noticed her holding a pendulum over a few dresses which had been laid on the bed. Her face bore a serious expression. I remember the scene vividly even now. I was wondering if that was a personal ceremony. It indeed was! She was just choosing what to wear that day.

Louwrien did her best to organise meetings with prospective collaborators in the initial stages of the planning of the WFSM. In 1999, she introduced me to Marina Abramovic. Marina was an internationally renowned performing artist from Belgrade, which was a part of former Yugoslavia. At that time she was residing in Amsterdam. Later she settled in the USA.

One evening, after a daylong programme of visits in and around the city, we went to visit Marina at her home. She showed me around and in a big room, I saw a large, empty table at the centre. She said that all works of art started within a blank space. To me, the statement meant that emptiness was the source of all creation, in the context of Buddhist mandala meditation. This meeting was memorable. Since then, we have become very good friends. I continue to have regular contact and collaborations with her, particularly in the matters of art and culture.

During my visit to Amsterdam in 2004, Marina introduced me to her friend Alessia Bulgari from Italy, who too became a good friend. In fact, she proved to be 'a friend in need is a friend indeed' as I will describe in a later chapter.

In 2004, I was invited to the Prince Claus Award ceremony, held in the Citizens Hall of the Royal Palace in Amsterdam. Among the awardees, those I remember most vividly are Mahmoud Darwish, for his literary achievements; the Bhutan Archery Federation, protector and promoter of a living tradition in Bhutanese culture; and Omara Khan Massoudi of Afghanistan, who steadfastly dedicated himself to the protection of Afghanistan's cultural heritage during the initial days of the Taliban regime, despite many dangers.

His Royal Highness Prince Johan Frisco, honorary chairman of Prince Claus Fund for Culture and Development said, 'The choice of the theme "Positive Results of Asylum and Migration" is appropriate at a time when almost all one hears and reads regarding migration has negative connotations. We sometimes forget that in their successful development, many countries relied extensively on migration. Even the Dutch Golden Age would have been less golden without it.' A dinner was hosted in the evening where I was seated at the same table as His Royal Highness Prince Constantijn, co-honorary chairman of the Fund. His easy manners and keen interest in the topics related to the theme of the event made the evening very pleasant.

In 1998, I led a group of monks from Drepung and Sera to Leipzig and Schneverdingen. The purpose of this tour was to prepare for the WFSM in Europe, familiarise Tibetan monks with Western civilisation and also to attend a major teaching by His Holiness in Schneverdingen, sponsored by the Tibetan Centre in Berlin which, as mentioned earlier, was established by Geshe Thubten Ngawang, a friend from my days in Tibet. Before the teaching commenced, His Holiness visited a pleasant, small retreat called 'Semkyeling' (which means 'Boddhichitta land' in Tibetan) situated outside of Berlin.

Immediately after His Holiness's arrival in Semkyeling, there was a reception ceremony with tea and ceremonial rice preparation during which I introduced all the monks to His Holiness. One evening, the monks presented a programme of chanting and monastic dance. The monks and I attended the teaching by His Holiness. After the teaching, the monks and I visited Austria to see the Mozart Museum.

After the passing away of Geshe Ngawang in 2002, I had no interaction with the Tibetan Centre, in Berlin. I heard it was renamed as 'Tashi Dargye'.

Louwrien continued to be active and organised a second international conference on 'Art Meets Science and Spirituality in a Changing Economy' in September 1996 in Copenhagen. Scientists, artists and scholars from different countries participated. Among them were David Bohm and Marina Abramovic. The same Marina who had shown me her empty table was eating an onion, this time on screen. The camera focused on her as she held an oversized onion. Her nails and lips were painted red. As she took large bites of the raw onion, her eyes, naturally, started watering. Simultaneously, she talked of how she was tired of things like taking planes, waiting, making decisions, pretending to be interested in conversations about art at openings and 'being ashamed of my nose being too big' and so on. As her list of complaints went on, she continued to tear into the onion aggressively and tears streamed down from her eyes. Her lipstick smeared and smudged. Once again she brought out the physicality of pain along with inner reflections, both emotional and spiritual. I found that very interesting.

After the conference, I had a few days of leisure and had the pleasure of meeting Lakha Rinpoche and the late Tarab Rinpoche, both of whom were two important tulkus from my college, Loseling of Drepung Monastery in Tibet. Lakha Rinpoche was a few years senior to me. He had set up a Buddhist Centre in Copenhagen. He gave me very good homemade thukpa and told me of an interesting dream he had some time before his disrobing and marriage. In his dream he saw his very strict teacher, who had passed away, telling him about his would-be wife. He was told that good things would come of marrying that woman.

The late Tarab Rinpoche was also senior to me. He also invited me to his centre and asked me to give a talk to his disciples. Although he was a Gelukpa lama, the main teaching in his centre was Chod, a practice that was mostly done by followers of Nyingma and Kagyu lineages. A session of Chod chanting was especially organised for me, with large, hand-held drums. I noted that there were no objects or images to identify his practice with any particular lineage of Tibetan Buddhism. He had held a position of director in Tibet House in Delhi. After his passing away, I heard his followers set up a trust in India to pursue his ideals.

In Tibet, we Tibetans sit cross-legged on the floor. Even now we do so. When I visited the meditation chapel of Prince Charles, I was struck by the fact that seating was on the ground. On the occasion of the Queens's Golden Jubilee in 2002, I was in London at the invitation of Phuntsog Wangyal of Tibet Foundation. I went there with a small delegation and presented a sand mandala to Prince Charles at High Grove on 3 June 2002. I had met Prince Charles once earlier during his visit to Delhi in 1993. His Royal Highness understood Tibet-related problems and expressed his concern and sympathy. That was when he gave his staff special instructions to show us his meditation chapel. We were taken around the park, where thc trees, vegetation and bushes were all kept in a semi-natural environment.

On that occasion, I visited the Buddhist Society of Britain. The authorities received me warmly and apprised me of their activities, some of which I already knew from their journal *The Middle Way*. They published articles about various aspects of the different Buddhist traditions. They also conducted courses on Dharma and related subjects. These courses were widely-known in London. I called on Prof. David Seyfort Ruegg to request guidance for future academic programmes. I learned that he was completing a translation of a treatise on the 'Eight Points of Importance in Madhyamika Philosophy' recorded by Gyaltsab Je, one of Tsongkhapa's two main disciples.

I also visited the British Library to do some reading. There I came upon some important documents – the correspondence between the Tibetan government in Lhasa and Agvan Dorzhiev regarding contact between the 13th Dalai Lama and the Czar of Russia – and managed to obtain copies of some of them. I also came across some interesting correspondence where the lama king Zhabdrung of Bhutan advised the Nepalese king to put an end to animal sacrifices during Kali puja.

I had been to England earlier also. In April 1988, the Global Survival Conference hosted by the Archbishop of Canterbury brought nearly 200 spiritual leaders and parliamentarians to the historic university city of Oxford. I had met the archbishop once earlier at a reception in the British High Commission in Delhi. He was a great figure in the world's major religions. At the reception, he interacted gracefully with guests. I was particularly impressed by his outstanding physical presence.

Cardinals, swamis, bishops, rabbis, imams, monks and elders participated in the conference; His Holiness the Dalai Lama and Mother Teresa graced the occasion with their presence. The idea was to explore the possibility of dialogue that included the perspectives of all these leaders. I had gone there as a member of the Global Forum Council which was founded in 1985.

In the United States, I have a second home in New York. Whenever I visit New York, I stay at Natalie's. She organises a gathering by inviting many of her friends. There is chanting and then I speak. Natalie is among the first group of students of Geshe Wangyal, perhaps the first Tibetan Buddhist teacher in the USA.

Joshua and Diana are also from that group. Since 2014, I have been regularly visiting the centre they manage in New Jersey.

I feel there are many like-minded people across the world and I was fortunate to have an opportunity to meet some of them. I had interesting experiences and learnt from them, too.

Part IX

A NEW CHAPTER

48

Beginning a New Chapter

In 2011, soon after the Tibetan new year, I was in Mundgod and had organised a workshop on the environment. Tibet House had always taken the lead in raising awareness about the environment, as His Holiness placed a lot of emphasis on environment protection. I had contacted people in the Tibetan community and put together a group called Green Force. I used the logo on interdependent-ness that we had used for the Buddha Jayanti Park event, where we had installed a statue of the Buddha seated in the earth-touching mudra.

On my return from Mundgod, I went to my office in Tibet House the next day. Alessia had come to see me. She had travelled with me to Kalimpong and Darjeeling before I had gone to Mundgod. I had had to go there for the governing body meeting of the Namgyal Institute of Tibetology.

I went to my office in Tibet House and sat down. There was a cup of hot coffee waiting for me and a letter from the Private Office. I opened the letter. It said in polite tones that I had contributed much to the development of Tibet House and that my service was appreciated, but I should now hand over the responsibilities to the new geshe. It gave a 'not later than' date for handing over. The letter was also kind enough to say that I could continue to stay in one of the rooms in Tibet House or that I could be provided a room in the building complex that had been developed for His Holiness and His establishment. Called 'phodrang' in Tibetan (meaning 'palace'), the complex was where tulkus and rinpoches stayed when required.

I faced a blank. And I faced Alessia! I had never made alternate plans for myself, other than being of service to His Holiness, so I was at a loss. Alessia was watching me and trying to understand the situation. I told Chungkey, my secretary, that the letter was from the Kuyig and about my departure from Tibet House. She started crying. She was keen to go and seek explanations from them. But I was not for that. As I have repeatedly said, I did not want to ask His Holiness for anything personal. And if this was what was demanded of me, so be it.

I replied saying I would hand over the charge very soon. I told them that I did not wish to stay in Tibet House but would definitely like a room in the complex of His Holiness. I would find it useful to have a room there when I went for the teachings given by His Holiness. I am still awaiting a reply to my letter.

I had worked on the promotion of harmony through Tibetan art and culture all my life. I was seventy years old at that time. To change course would not be possible and was also not to my liking. Alessia supported me. She understood my commitment to the cause I had espoused all along.

Anyway, I cleared my desk as soon as I could and within a week left for Chennai where I had a prior appointment for an ayurvedic treatment. Chungkey found a house for me in Gurgaon to move into and looked after the logistics. Alessia made arrangements forevery possible expense of mine. It may not be out of place to mention that Tibetan monks were quite rich by then. But I had negligible savings to my credit. Till that moment I had not realised I should have personal savings. I told Alessia that my requirements were minimal. Whatever she could, she should donate to the trust I had created so that I could continue my work.

That was the story of Alessia that I wanted to share. I am indeed grateful for her friendship and I am thankful to Marina for introducing me to her. She continues to be in touch with me. And even today I continue to serve His Holiness, without the banner of Tibet House, thanks in large measure, to Alessia.[1] It may also be worth mentioning that every time I needed some kind of personal issue addressed, Alessia was there. Chungkey wonders if there is a connection with my gifting her a white Tara thangka and her being present at all troublesome moments of my life thereafter.

I must tell you why I had fixed up to go to Chennai for ayurvedic treatment. An incident that took place on the morning of 16 June 2005 affected my life forever. And since then, I have been trying out different treatments, hoping something would work. I have, of course, tried Tibetan medicine, too.

I was in Estonia for an event and the organisers were to pick me up early in the morning. While stepping out of the shower, I slipped and injured the nail of my big toe. There was blood everywhere. And I couldn't even manage to get up. Somehow I dragged myself to the telephone and managed to call the reception. They sent people who provided some first-aid before taking me to a hospital where the injury was treated and bandaged. And I found myself wheelchair-bound!

Upon getting back to Delhi, I went to Moolchand Hospital to get the dressing changed. After a few days, I suffered from fever and had an upset stomach. I asked the doctor whether the injury of my toe had anything to do with the fever and upset stomach. As doctors normally do, he immediately suggested many tests and what emerged, though unlinked to the accident, did require me to spend several days in intensive care at Holy Family Hospital. It turned out that there was a problem with my liver, which had been compounded by my diabetes. Even after getting discharged, for some time I had to undertake repeated trips to the hospital. With the kind arrangements by my good friend, the late Ravindra Varma, I spent some time recuperating in a pleasant room at the Vishwa Yuvak Kendra. Until the time of writing this, my health problems have persisted and I am learning to live with the condition. As I take several medicines, I have got into the practice of throwing away the doses I missed to save myself from confusion later.

I was going to Chennai for Ayurvedic treatment, hoping to find some solution there.

49

A Dream

Some time ago I had a vivid dream in which I requested His Holiness for a teaching of *Lam-rim Chen-mo*, the great treatise of Lama Tsongkhapa, and initiations of the three principal deities of the Gelukpa tradition, to which He agreed. He also said that He had already made preparations for the teaching of the mind training text *Wheel of Sharp Weapons*.[2]

When I met with His Holiness the Dalai Lama next, I narrated the dream to Him and made a formal request for the teachings, to which he readily consented. So, on 24 February 2005, the first day of *Lam-rim* teaching, I, as the main sponsor,[3] escorted His Holiness from His residence through the courtyard to the main temple in Dharamsala. I made an offering of a mandala and a yellow Pandita hat to His Holiness. I had especially commissioned this hat and had it tailored by His official tailor. He put on the hat immediately. I felt immensely gratified. On the second day, His Holiness, during the course of the teaching said, 'I don't know how big an offering Doboom Rinpoche has prepared, but judging from his big belly, he may have a big offering!' Everyone had a hearty laugh. I know this was His Holiness's unique way of announcing that He recognised me as the one who had requested the *Lam-rim* teaching. Then, He said, 'I wouldn't accept a single rupee as offering for the teaching.'

The teaching continued for 14 days. On the last day of this particular teaching, His Holiness gave an initiation of thousand-armed Avalokiteswara during which He asked me to throw the flower on the mandala on behalf of all the participants. The flower fell on the north side which was Amoghasiddhi's domain. His Holiness said it was a good omen, a sign of fulfilling all the missions. I felt satisfied and blessed that His Holiness recognised me as the main person to request this teaching. So it came as a surprise when I found the official magazine of Dharamsala, *Sheja*, stating that a person from Switzerland was the main person. Journalistic indiscretion or internal politics – I did not find out!

On 8 June 2004, His Holiness called me to the Radisson Hotel. He talked about the importance of Buddhist learning programmes and also expressed His anxiety about the future of Tibetan establishments in India. Earlier, I had an idea for a Buddhist Cultural Centre which would be secular in nature. I briefly mentioned this idea to Him. He said to me that Bengaluru should be an ideal place for such a Buddhist Centre. At that point, it was time for Him to leave for airport. After that I made several trips to Bengaluru, visiting possible sites and making contacts at various levels in the government to find a suitable place. I had registered a trust in 1996, inspired by the House of World Culture in Berlin. I planned to make the trust a forum for this idea rather than using an existing institution linked to His Holiness's name. I am against using His Holiness's name unnecessarily, as it will be a great disservice to Him if it does not live up to His expectations. During a later audience, His Holiness told me that he had given the responsibility of establishing a Buddhist Dharma Centre in Bengaluru to Lama Zopa Rinpoche. This gave me both a sense of relief as well as a loss, due to missing an opportunity to initiate a creative venture.

In October 2004, His Holiness gave a teaching to a large group of Korean Buddhists. This time He preferred to have these teaching sessions in Delhi's Tibetan Youth Hostel in Rohini. The teaching lasted for four days and His Holiness wanted me to help the two Korean translators with technical Buddhist terms. So I sat with the two girls at the teachings. Their Tibetan knowledge was quite good. Acharya Shantideva's *Boddhicharyavatara* was the text used for the teaching. I understood that the translation of this text in Korean language was as effective as the Tibetan version of the text. I observed that the translators as well as a few in the audience were in tears just hearing the verses. It was quite satisfying and an honour for me to be of some use at this teaching.

On 30 October, the last day of the teaching, I had a quick audience with His Holiness and took the chance to seek advice directly from Him about the artifacts that originally belonged to Dzongkar Choede Monastery in Tibet. They wanted them back. Tibet House had some role in getting them from Nepal to India in the 1960s and had preserved and conserved these artifacts for over three decades. However, in the main register of Tibet House, 'Zobuk' (the inner storeroom of His Holiness) was mentioned as the source against each item. Because of that I could not take any action. I took the matter to the governing body, but no solution could be reached. The monastery was by then well established in Karnataka in south India and I felt that it was the right place for the artifacts to be preserved. However, the governing body of Tibet House had taken a position which may have been legally correct but did not seem right. As I began to explain my feelings to His Holiness, He immediately approved the idea of handing the artifacts over to the Dzongkar Choede Monastery in Karnataka.

There have been many occasions when I have been with His Holiness and have benefitted from His views. One such occasion was about a major controversy, coming from the time of the 13th

Dalai Lama, about which He took me into confidence. That was when I was working in LTWA. The point is that I was one of the few people with whom His Holiness shared His opinion on the matter.

50

Taken Away

Praise or abuse, to the ocean
No difference it makes; but
To a few readers, these statements of reality
In verse, will hopefully, some difference make.
(Ocean Maxims 37)

And so I have told the story of my life. There are several reasons why I wanted to tell it. In its simplest sense, it is a record. A record for people to know how we actually lived in Eastern Tibet and how we moved on horses and mules to Central Tibet; how we sat in a courtyard of the monastery and learnt and how many of the students struggled to find their way back to their room in the dark; how we came to India using snow covered rocks as landmarks to show us the way and how we travelled in all our monastic finery to keep our luggage light; how we lived in transit camps and imagined that, as everything else, this too was temporary; and how each of us chose our futures here in India and now live as one among the Indians.

This is an experiential account of a lama. In the early twentieth century, lamas were perceived as unusual beings having a wonderful time in the monastery, training in Buddhist studies, meditating and so on. While some part of that was true, my purpose of writing about my experiences is also to show the ordinariness of the life of a lama. In the early twentieth century, there was mystery and curiosity about Tibetan Buddhism, particularly in the West. The books written in those times kept the mystery and myths alive. There were many books that gave exaggerated accounts about Buddhism with made-up incidents. The romance of Tibet and Tibetan Buddhism was further reinforced by the fact that some remarkably genuine initiates emerged in that period, with incredible learning and mystical powers.

One of these initiates was the well-known lama, Anagarika Govinda. He was born to a German father and a Bolivian mother. He enlisted in the German army during the First World War but he contracted tuberculosis and so was discharged. In those days, treatment for tuberculosis was lengthy and arduous. During his extended stay in the sanatorium, he studied philosophy and other related subjects, and came across Buddhism. He was so influenced by it that by the age of eighteen, he was a devout Buddhist. He travelled to Sri Lanka initially and then to Tibet where he embraced Tibetan Buddhism. He was a good-looking and learned man who wrote many good books on Buddhism. These books were learned and rigorous, and he came to be known as a lama. His scholarship and his life story are both awe inspiring.

There was also a nun named Alexandra David-Neel who was half Belgian and half French. In addition to imbibing Buddhist philosophy, she was an adventurous woman who travelled to Tibet disguised as a beggar when it was a forbidden place for foreigners and even wrote a book titled *Magic and Mystery in Tibet*. She went on to write several books and gave many teachings. She even set up a centre called 'Samten Dzong' in Provence, France. When I was in the Private Office of His Holiness, they requested for a monk to be sent there.

The purpose of recounting all this is to show how the mystique attributed to Tibetan monks was fuelled by extraordinary people. Subsequently, there has been a lot of literature generated and Buddhism has travelled more deeply into the West, thus demystifying the life of Tibetans and Tibetan monks. My account is one more in that line.

Let me illustrate my point with a story. In the 1970s, a group of five lamas went abroad. They stayed in the house of a good hostess. Excited, she called up her friend and said, 'Look, I have five lamas staying in my house!'

Her friend was even more excited. 'How do you keep them in your house?' she asked.

'Oh,' replied the hostess very proudly, 'you know it is not very difficult, only the language…'

'Do they sleep on the floor?' asked the friend interrupting her.

'No, no, on the bed…'

After a few minutes of conversation along similar lines, they realised the friend had thought the hostess was talking of llamas.

What I want to emphasise, particularly to my younger readers, is that Tibetans are human beings, lamas are human beings and so are Rinpoches. There is nothing extraordinary about them. By following a certain path, the path shown by the Buddha, because of our environment and the company we keep, some changes need to come from within.

Having said that, I must also recount occurrences which are not so ordinary. I would not call them miracles, but they are different from common occurrences. I do not remember ever having thoughts of harming any living being, even the smallest of animals or insects. I think I had the feeling that they had the same kind of emotions as we do. I am fond of watching insects and birds building their nests. I can spend hours watching a spider weave its web or a bird build its nest. I have enjoyed watching the way bees collect honey. I find it fascinating, even when I see such shows on the television nowadays.

Chungkey is ever alert to kill any mosquito that is hovering around me ever since I had to be hospitalised with dengue in August 2016. I get very upset when she does that. So I spend a lot of time spraying the room with air fresheners. I may be wrong but I feel the smell puts off the mosquito and it flies away. Maybe it also causes its death eventually, but that I cannot tell, perhaps not even avoid.

Once I was walking down the streets of Lhasa, while I was studying in Drepung. I saw a copy of the *Abhidharmakosha* by Vasubandhu. I bought it and went back to the monastery. It was a good two to three hour walk to the monastery. I placed the book on the altar and went about my chores for the day. A few nights later, my attendant told me I was chanting in my sleep and when he told me what I was chanting, it turned out to be the first few verses of the *Abhidharmakosha*. I had not tried to memorise or learn the verses. How I knew them, I do not know.

Similar things have happened with smaller texts several times. Once a lama came to see me. He gave me a text for guru puja. It was about five to six pages. I even remember the colour of the paper on which it was printed. I do not remember memorising it, but I can still remember it. Once I was given a book titled *Clear Explanation of Dharmakirti's Pramanavarttika*. Dharmakirti was a follower of Dignaga. I not only knew the text, but had a superficial understanding of it, too. I had not read the book earlier.

In 1959, when we were living in Drepung Monastery and the Norbulingka Palace was being shelled, the talk was that the next target would be our monastery. We planned to escape and quickly packed our belongings. I was asked to wear my best clothes so that they would be safe and the luggage would be lighter. My attendants were planning to go to southern Tibet for they felt the Chinese would not go that far. They had planned for us to spend some time in a monastery and then return to Lhasa. I looked around to see what I could take. I took my prayer book. Then my eyes fell on the book to learn Hindi, a self-learning guide published in Kalimpong. I do not know why I picked that up. It was among my meagre belongings and when we landed up in India, it came in very handy!

When we reached Tawang and Bomdila, I started looking into the Hindi book and the first page said *ka, kha, ga, gha, na* and so on. I thought it would be very easy for in Tibetan our letters are *ka, kha, ga, nya*. We have four letters and Hindi has five. I would ask in Missamari, where we had a transit camp, '*Bazaar kahan hai*?' (Where is the bazaar?) and people would be so impressed with me! When I picked up that book, I was under the impression that we would be going to some monastery in southern Tibet, so actually I had no need of it. But it became really useful in India.

When I look back, I realise that all these out-of-the-ordinary things were a part of the flow. I am often asked how religion has guided me. It has not guided me – it has been a natural flow. If it is conscious, then it is not a flow, we are making it happen. Everything was with the flow, not necessarily one leading to another, but there were definitely some connections. Sometimes the connection was apparent from one period to the next, at other times it was a little delayed and came to light after a period of time. Perhaps that is why when I look back, I find my life fulfilling. I do not have the feeling that I have not accomplished anything. I am satisfied, not with anything specific, but in totality. There was no period in my life that was terrible. I am often asked the question, 'Which was the worst period in your life?' There was no such period. Each and every time I have learnt something and I see something good in every period.

Some people say the camp at Buxa was terrible – the food was bad, the heat was oppressive especially since we were coming from Tibet, a cold country, the place was not good and so on. But I did not have any problems. In fact, in some ways I feel that period was good for me, perhaps because I did not have to suffer much. There were others who worried about food, about the rations being misused and so on. Some people stayed there for eight to nine years. As I said, I had a good time. Whenever I felt hot, I would take a dip in the small river close by – everything was a flow, like a river.

This leads me to explain the title of my memoirs. Taken away – these two words I think, capture the essence of my life. I was taken away from my parents even before I knew anything. My horse, one of the few beings I was very attached to, was taken away from me when I went to study in Lhasa. My country was taken away from me. Doboom Ritro, established by the second Doboom, was taken away from me. And if you follow my life into the recent past, even my directorship of Tibet House was taken away from me!

After coming to Tibet House, my daily routine had become that of a typical junior babu. In India, junior babus would come with their tiffin boxes and spend the one hour of their official lunch break, eating that lunch. They would come on time. They would leave on time, at five. They worked for their salary – nothing more. The time restrictions did not apply to me, nor the salary. And, of course, my dress code was different!

I felt I was doing a duty given by His Holiness who is my root guru. In Buddhism, the root guru is the main guru, the basic or fundamental guru. So in that way I don't differentiate between spiritual practice and doing a duty. I don't see them separate because that is my attitude. I can claim that I was trained in this way, that the basic attitude should be clear and we should hold to it firmly and, premised on that, react to daily challenges. Such an attitude keeps whatever we do within the boundaries of the essential goal. On certain occasions we need to take a stronger position and not bow down to everybody who comes with orders, supposedly from higher-ups.

In Buddhism it is said, *pragya* (wisdom) and *upaya* (skilfulness) go together. They are like two wings of a bird. If we are not skilful, we will neither be able to serve others nor overcome the pitfalls that lie our way along a certain path known to people. So one interesting lesson life has taught me is that there is politics everywhere. We have to learn not to be affected by it. I have realised that everyone tries to be close to or appear to be close to

His Holiness. This gives them power and some reflected glory. But to the others, it can give angst.

I have had the good fortune to be very close to His Holiness right from the days in Lhasa when He remembered me as a 'plump boy' till recently when he walked straight towards me before giving a teaching in Gyudmed Monastery, calling me His friend. Once there was a professor from Estonia, Prof. Linnart Mäll, who told me he had asked His Holiness who his best friend was. His Holiness replied, 'Doboom,'. Prof. Linnart Mäll was an expert in Prajnaparamita and had invited me to Estonia.

I have dedicated my life to His Holiness, deeming service to Him as my path of spiritual practice. I am also sure His blessings have been with me as I had the opportunity to interact with some of the most influential people in India and a few abroad. I received invitations from numerous institutions including foreign universities to join them. As I said, my basic attitude dictated my choices, in good as well as unfair times.

I must admit I have faced difficult times and inelegant times. I think it is important to mention that, so that readers do not think everything was a bed of roses. In a monk's life too, tremendous trivialities play a role and to manage them is a challenge. It may seem strange that a monk gets a salary, but that is how each of us meets our daily needs – with the salary we get. Vested interests did not institutionalise processes so that they could keep control in their hands. In Tibet House, among other things, the salary of the director was never discussed, let alone subject to any raise. One day Chungkey, my secretary, told me she would soon be getting paid more than me. I had an opportunity to laugh!

The problem was not that my salary was lower than that of my secretary. The problem was that a few people in power and close to His Holiness were not decentralising and institutionalising the organisational activities. This is not healthy for any system. This causes the emergence of a parallel administration which is not always in keeping with the central ideology or thinking.

It also builds a coterie of self-seeking individuals with their own groups of sycophants. Often, the focus shifts from doing the job or tackling the issue at hand to satisfying and keeping the coterie in good humour.

Several times I have been invited by His Holiness to an event or a tour, only to find the organisers reluctant to let me join. I have mentioned these incidents in my story. If I do not touch upon them, my memoirs will not be complete. Such things require mention. But I do not suffer from any negative emotion because of what has happened. There are two reasons for that.

First, way back, when I joined the Private Office of His Holiness, I had decided that I would never ask Him for a personal favour. Second, it is my attitude. I never dwell on anything for long and let it fester and become a wound. My approach is to not obsess over the incident in my mind. If I have to meet the people who have done the wrong, I do not shun them. I do not dislike them. I talk to them normally. Ideally, they say, we should forgive. I do not think I have reached that stage. I just do not let it bother me. I do not hide my negative feelings. I do not pretend that I do not have any negative feelings. I just let them be, then the feelings do not grow larger than life. I move on.

I also look at things from different perspectives. What would I have done if I had not been taken away from my parents or my country? Maybe I would be a nomad in Tibet. One of my childhood friends, who was a monk with me, is a nomad now. In such a scenario, I would not have seen the world. I have learnt a lot from different cultures and different societies and different people. I have learnt the broadmindedness of science and accepted the different beliefs and ways of thinking.

I could have been in some big monastery, even sitting on a big throne as I hear lamas in Tibet and also in the West, are now doing. But then I would not be able to speak what was on my mind. I do not think I would have been happy that way.

I never knew of a life other than monkhood. I have lived only that life. I received a lot of care and love during my childhood years and enjoyed the simplicity and proximity with nature. I think they built my foundation for the future.

I do not think there can be any guidelines to move on in life. I think it depends on the individual. People break it down into steps, like a guide for travel to a foreign country, for example. Go to the embassy and get a visa, then buy a ticket and finally leave for the airport. I do not think this journey of life can be broken down into such easy stages. As we get familiar with the teachings, we begin to ask, 'What is the purpose of life?' It is a big question, everybody asks it – it is perhaps the process of evolution. I cannot claim to know the purpose of life, but I do have some idea. I think the purpose of life is to be useful to others. Not only other sentient beings but all of the environment. As we say, to both the container and the contained. Here container is the earth. Even though we read about the many galaxies and the Goldilocks zones and so on, I think only of the earth and its inhabitants. To be useful to all the sentient and non-sentient beings, be it a small insect or a plant, that is the only way to go on. That is the purpose of life.

Some people understand nirvana as equivalent to stopping an individual's existence. In Buddhism there are many descriptions of nirvana. For example, it is said that nirvana is like extinguishing a lamp when the oil is finished and the wick burns out. This is another way of saying, live for yourself. If the purpose of existence is only for yourself, then this kind of nirvana can be understood as your final goal. My understanding is that the purpose of existence is to be useful. We all have a natural inclination to be happy, to desire comfort and joy and pleasures, and to want to escape from harm. That means others too must be like us, desiring happiness, joy, pleasures and wanting to escape from harm. I feel that should be our guiding principle.

For an animal, another animal is either a threat or food. I see videos and instances of animals helping each other. Rare cases, perhaps. They are exceptions. I saw a video of a tigress rearing a fawn. Maybe she thought that it was her baby. Or maybe she felt love, I do not know. But these are rare cases and are also not viable in the long run. This tigress was protecting the fawn but another tiger saw it and attacked it. So such situations cannot last for long.

I feel human beings are different. We can create lasting situations of love and camaraderie. That comes with equanimity. In Buddhism we have the four immeasurables – *maitri* or loving kindness, *karuna* or compassion, *mudita* or empathetic joy and *upeksha* or equanimity. Upeksha can also be the first, depending on where we begin, for it is with equanimity that we develop kindness, compassion and innate joy.

So I think the purpose of being useful is useful. That is the only way to go on.

It is the process and the goal.

On ships or on boats in the ocean,
All pray and wish safe return to the shore;
Taking any path to enlightenment,
Endeavour to reach the shore of Bodhi.
(Ocean Maxims 19)

A Peep behind the Screens

I thought of my role as that of a ventriloquist's dummy. But a dummy, by definition, does not think, does not have preconceived notions and is not articulate. I realised it was not going to be that simple.

Our venture of writing Lama Doboom Tulku's life story for him developed a certain texture because of one important reason. I had my own vision and images in my head – of a Buddhist monk, a Rinpoche, a Tulku, former director of Tibet House, organiser of the World Festival of Sacred Music. But Lama Doboom Tulku was presenting himself as he was, as an individual, as an honest and straightforward person. He was not trying to match my image of a Buddhist monk. Sometimes my perception of who he was did not match his. Those times were important for they made me pause and, perhaps, revealed more about the person on whose behalf I was writing.

Sailing about in his maroon robes, Lama Doboom Tulku could be spotted often in and around the India International Centre. His ready laughter, his love for cheese straws that he enjoyed in the IIC lounge, his cold office room in Tibet House decorated with beautiful and artistically arranged artefacts, the jasmine tea he served, his slow and deliberate manner of speech … he gave the impression that he did not live in our world of tremendous trifles. Perhaps that is why when someone asked him a little mischievously in a gathering he was addressing, 'Have you been to Shambala[4]?' he responded with a serious expression on his face, 'They did not give me a visa.'

I have worked with him on several occasions, particularly during the World Festival of Sacred Music. He would stare into space as I showed him a copy. He generally asked me to read out what I had written and rarely read the copy himself. Often, he would give the impression that he was not listening but suddenly he would pick out a word, a seemingly insignificant one, and show that he had actually been paying attention to even small details. Once I had written, 'They had decided to go south of Tibet'. He stopped the reading and asked, 'Wouldn't southern Tibet be more precise?' He is such a good listener that he gives the impression that all the wisdom came from the one he was listening to.

Rinpoche, as he is addressed, is very creative. Always alert to the beautiful, he visualises details with elegance. When I was trying to work on his maxims – four-line verses on the ocean, the moon, the earth and stone – I found he used simple words with not-so-simple undertones.

Once, when we were working on this book and were talking of his prayer and meditation schedule – which takes three hours in the morning – I asked him, 'If ever you were working on something and things were not going in your favour, to whom and how do you pray for blessings?' He did not understand my question. After I had explained it several times, he still nodded his head with a kind of bewildered expression and finally, still unsure of whether that was the answer to the question I had asked, said, 'You never pray for yourself. Prayers are always for others.'

On that day, I did not continue further.

Another day, he was talking of how he was unceremoniously removed from Tibet House. It seemed to have hurt him deeply. I asked him for more details. I was expecting him to say something on the lines of how he has forgiven those who troubled him. You know, along the goody-goody lines of, 'Forgive them for they know not'. Instead, he said that the occasion had to be mentioned in his memoirs. He said, 'Don't try to be over nice and use nice words. Don't blame anyone, but to say what happened is my duty.' He continued with no change of expression, 'Forgiveness is a big claim. I cannot claim that. But it is true that I do not hold any negative feelings.'

That day too, I decided I needed a new pen.

Lama Doboom said he wanted to write his life story, among other reasons, to demystify the life of a Tibetan monk. He was being true to his purpose.

We enjoyed the rustic landscape and life in the Tibet of his times. We enjoyed the poetry and literature in Tibetan, to which I would otherwise have had no access. We enjoyed stories of travels and encounters with different people. We enjoyed life in a monastery and life as a monk (vicariously, for me). We enjoyed Chungkey's attention to keep the tea and snacks, not to mention lunches, coming regularly.

And then I sneaked in the question, 'But what is the purpose of this life?' He seemed amused, partly by the question and partly that I should ask it. 'To be useful. It is the process and the goal of human life,' he said.

Since I belong to the category of people who pray for themselves, the prayer that moves my lips is that the book should represent Lama Doboom Tulku, as he is, as he finds himself – no judgement, no regret, no pride. A plain acceptance, and discovery with each moment.

Even as the manuscript was being edited, Rinpoche's health worsened. Is it poetic irony that he was taken away by his multiple illnesses before the book was published?

Early on the morning of 29 January 2024, Rinpoche Lama Doboom Tulku breathed his last. He had spent the past six or seven years trying to convince me that though a monk, he was an ordinary person. He forgot to do so after 29 January when he lay in deep meditation or *thukdam* for a week after his last breath. Thukdam is a Buddhist phenomenon where the realised monk's consciousness remains in the body even after his passing. So decomposition of the body does not begin. On 4 February, the last rites were held in the grounds of Tehor Khangtsen, Mundgod, in a grand ceremony and the relics taken to his residence in Drete Dhargyon in Mundgod, Karnataka.

It is customary to pray for the swift return of realised lamas whose lives are dedicated to bring spiritual betterment to the people. A special swift return prayer has been composed by His Holiness the Dalai Lama. Kyabje Khensur Tokden Rinpoche and Kyabje Za Choeje Rinpoche have also composed swift return prayers for Lama Doboom Tulku.

The prayers are being chanted.

Till then…

Sudhamahi Regunathan
12 February 2024

With His Holiness in Dharamsala, 25 January 2023

Notes

PART I TEHOR (1941–54)

1 Lama Doboom Tulku, *Words Well Spoken: Maxims of Earth and Stone* (Karnataka: Magenta Press, 2012).

2 Those belonging to the Kham region were called Khampas. The area is known today as Yushu Tibetan Autonomous Prefecture in Qinghai Province.

3 A khatag is a ceremonial scarf used in Tibet and Mongolia when greeting visitors. Khatags are offered in the Tibetan Buddhist tradition to religious images and statues, holy sites, lamas and also used in certain rituals. It symbolises respect to the recipient.

4 A 'geshe' literally means 'virtuous friend' or 'kalyana mitra' in Sanskrit. A Tibetan Buddhist academic degree for monks and nuns is also called geshe. Here I use the word to mean 'kalyana mitra', describing Kalsang Tenpa.

5 Doboom was also the name of the hermitage where the Dobooms lived. It literally means 'stone vase'.

6 A tradition worth mentioning – the followers of a monk often request a high ranking and famous lama to write a long-life prayer for the monk. This prayer for the second Doboom was written by Serkong, who traced his lineage to Ananda, the Buddha's closest aide. My long-life prayer was written by Phurchok, the reincarnation of the tutor of the 13th Dalai Lama.

7 Officially, my year of birth is recorded as 1941.

8 There are four major sects in Tibet – Nyingma, Kagyu, Sakya and Geluk.

9 The game is somewhat similar to the modern-day Snakes and Ladders, except that every move had a spiritual meaning in the game we played. Later someone tried to redesign the game in India, but there were no takers.

10 The Buddha is also referred to as a Mahapurusha. There are 32 lakshanas or physical features that are traditionally used to describe a Mahapurusha.

11 The community of monks and nuns following the Buddha.

12 Boddhichitta is the inspiration to get Buddhahood.

13 Sadhana here is not the name of a text. It is a method of achieving Buddhahood.

PART II LHASA (1954–59)

1 In Venerable Olande Ananda's words, 'I called Lama-ji from the Dargye area. He asked me, "What do you see?" I replied saying I saw rocks, rubble and ruins. "That was my Ritro," replied Lama-ji.'

2 The administrator who was in charge of the discipline of the monks.

3 Tibet was divided into three regions – Kham, Amdo and the central and northern region. People in Amdo had better schools. His Holiness the Dalai Lama is from Amdo. Elsewhere there were a few private schools run by families, which not many people got to attend. There were some monasteries in Kham where they taught not just religious studies but general subjects like literature, medicine, astrology and so on.

4 There were four degrees, beginning with Dorampa, then Lingtse, followed by Tsokrampa and finally Lharampa, which was the highest. The abbot decided in which category the student was, depending on the overall performance of the student.

5 Lama Tsongkhapa was an important philosopher of the Gelukpa tradition and a prolific author.

6 Pothis are manuscripts written on rectangular sheets of rough, handmade paper. A loose collection of such papers was tied together in a bundle with generally a cover page and a back page. This was known as a pothi.

7 My English translation of the original Tibetan.

8 People thought it was called Tsangpo because it came from the Tsang region of Tibet. In the 1970s, when I visited Joseph Gergen – a Ladakhi whose home was in Srinagar, who had compiled and published his father's notes on Ladakh history – he told me the name was actually Tshangbu, where 'tshang' stands for Brahma, and 'bu' means 'putra' or son.

9 Milarepa belongs to the Nyingma tradition.

10 It is the highest geshe degree of scholarship conferred within the traditional Tibetan monastic system in the Gelukpa School.

The curriculum requires 15–20 years of intensive study. The four categories are the Dorampa, Lingtse, Tsokrampa and Lharampa.

11 Yamantaka is a deity who is considered to be the destroyer of death.

12 Ceremonial Buddhist tantric ornament.

PART III IN TRANSIT

1 The book contains the essence of perfect sayings which deal with interpretative and definitive meanings of Buddha's teachings in both Madhyamika and Vijnanavada systems.

2 Chuba refers to the attire of both men and women in Tibet. In Nepal it is called 'bhaku'. The manner of wearing the chuba differs from region to region.

PART IV INDIA: SETTLING DOWN, FINDING GROUND

1 There are two collections of scriptures for Tibetan Buddhists – the Kangyur and the Tengyur. The Kangyur is a collection of Buddhist scriptures translated from Sanskrit into Tibetan. They are believed to be the Buddha's words. The Tengyur is predominantly a collection of commentaries on the texts, also translated from Sanskrit into Tibetan.

2 A British post continued by the Indian government.

3 'Kha' means mouth, entrance or approach.

4 Sambhogakaya is explained earlier, in Chapter 2.

PART V STUDIES

1 Each monastery has a debating courtyard where much of the teaching and learning takes place. It is also called Dharma Court or 'chora'.

2 Later renamed as Sampurnanand Sanskrit Vishwavidyalaya.

3 Jigme Taring was the eldest son of Raja Taring, the Maharaja of Sikkim. He married Rinchen Dolma, daughter of Tsarong, an aristocratic family in old Tibet. They were popularly known among Tibetans as Taring Pala and Amala.

4 'Khen' is the short form of 'Khenpo', which means 'abbot'.

5 He was of my age. He passed away in 2011 in New Zealand.

PART VI WORKING LIFE

1 Venerable Panchen Otrul Rinpoche is now the spiritual director of Jampa Ling Tibetan Buddhist Centre in West Cavan, Ireland.

2 Short form of Kuger Yigtsang, which is the Private Office of His Holiness the Dalai Lama.

PART VII TIBET HOUSE

1 Bon is understood as the pre-Buddhist Tibetan religious practices, in general.

2 Prof. Sundar Sarukkai explained that for scientists, energy packets are part-less as they have no weight, that there is scientific evidence for time having substance, and that space was dependent on matter as a concept, and its qualities may be known in terms of its curvature, which was measurable.

3 Vijayalakshmi Pandit was a member of the Tibet House governing body. I met Rajiv Gandhi for the first time when she passed away.

4 It was edited by Sudhamahi Regunathan.

5 Today this post is called Sekong or president.

PART VIII PEOPLE AND PLACES

1 A gonpa or gompa may be understood as a place of learning and meditation.

PART IX A NEW CHAPTER

1 Alessia came to see me when I was very unwell and stayed for a while till I needed to be flown down to Mundgod in a chartered ambulance in January 2024. She organized my chartered flight.

2 In Tibetan *Theg-pa-chen-pohi-blo-sbyong mtson-cha-hkhor-lo* by Dharmarakshita.

3 A sponsor is one who makes the first request and shares the expenses which means giving tea and bread to everybody. These days many people make requests and their contributions are clubbed together.

4 Shambala is a mythical Buddhist kingdom where all people are said to have attained enlightenment.

About the Authors

Venerable Doboom Lobsang Tenzin Tulku was born in 1942 in Kham in eastern Tibet. At the age of two or three, he was recognised as the reincarnation of the second Doboom Tulku. In 1953, Doboom Tulku entered Drepung Monastery in Lhasa, where he studied Buddhist philosophy until the Chinese invasion of Tibet in 1959 forced him into exile in India at the age of seventeen. He resided at the lama camp at Buxa Duar, West Bengal, until he joined the Institute of Higher Tibetan Studies in Sarnath in 1969. After obtaining the Geshe Acharya degree in 1972, he worked as a librarian at Tibet House in New Delhi, until he joined the Library of Tibetan Works and Archives in Dharamsala as a librarian and research assistant in 1973. By 1981, having gained more experience, he returned to Tibet House, New Delhi, to serve as director, with the mission of promoting Tibetan cultural heritage through Tibet House's diverse range of programmes. Doboom Tulku served as director of Tibet House for thirty years.

Doboom Tulku has also worked with His Holiness the Dalai Lama's Private Office and has accompanied His Holiness the Dalai Lama on visits to the USA, the USSR, Japan and Mongolia, among others. He has written widely on topics ranging from Tibetan medicine to Buddhist meditation and the Chittamatra (Mind Only) school of philosophy. In 1996, he founded the World Buddhist Culture Trust to bridge the gap between cultures and promote religious dialogue and harmony on the basis of universal compassion. He also had a personal interest in the effects of music for spiritual practice and worked hard at setting up the World Festival of Sacred Music, which became a global event.

Sudhamahi Regunathan is the former vice-chancellor of Jain Vishva Bharati Institute (Deemed University), Ladnun, Rajasthan. She is an author and a translator. Her books include *Siku: Faith and Conversion – Donyipolo Movement in Arunachal Pradesh*, *Rishabhayan: The Story of the First King*, *The Colours of Desire on the Canvas of Restraint* and *From One Birth to Another: Stories from Jaina Literature*.